Adventure Guide to

The Florida Keys
& Everglades National Park

3rd Edition

Joyce & Jon Huber

HUNTER

Hunter Publishing, Inc.
130 Campus Drive, Edison NJ 08818
☎ 732-225-1900, 800-255-0343; fax 732-417-1744

Ulysses Travel Publications
4176 Saint-Denis, Montréal, Québec
Canada H2W 2M5
☎ 514-843-9882, ext. 2232; fax 514-843-9448

Windsor Books
The Boundary, Wheatley Road, Garsington
Oxford, OX44 9EJ England
☎ 01865-361122; fax 01865-361133

ISBN 1-58843-119-3

3rd Edition © 2001 Joyce & Jon Huber

Photo credits: (front cover) *sailboat, roseate spoonbill* and *angelfish* by
Jon Huber; *fishing sunset* courtesy Florida Keys TDC.
Maps and most illustrations by Joyce Huber.

Preface

The Adventure Guide to the Florida Keys & Everglades National Park details how and where to enjoy varied sports and activities that are often skipped over by travel guides. We find most visitors to the region define themselves by what they do, recreation-wise. A few confess to just wanting to lie back and do nothing; for them we've included all the great resorts with glorious beaches and spas. But the true flavors of this special area can only be tasted by those who venture out of their everyday lives to become scuba divers, snorkelers, canoers, bird watchers, sea kayakers, deep-sea or fly fishermen, swamp hikers and sea sprites. We've included maps, directions and details on a variety of outdoor adventures. And to assure future generations some fun, we've added EcoTips, a collection of earth-friendly ways to leave the area a little better than you found it.

Acknowledgments

The enthusiasm and assistance of the following people made an invaluable contribution to this guide.

Special thanks to Lissa Dailey, Toni Carbone and Michael Hunter of Hunter Publishing; Andy Newman of Stuart Newman Associates; Nadia and Jim Spencer of Key Largo; Bill Keogh, Big Pine Kayak Adventures; Christian Schoemig, Sky Dive Key West; Brad Lange, Flying Fish Flight School; Barbara Fox and Laura B. Quinn of the Florida Keys Wild Bird Rescue Center; Larry and Carol Mulvehill; Bob Epstein, Wildwater Productions; Bill Anderson, Old Island Restoration Foundation; Ed Carlson, National Audubon Society; Jean, Douglas, and Oliver Prew; Dr. Stephen L. Brenner, who stitched us back together after researching the last edition; Josh Neiman, Discovery Glassbottom Boat Tours; Barbara Swab and Frank Holler and Paul Seiswerda, New York Aquarium, and Dee Scarr, Touch the Sea, for their eco-tips on fish handling.

Contents

The Florida Keys

N.W. Cape

White
Ba

Middle
Cape

East Cape

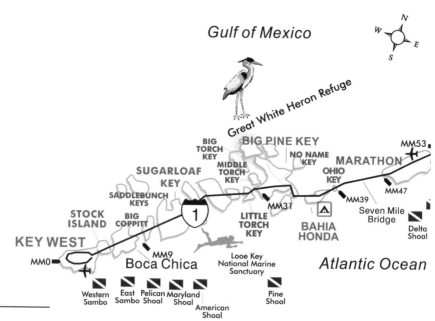

Gulf of Mexico

N
W • E
S

Great White Heron Refuge

BIG
TORCH
KEY

BIG PINE KEY

NO NAME
KEY

MM53

MARATHON

SUGARLOAF
KEY

MIDDLE
TORCH
KEY

OHIO
KEY

MM47

SADDLEBUNCH
KEYS

MM39

Seven Mile
Bridge

STOCK
ISLAND

BIG
COPPITT

MM31

LITTLE
TORCH
KEY

BAHIA
HONDA

Delta
Shoal

KEY WEST

MM0

MM9

Boca Chica

Looe Key
National Marine
Sanctuary

Atlantic Ocean

Western
Sambo

East
Sambo

Pelican
Shoal

Maryland
Shoal

American
Shoal

Pine
Shoal

← 70 Miles to Fort Jefferson

Florida City
**Florida City
Homestead**

Visitors Center
Park Headquarters

**Everglades
National
Park**

water
y

Flamingo

Florida Bay

Card Sound Rd

Biscayne National Park

_Card
Sound_

Ocean Reef Club

5 Crocodile
Lake

Carysfort
Reef

_Barnes
Sound_

_Blackwater
Sound_

MM 106

KEY LARGO

_Largo
Sound_

The Elbow

John Pennekamp
State Park

MM100

Rock Harbor

French Reef

Tavernier

MM92

Plantation Key
Windley Key
Whale Harbor

Straits of Florida

Molasses Reef

Pickles Reef

Upper
Matecumbe

MM83

Conch
Reef

ISLAMORADA

Lower
Matecumbe

MM80

Little Conch

Davis
Reef

Bibb/Duane

LONG KEY

MM73

Crocker
Reef

CRAIG KEY

Layton

Alligator
Reef

Mm58

DUCK KEY

**CRAWL
KEY**

GRASSY KEY

Tennessee
Reef

Key Colony
Beach

East Turtle
Shoal

Atlantic Ocean

Coffins
Patch

Watherwoman
Shoal

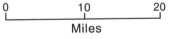

0   10   20

Miles

Map © Joyce Huber

Key West Attractions and Points of Interest

1. Audubon House
2. Charter Fishing Boats
3 & 33. Conch Train Depots
4. De Poo Hospital
5. East Martello Museum and Gallery
6. Florida Keys Memorial Hospital
7. Golf Course
8. Hemingway House

9. Hospitality House
10. Key West Beaches
11. Key Plaza Shopping Center
12. Mel Fisher's Treasure Museum
13. Key West Aquarium
14. Key West Chamber of Commerce
15. Key West City Cemetery
16. Key West International Airport

Map © Joyce Huber

Planning Your Trip

A unique range of recreational choices combined with a sub-tropical climate attract more than six million visitors to the Florida Keys and Everglades each year. Whatever the outdoor adventurer has in mind, there seems to be a perfect place for it in this part of the world. Activities exist for every age, fitness, and experience level.

Whether you choose to settle in the upper or lower Keys you will be near enough to explore the mysteries and surprises of all the islands. Everglades National Park's main visitor area is a day-trip from Key Largo. The Ten Thousand Islands region, favored for fresh-water fishing and canoe camping, is a 95-mile drive from Miami.

When to Go

The Florida Keys' high season has traditionally run from December through May, though many divers and snorkelers prefer the calm and warmer waters of late spring and summer. In winter, skies are predictably sunny, and air temperatures range from 75° to 85° F. Fall brings the chance of a hurricane, but offers lower hotel rates and often beautiful weather.

Salt-water fishing is big all year. Comfort-wise, angling the backcountry is best in winter, but good fly fishing in the bays and Gulf of Mexico is more dependent on a full or new moon than the season. This high-tide period occurs twice a month and is published in the tide tables (available in your daily newspaper or online at www.marineweather.com or www.harbortides.com).

Key West's attractions are best seen during winter and spring. During summer, though trade winds offer a bit of relief to the other islands, Key West's maze of city buildings blocks the breezes, causing uncomfortably hot days during July and August.

Visit Everglades National Park from December through March, the dry season. The rest of the year brings torrential downpours and mosquitoes that cloud the air and cluster in gobs on your skin. We found bugs a problem as late as mid-November, particularly in Flamingo.

Adventure Tours

Full- and half-day sailing, fishing, and snorkeling tours are offered throughout the area. (See specialty chapters for listings.) Dive shops throughout the US offer group trips covering transportation, diving and accommodations. Snorkelers often may join for a lower rate. Every major resort in the Florida Keys offers a dive-accommodation package, as do many of the Keys dive shops (see *Scuba, Snorkeling* and *Where to Stay* chapters, pages 145 and 209, for listings).

Money-saving vacation packages for air, hotel and car rental can be arranged through your travel agent. Accommodation-only packages are offered direct from many of the resorts.

Everglades National Park rangers lead guided nature walks and canoe-camping trips.

Handicap Facilities

Most large resorts feature full handicap facilities. State and national parks have wheelchair-accessible trails, tour boats, accommodations and restaurants.

The following dive operators offer certification and dives for the handicapped, depending on degree of handicap and skill of the diver:

Key West Diving Society Inc.
Stock Island, MM 4.5
☎ 305-294-7177

Dive Key West
3128 N. Roosevelt Blvd.
Key West
☎ 305-296-3823

Lost Reef Adventures
Land's End Village
261 Margaret St.
Key West
☎ 305-296-9737
www.allcoastal.com/lostreef/

Looe Key Dive Center
MM 27
Ramrod Key
☎ 800-942-5397 or 305-872-2215, ext 2

Strike Zone Charters
MM 29.5
Big Pine Key
☎ 800-654-9560 or 305-872-9863

John Pennekamp State Park
Key Largo
☎ 305-451-1202

Theater of the Sea has wheelchair ramps into the attraction area and swim-with-the-dolphin pools.
MM 84.5
Islamorada
☎ 305-664-2431

For updated information, contact the individual resorts and facilities.

Getting There

■ To the Florida Keys

All major national and international airlines fly into Miami International Airport. Connecting scheduled flights land in Marathon and Key West. No regularly scheduled public transportation travels to Everglades National Park.

Airlines Serving Key West Airport

General flight information	☎ 305-296-5439
American Eagle	☎ 800-433-7300
Cape Air	☎ 800-352-0714
Continental Connection	☎ 800-525-0280
at Key West airport	☎ 305-294-1421
Delta/Comair	☎ 800-354-9822
Website	www.fly-comair.com
Air Canada	☎ 800-776-3000
USAir Express	☎ 800-428-4322
Virgin Atlantic	☎ 800-862-8621
Website	www.virgin.com

Airlines Serving Marathon Airport

American Eagle	☎ 800-433-7300
USAir Express	☎ 800-4284322

By Road

To reach the Keys **from Miami International Airport**, take LeJeune Road south to 836 West. Then take the Florida Turnpike extension south to US 1 and the Keys. Card Sound Road offers an alternative route to Key Largo.

From the west, come across I-75 (Alligator Alley) to the Miami exit and south to the Turnpike Extension.

From the north, take the Florida Turnpike south along the east coast down to just below Ft. Lauderdale and Exit 4 Homestead/Key West. This is the Turnpike Extension that meets US 1 in Florida City, which takes you to Key Largo, some 25 minutes south. **From Tampa**, take I-75 south to Naples, then east to Miami and the Turnpike Extension or 41 South, then east to the Turnpike Extension, then south to US 1.

If you prefer a bus, the **Greyhound Keys Shuttle** serves the Florida Keys from Miami International Airport. ☎ 800-231-2222, www.greyhound.com. See below, page 7, for details.

Emerald Transportation Company offers personalized door-to-door service to and from all airports and the Florida Keys. Executive cars, vans, limos, or charter buses are available, ☎ 800-524-7894, local 305-852-1468. **Keys Shuttle** features door-to-door service from Ft. Lauderdale and Miami International Airports to Marathon, Islamorada and Key Largo. ☎ 305-289-9997.

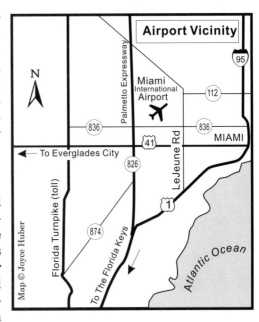

Mile Markers

Mile Markers (MM) are used throughout this guide to reference locations in the Florida Keys. The markers appear on the right shoulder of the road (US 1) as small green signs with white numbers and are posted each mile beginning with number 126, just south of Florida City. Mile markers end with the zero marker at the corner of Fleming and Whitehead streets in Key West.

Awareness of these markers is useful, as Keys' residents use them continually. When asking for directions in the Keys, your answer will likely reference a mile marker number.

Distances from Miami

Key Largo (MM 110-MM 87); MM 110 is about 58 miles from Miami

Islamorada (MM 86-MM 66); MM 86 is 76 miles from Miami

Marathon (MM 65-MM 40); MM 65 is 111 miles from Miami

Big Pine Key (MM 39-MM 9); MM 39 is 128 miles from Miami

Key West (MM8-MM 0); MM 8 is 159 miles from Miami

■ To the Everglades

Flamingo

From Miami Airport, take LeJeune Road south to 836 West, then Florida's Turnpike south to the Overseas Hwy. (aka US 1). Turn right off US 1 in Homestead onto State Hwy. 9336. An 11-mile ride will bring you to the Everglades National Park entrance and the Main Visitor's Center. From there it is a 38-mile trip along the Main Park Road to Flamingo. There are no services along the Main Park Road.

Everglades City & the Gulf Coast via the Tamiami Trail

Departing Miami Airport, take LeJeune Road south to 836 West, then Florida's Turnpike south to the Tamiami Trail (Route 41) westbound. Expect a 45-mile ride to Shark Valley and the Miccosukee Indian Reservation. To reach the Gulf Coast Ranger Station, Everglades City and the Ten Thousand Island region, continue an additional 40 miles along Route 41 West to Route 29 South. Then go three more miles to the ranger station. Total distance from Miami to Everglades City averages 95 miles.

■ Public Transportation & Rentals

At Miami Airport: Avis, Budget, Hertz, National and Value. If possible, book rental cars in advance of your trip. In season you may be forced to rent more car than you had planned.

Rental Cars

Alamo	☎ 800-327-9633 or local 305-294-6675
Avis	☎ 800-331-1212 or local 305-296-8744
Budget	☎ 800-527-0700 or local 305-294-8868
Dollar	☎ 800-421-6868 or local 305-296-9921
Hertz	☎ 800-654-3131
National	☎ 800-328-4567
Value Rent-A-Car	☎ 305-296-7733

Taxis

Miami

Airport Transportation	☎ 453-0100, US 800-749-5397
Checker Cab	☎ 305-888-8888
Yellow Cab	☎ 305-444-4444
Diamond Cab	☎ 305-545-7575

Key Largo - Tavernier

Sailboat John's	☎ 305-852-7999
Island Taxi	☎ 305-664-8181

Airport Trans	☎ 305-453-0100
A Kokomo Cab	☎ 305-852-8888
Upper Keys	☎ 305-453-0100

Marathon

Island Taxi	☎ 305-743-0077
Paradise Taxi	☎ 305-293-3010

Big Pine Key

Island Taxi	☎ 305-872-4404

Key West

Gary's	☎ 305-289-9840
Maxi Taxi	☎ 305-294-2222
Pink Cabs	☎ 305-296-6666
Sun Cab	☎ 305-296-7777
Yellow Cab	☎ 305-294-2227

Everglades City Area

Naples Taxi	☎ 305-775-0505

Trains

Amtrak	☎ 800-872-7245
Metrorail (Miami)	☎ 305-638-6700

Buses

Greyhound Keys Shuttle buses depart Miami airport at 6:20 am, 12:20 pm and 6:50 pm. The airport-vicinity bus station is at 4111 NW 27th St., Miami; ☎ 305-871-1810, or 800-231-2222. Travel time to Key West is 4½ hrs.

The Greyhound Keys Shuttle departs Key West Airport at 8:45 am, 11:30 am and 5:45 pm. ☎ 305-296-9072.

Greyhound offers bicycle boxes for $15 at Miami and Key West terminals. You must disassemble your bike.

The Homestead terminal is at 5 NE 3rd Road, Homestead FL 33030. ☎ 305-247-2040.

By Bicycle

Cyclists are advised to transport their bikes by car from the airport to the Everglades or the Keys. Florida's Turnpike does not allow bicycles, while US 1 is devoid of a shoulder in some sections and dangerous for road riding. Greyhound will transport your bike to points along US 1 if the bicycle is boxed (see *Cycling* chapter). Rentals are widely available.

■ By Boat

Boaters can reach the area by the Intracoastal waterway or outside via the Gulf or Atlantic. The Intracoastal Waterway is limited to shallow draft vessels (5 ft or less). Deep draft boats en route to Key West follow Hawks Channel, which passes between the outer reefs and the Florida Keys. The Coast Guard monitors VHF 16. All channels are well marked. Dock space is readily available. Reservations may be required at some marinas during high season for overnight stays.

Marinas

Key Largo

Pilot House Marina

13 Seagate Blvd.
Key Largo FL 33037
☎ 305-451-3452, fax 451-0225;
E-mail: FLPHM@aol.com

Curtis Marina

MM 93, Bayside
Key Largo FL 33037
☎ 305-852-5218

Garden Cove Marina

MM 106.5, Oceanside
Key Largo FL 33037
☎ 305-451-4694

Italian Fisherman Marina

MM 104, Bayside
Key Largo FL 33037
☎ 305-451-3726

Key Largo Harbor Marina

MM 100, Oceanside
Key Largo FL 33037
☎ 305-451-0045

Marina Del Mar Marina
MM 100, Oceanside
Key Largo FL 33037
☎ 305-451-4107

Marriott Bay Beach Marina
MM 104, Oceanside
Key Largo FL 33037
☎ 305-453-0000

Molasses Reef Marina
MM 99.5, Oceanside
Key Largo FL 33037
☎ 305-451-9411

Rock Harbor Marina
MM 97, Oceanside
Key Largo FL 33037
☎ 305-852-2025

Rowells Marina
MM 104, Bayside
Key Largo FL 33037
☎ 305-451-1821

Islamorada

Bud & Marys Fishing Marina
Mile Marker 79.8, Oceanside
Islamorada FL 33036
☎ 305-664-2461, fax (305)-664-5592
E-mail: bnmfm@budnmarys.com

Coconut Cove Resort & Marina
84801 Old Hwy.
Islamorada FL 33036
☎ 305-664-0123, fax 305-664-4498
E-mail: coconut@coconutcove.net
Five acres directly on the Atlantic Ocean. Efficiency cottages.

KT'S Marina Bait & Tackle
MM 68.5, Oceanside
Islamorada FL 33063
☎ 305-664-4509, fax 305-664-0132
E-mail: ktmarina@aol.com

Treasure Harbor Marina

200 Treasure Harbor Marine Drive
Islamorada FL 33036
☎ 305-852-2458 or 800-FLA-BOAT, fax 305-852-5743
E-mail: info@treasureharbor.com
Rents power and sailing yachts, captained or bareboat, from 19 to 41 ft.
Dockage is free to charter parties.

Marathon

Capt. Hook's Marina and Dive Centers

11833 Overseas Hwy.
Marathon FL 33050
☎ 800-CPT-HOOK or 800-278-4665, fax 305-289-1374
E-mail: grange@marathonkey.com

Big Pine Key

Dolphin Resort and Marina

MM28.5, Overseas Hwy.
Little Torch Key FL 33042
☎ 800-553-0308
E-mail: dolphinresort@earthlink.net

Sugarloaf Marina

Sugarloaf Shores FL 33044
☎ 305-745-3135

Key West

Oceanside Marina

5950 Peninsula Ave.
Key West FL 33040
☎ 305-294-4676, fax 305-292-4995
Key West's largest marina. "Wet slips" can handle vessels to 150 ft.

Seahorse Marina

5001 5th Ave.
Stock Island Key West FL 33040
☎ 305-292-9880
E-mail: info@seahorsemarina.com
Located just past Cow Key Channel on Stock Island, Key West.

The Galleon Resort & Marina

617 Front St.
Key West FL 33040
☎ 305-296-7711 or 800-544-3030, fax 305-296-0821.
E-mail: info@galleonresort.com

A & B Marina

700 Front St.
Key West FL 33040
☎ 305-294-2535 or 800-223-8352,
E-mail: abmarina@aol.com
Walking distance to Old Town restaurants, shopping, night life and Mallory Square.

Aaron's US 1 Marina Boat Rentals

MM 42 US 1
Stock Island FL 33040
☎ 305-296-0075

Garrison Bight Marina

Garrison Bight Causeway
Key West FL 33040
☎ 305-294-3093

Geiger Key Marina

5 Geiger Rd.
Key West FL 33040
☎ 305-296-3553

Key West Conch Harbor

909 Caroline St.
Key West FL 33040
☎ 305-292-1727

Key West Sailing Club

PO Box 828
Key West FL 33041
☎ 305-294-9125

Key West Yacht Club Marina

2315 N Roosevelt Blvd.
Key West FL 33040
☎ 305-296-3446

Land's End Marina

201 William St.
Key West FL 33040
☎ 305-296-3838

Robbie's Full Service Marina

Shrimp Rd.
Stock Island FL 33040
☎ 305-294-1124

Safe Harbour Marina
6810 Front St.
Key West FL 33040
☎ 305-294-9797

Sunset Marina
5601 College Rd.
Key West FL 33040
☎ 305-296-7101

Truman Annex Marina
201 Front St.
Key West FL 33040
☎ 305-293-9378

Public Boat Ramps

Upper Keys

Blackwater Sound, MM 110, Bayside

Harry Harris Park, MM 92, Oceanside

Indian Key Fill, MM 79, Bayside

Marathon, MM 54, Bayside

Lower Keys

Spanish Harbour, MM 33.7, Bayside

Cudjoe Key, MM 10.8, Bayside

Stock Island Ramp, Bayside

Key West, end of A1A

NOAA Charts

11451: For small craft – Miami to Marathon and Florida Bay

11465: Intracoastal Waterway from Miami to Elliott Key

11463: Intracoastal Waterway from Elliott Key to Islamorada

11462: Fowey Rocks to Alligator Reef

11452: Alligator Reef to Sombrero Key

11550: Fowey Rocks to American Shoal

11449: Islamorada to Bahia Honda

11448: Intracoastal Waterway – Big Spanish Channel to Johnson Key

11445: Intracoastal Waterway – Bahia Honda to Key West

11441: Key West Harbor and approaches

11447: Key West Harbor

Gulf Coast

11429: Naples to Pavilion Key

11431: Pavilion Key to Florida Bay area

Bare Boating & Crewed Yacht Vacations

Fully-equipped live-aboard motor yachts and sailboats for day trips, overnights or extended vacations, with or without crews, can be chartered from any of the following:

Atlantic Coast

Cruzan Yacht Charters

3375 Pan American Drive
Coconut Grove FL 33133
☎ 800-628-0785 or 305-858-2822, fax 305-854-0887.
Write to: PO Box 53, Coconut Grove FL 33133.

Cruzan, operated by Captain Danny Valls, offers a large selection of sail and power bare boats from 30 to 50 ft for half- or full-day, weekend or weekly cruises to Biscayne National Park, the Florida Keys or the Bahamas. Captained day and moonlight cruises may be arranged for two to 12 passengers. Sample rate for a party of six aboard a 50-ft captained sailboat starts at $3,700, not including food, drinks or port taxes. Visa and MasterCard accepted.

Treasure Harbor Marine Inc.

200 Treasure Harbor Drive
Islamorada FL 33036.
☎ 800-FLA-BOAT, 305-852-2458, fax 305-852-5743.
E-mail: info@treasureharbor.com

Treasure Harbor Marine features day sailboats and live-aboards. High-season prices range from $110 per day for a 19-ft day sailor to $330 per day for a 44-ft uncrewed yacht. By the week, from $395 to $1,700. Captains available; call for rates. Lower rates apply between April 1 and November 14.

Gulf Coast-Everglades 10,000 Island Area

Gulf Shores Marina

3470 Bayshore Drive
Naples FL
☎ 941-774-0222
E-mail: info@gulfshoresmarina.com

Cedar Bay Marina
705 E. Elkcam Circle
Marco Island FL 34145
☎ 941-394-9533 or 800-906-2628,
E-mail: info@cedarbaymarina.com

■ By Private Plane

There are some restrictions for private aircraft flying into the Keys. Light planes must have 12-inch registration numbers and a mode C transponder. A flight plan is required for some areas. Before entering the area contact the **Aircraft Owner's and Pilot's Association** for a current briefing; ☎ 301-695-2140 or write **AOPA Flight Operations Department**, 421 Aviation Way, Frederick, MD 21701. For water landings additional information may be available from the **Seaplane Pilot's Association** at ☎ 301-695-2083 or the **Key West Seaplane Base**, ☎ 305-294-6978, fax 305-292-1091. The Miami sectional map covers the area.

What to Bring

■ Clothing

During winter, pack a light jacket, long-sleeved shirts and long pants. Temperatures occasionally drop to the 50s. Shorts and tee shirts cover most fashion needs, though one dressy outfit may prove useful.

Scuba divers visiting the Keys between December and March will find a shortie or lightweight wet suit appropriate. Water temperatures drop to the 70s. Winter snorkelers will be most comfortable with a lycra wetskin or light wet suit.

In the Everglades, long pants and long-sleeved shirts offer some protection from bug bites. During summer, mosquitos will bit you no matter what. Bring sunglasses and a hat that will shade your face.

■ Gear

See individual adventure chapters for details. If you are joining a special-interest tour group, avoid mix-ups by labeling all you bring. Colored plastic tape and permanent markers are waterproof.

Dive packages often include use of tanks and weights. Bring or plan to rent everything else. Snorkeling equipment is usually provided by the boat-tour and seaplane operators, but bringing your own insures a comfortable fit (see *Scuba* chapters).

Charter and party boats provide fishing gear. Just bring a cap with a wide brim. The marina stores are well-stocked with tackle and other

Route 29 cuts through Big Cypress National Preserve (© Jon Huber).

gear. Polarizing sunglasses such as Cabela's, Corning Serengeti Strata or Rayban are best for spotting fish in the mangrove flats.

Hikers wishing to explore off-the-beaten-track trails should wear submersible shoes. Bring the type with a non-slip sole that won't tear on sharp rocks. Aqua socks or strap-on kayaking sandals are perfect for sloshing around mangrove islands, beach combing and walking on coral rubble.

■ Sundries

Mosquito repellent is necessary, especially in summer. Resort areas in the Keys are thoroughly doused with pesticides each evening by a low-flying DC-3 (don't look up when you hear it coming), but state and national parks are considered natural areas and the mosquitoes are left unharmed. One gentle repellent that some find useful is Avon Skin So Soft. Off - Deep Woods is more potent and works well against mosquitoes and other stinging insects. Autan, if you can find it, is excellent. Deet is also effective.

Shopping centers selling everything are scattered throughout the Keys, and during winter months the camp store and restaurant at Flamingo are open. But off-season (March 15-Nov. 15), campers heading to the Everglades should pack some of everything needed.

Credit Cards

Except at some small motels, all major national and international credit cards are widely accepted throughout the Florida Keys. ATMs are found in the populated areas of the Keys. Personal checks are accepted in some stores with ID – a driver's license and a major credit card. You need a major credit card to rent a car.

*With rare exceptions, restaurants and stores in Everglades City do **not** accept credit cards.*

Banks

■ Main Offices

Barnett Bank of the Keys, 1010 Kennedy Drive, Key West. ☎ 292-3860

First State Bank, 1201 Simonton St., Key West. ☎ 296-8535

First Union Bank, 422 Front St., Key West. ☎ 292-6600

Nations Bank, 5401 Overseas Hwy., Marathon. ☎ 743-4121

TIB Bank, 994 Overseas Hwy., Key Largo. ☎ 451-4660

■ Foreign Currency Exchanges

Barnett Bank of the Keys. All Florida Keys locations: Key Largo, Tavernier, Islamorada, Marathon, Marathon Shores, Summerland Key, Key West.

First National Bank of the Florida Keys. All locations: Islamorada, Marathon, Marathon Shores, Key West.

Kelly's Motel. MM 104.2, Key Largo. ☎ 305-451-1622 (from foreign to US currency only).

Citgo Station. MM 92, Key Largo.

Key West Currency Exchange. 1007 Truman Ave., ☎ 305-292-0005.

Insurance

Standard **Blue Cross and Blue Shield** policies cover medical costs while traveling. Lost luggage insurance is available at the ticket counter of many airlines. If you have a homeowner's policy, you may already be covered. Some credit cards also cover losses while on vacation. Membership in the **American Automobile Association** covers unexpected road emergencies for auto travelers.

Inexpensive insurance for rental car mishaps is available from the rental agencies and is well worth the price.

Visitors from Great Britain may obtain traveler's coverage from **Europ Assistance**, 252 High St., Croydon, Surrey CRO 1NF, ☎ 01680-1234.

Scuba divers can get health insurance to cover accidents or emergencies that are a direct result of diving for a low annual fee from **Diver's Alert Network (DAN)**. A stay in a recompression chamber can amount to thousands of dollars and is often not covered by standard medical insurance. For information, stop in your local dive shop or write to DAN, PO Box 3823, Duke University Medical Center, Durham NC 27710, ☎ 919-684-2948.

Helpful Phone Numbers

Florida Keys travelers can take advantage of a new visitor assistance program (once they arrive at their destination) by calling ☎ 800-771-KEYS. A live, multilingual operator is available 24 hours a day, seven days a week, to answer any questions visitors may have. The help operator can give directions to lost motorists, either in the Keys or en route, and provide information on local medical facilities and auto repair centers.

Emergency (Police, Ambulance, Fire), ☎ 911

Mariners Hospital, MM 89, ☎ 305-852-4418

Fisherman's Hospital, MM 48.5, ☎ 305-743-5533

Florida Keys Health Systems, MM 5, ☎ 305-294-5531

Everglades National Park, ☎ 305-247-7700

Shark Valley, ☎ 305-221-8776

Gulf Coast, ☎ 941-695-3311

Biscayne National Park, ☎ 305-230-7275

Weather, ☎ 305-296-2741

Marine Patrol, ☎ 305-743-6542

Coast Guard

☎ 305-743-6388 or 743-6778

Miami area, ☎ 305-661-5065

Key West, ☎ 305-296-2011

Customs

Miami area, ☎ 305-536-4126

Key West, ☎ 305-296-4700

Chambers of Commerce/Visitor Information

Everglades City, ☎ 941-695-3941, fax 941-695-3172

Key Largo Information, ☎ 305-451-1414, 800-822-1088

Islamorada Information, ☎ 305-664-4503

Marathon Information, ☎ 305-743-5417

Lower Keys Information, ☎ 305-872-2411

Key West Information, ☎ 305-294-2587

Florida Keys & Key West Visitor's Bureau, PO Box 1147, Key West FL 33034; in the US, ☎ 800-FLA-KEYS; from outside the US, ☎ 305-296-3811; www.fla-keys.com.

Everglades National Park, 40001 State Road 9336, Homestead FL 33034; ☎ 305-242-7700; www.nps.gov/ever.

For the Ten Thousand Islands Region contact **Everglades Area Chamber of Commerce**, PO Box 130, Everglades City FL 33929; ☎ 941-695-3941; www.florida-everglades.com.

Introduction to the Keys & Everglades

Two worlds of beauty welcome visitors to the Florida Keys and Everglades – the only living coral reef system off the continental United States, and North America's last remaining wilderness swamp. Together they preserve some of America's most valued and unusual natural resources.

In fact, the entirety of the Florida Keys has been designated a National Marine Sanctuary and the Everglades is recognized as an International Biosphere Reserve and a World Heritage Site. Overall, the area encompasses five national parks – Everglades, Big Cypress, Biscayne, Dry Tortugas (formally Fort Jefferson National Monument) and the Florida Keys.

The Shipwreck Trail, managed by the Florida Keys National Marine Sanctuary, protects nine historic wreck sites, each marked with a spar buoy and accessible by private boat or dive shop charters.

With the exception of Dry Tortugas National Park, you can drive through and see the entire Florida Keys and main park area of the Everglades in three days. But to really savor this exotic environment it's best to put on your hiking shoes and head for the nature trails. Then tour the sea and waterways – go fishing, paddle a canoe, sign up for a glass-bottom boat tour, snorkel or dive the reefs, sail, birdwatch or join an Everglades slog (wet hike through water and mud).

The Florida Keys

Key Largo, the jump-off point to the Florida Keys, lies 42 miles south-southwest of Miami. The largest of the island chain, Key Largo features **John Pennekamp Coral Reef State Park**, the first underwater preserve in the United States, and the adjacent **Key Largo National Marine Sanctuary**. Key Largo also boasts the world's only underwater hotel. From Key Largo, the Keys arc southwesterly towards Cuba.

All points, from Key Largo to Key West, connect to the mainland and to each other by a cement and steel wonder, The Overseas Highway, a continuation of US 1, which follows the road bed of Henry Flagler's seagoing railroad, built in 1912 but destroyed by an unnamed hurricane in 1935.

This "highway that goes to sea" features 43 bridges and connects Key Largo to Islamorada, and the purple isles – Plantation Key, Windley Key and both Upper Matecumbe and Lower Matecumbe Key.

Known as the sportfishing capital of the world and heralded for its angling diversity, **Islamorada** features the Keys' largest fleet of offshore charter boats and shallow-water "backcountry" boats.

Marathon Key, the heart of the Florida Keys, houses the local **Museum of Natural History** and two golf courses. A drive across the Seven Mile Bridge from Marathon leads to the **Lower Keys** and Key West.

Crossing the Bahia Honda Bridge affords sweeping views of the Straits of Florida and the Gulf of Mexico. It brings you to **Bahia Honda State Park**, which features one of the top 10 beaches in the US.

Big Pine Key is noted for the **Looe Key National Marine Sanctuary**, a spectacular underwater park, and the **Key Deer Refuge**. **Key West**, the nation's southernmost city, marks the final stop on the Overseas Highway. Situated closer to Havana than Miami, Key West exerts a charm all its own, with quaint, palm-studded streets, century-old gingerbread mansions and a relaxed citizenry of self-styled "Conchs."

Resorts, recreational facilities, restaurants, and shopping areas pave the way from Key Largo to Key West.

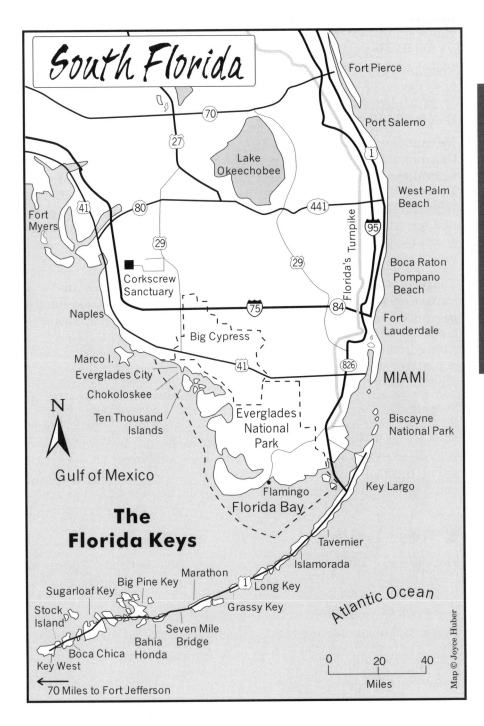

South Florida

Fort Pierce

70

27

Port Salerno

1

Lake
Okeechobee

West Palm
Beach

80

441

95

Fort
Myers

41

29

29

Boca Raton
Pompano
Beach

Florida's Turnpike

Corkscrew
Sanctuary

Naples

75

84

Fort
Lauderdale

Big Cypress

41

826

MIAMI

Marco I.

Everglades City

Chokoloskee

N

Ten Thousand
Islands

Everglades
National
Park

Biscayne
National Park

Gulf of Mexico

Flamingo

Florida Bay

Key Largo

The
Florida Keys

Tavernier

Islamorada

Marathon

Sugarloaf Key

Big Pine Key

1

Long Key

Stock
Island

Grassy Key

Atlantic Ocean

Seven Mile
Bridge

Boca Chica

Bahia
Honda

Key West

0   20   40

← 70 Miles to Fort Jefferson

Miles

Map © Joyce Huber

■ Florida Keys National Marine Sanctuary

Planning Office
9499 Overseas Hwy
Marathon 33050
☎ 305-743-2437

Future generations of visitors may expect to enjoy the continued pristine majesty of the Florida Keys' colorful living reefs thanks to a 1990 federal law designating the entire island chain as a National Marine Sanctuary. This status allows the designation of reef rejuvenation zones and fish nurseries – areas where diving and fishing are prohibited for selected time periods. These sheltered areas allow corals to grow and fish populations to expand. Similar procedures have already proven successful in the Caribbean.

The reefs, which lie six miles offshore and parallel the islands from Key Largo to Key West, attract millions of divers and fishermen annually. In addition to these recreational opportunities, the coral reefs protect the islands by forming a critical breakwater that diffuses the energy of storm-driven waves. The reefs also provide sand for Florida's beaches; scientists estimate that fish nibbling on corals and calcareous algae produce more than 2½ tons of sand per acre annually.

Touring the National Marine Sanctuary rates as one of the Florida Keys' biggest delights. You can view the reefs via dive, snorkel or glass-bottom boat. Expect miles of fish and other reef residents to line up and look you over. They will swim up to your mask and curiously peer back at you through the glass-bottom boat panes. (See *Boat Tours*, *Scuba* and *Snorkeling* chapters, pages 50, 134, 160, for details.)

■ Reef Balls

Florida Keys students from the Coral Shores High School in Islamorada, with help from government, public and private agencies, launched an artificial reef program consisting of three "reef balls" in 15 ft of water off Key Largo near Molasses Reef.

Reef balls imitate the appearance and function of natural coral reefs, with openings and canals that provide favorable habitats for marine life. The students built the balls themselves during 1999; the balls weigh between 400 and 1,000 pounds.

Juvenile corals transplanted onto the balls have been flourishing. The primary goal of the program is educational, but the site is open to divers and snorkelers who want to learn about habitat enhancement and the growth of coral. Global Positioning System coordinates are N 25°, 01.316 and W 080°, 23.783.

■ Dry Tortugas National Park

PO Box 6208
Key West FL
☎ 305-242-7700

Almost 70 miles west of Key West lie the Dry Tortugas, a cluster of seven uninhabited islands surrounded by healthy coral reefs and renowned as a stopover point during spring bird migations.

Besides providing a showcase for magnificent wildlife, the islands are the site of **Fort Jefferson**, America's largest 19th-century coastal fort.

Accessible only by boat or seaplane, the islands feature a visitor center on Garden Key, open daily from 8 am to 5 pm, and safe anchorage in the Tortugas harbor. Contact the park for a list of private carriers. No water, food, fuel, supplies or accommodations are available at the park. Visitors to the park enjoy good fishing, bird watching, snorkeling and self-guided tours of the fort. Bird checklists are available from the park. (See *Aerial Tours*, page 45, and *Boat Tours*, page 50.)

Tours of the Fort center around the parade ground, which contains the ghostly remains of two huge buildings: the Officers Quarters and Soldiers Barracks, which were the first structures begun after the fort was established.

The Everglades

The Everglades region, a great wilderness nurtured by a shallow freshwater river, flows across most of Florida's southern tip. Just six inches deep, but 50 miles wide, its riverbed originates at Lake Okeechobee and moves southward. Along its course it gradually drops 15 ft before emptying into Florida Bay and the Gulf of Mexico. The Indians call it *Pa-hay-okee*, the river of grass, for the dense prairies of razor-toothed sawgrass that grow in the river. Warmed by the tropical sun, the river breeds algae and insects that nurture fish, turtles and snakes. These, in turn, feed alligators and wading birds. Mounds of higher ground support groves or "hammocks" of hardwood trees, the showcases of the Everglades.

Snowy egrets, Everglades (© Jon Huber).

In remote areas, crocodiles share this vast marshland with rare Florida panthers, cougars and the gentle manatee, an aquatic, plant-eating mammal dubbed the sea cow for its huge proportions.

Geographically, the Everglades region covers seven million acres. Bounded by densely populated resort cities along the east coast and fringed by a maze of mangrove islands which rise from the Gulf of Mexico on its southe and western shores, the area encompasses Everglades National Park, Great Cypress National Park, Indian villages along Tamiami Trail, Collier-Seminole State Park, the National Audubon Society's Corkscrew Swamp Sanctuary and the Fakahatchie Preserve.

■ Everglades National Park

40001 State Road 9336,
Homestead FL 33034-6733
☎ 305-242-7700

Everglades National Park comprises just a small part of the Everglades' watery expanse. Established in 1947, the park covers some 1.5 million acres. Despite the park's size, its fragile environment is vulnerable to surrounding agriculture, industry and urban development.

During summer, the rainy season, the park presents visitors with a hostile expanse of wet sawgrass prairies, muddy trails and clouds of buzzing insects. But come the dry period from mid-November through mid-March, the clouds of bugs diminish, while sloughs and trails transform into a welcoming environment for hikers, bird watchers, canoeists, and fresh-water fishermen. Alligators and wading birds become easier to spot as they move to deep watering holes near the trails.

Impenetrable mangrove islands, known as the **Ten Thousand Islands**, web the entire western Gulf shoreline. Between the islands and the mainland exists a flat river, the **Wilderness Waterway**. Favored for rugged canoe camping expeditions, this shallow watercourse begins at **Everglades City**, then winds for about 100 miles through shallow creeks and bays to **Flamingo**, an outpost on Florida Bay, the south tip of Everglades National Park.

■ Big Cypress National Preserve

HCR 61, Box 11
Ochopee FL 33943
☎ 941-695-4111
www.nps.gov/bicy

Some consider Big Cypress National Preserve the "real Everglades" because it more closely resembles the Hollywood sets. Unlike other National Parks, and despite environmentalists' concerns, it is the one area where air-boats, swamp buggies and other off-road vehicles are allowed (by permit). Hunting and trapping continue. Big Cypress is also considered one of the best areas for fresh-water fishing.

A vast swamp more than 1,100 square miles in size, Big Cypress was given Park status to protect its giant cypress trees from their earlier fate as gutters, coffins, stadium seats, pickle barrels and the hulls of PT boats. In 1974, over 570,000 acres were set aside as a National Preserve. In addition to the cypress swamp, the park contains pine islands, wet and dry prairies and mangrove forests. Here, an occasional Florida panther leaves impressive paw marks. Black bears claw crayfish from the sloughs, or rip cabbage palmettos apart for their soft fruits.

Eleven thousand acres of Big Cypress are owned by the Audubon Society. Known as the **Corkscrew Swamp Sanctuary**, this particularly lovely area is a breeding ground for the endangered wood stork.

■ Biscayne National Park

PO Box 1369
Homestead FL 33090-1369
☎ 305-230-PARK
www.nps.gov/bisc

Biscayne National Park, 21 miles east of Everglades National Park and six miles east of Florida's Turnpike (Exit 6, Tallahassee Rd.), became a national monument in 1968. In 1980 it was enlarged and designated a national park. Most of it lies underwater. The park boundaries begin below Key Biscayne and encompass the reefs, islands and subsea area from the mainland to 15 miles offshore. The south end is at the tip of the Key Largo National Marine Sanctuary. Biscayne encompasses the uninhabited northern section of Key Largo, Elliot Key, Sands Key, Boca Chita Key and some private islands to the north, the Ragged Keys. The entire area rates high for canoeing, kayaking, fishing, diving, snorkeling and wilderness camping.

The Intracoastal waterway runs through the park boundaries. To reach Biscayne's **Convoy Point Visitor Center** take either Florida's Turnpike to Exit 6, Tallahassee Rd., or travel nine miles east from US 1, Homestead, on SW 328th St. (North Canal Drive). Public boat tours leave from Convoy Point. Diving and snorkeling trips can be arranged at the ranger station. Anglers and boaters may launch their own boats at the Homestead Bayfront Park boat ramp next to Convoy Point. WaveRunners and Jet Skis are **not** allowed in the park.

Environments

In recent years we've realized technology's enormous impact on south Florida's parks and sanctuaries. The emergence of air-conditioning, scuba equipment and air travel during the 1920s and '30s laid the groundwork for south Florida's current status as a vacation and retirement capital.

During the first half of the 20th century, native deer, panther, bear, alligators, birds and fish were hunted to near-extinction; coral reefs were ripped up for souvenirs. Conch beds were harvested until they were bare. Huge turtles that nested on the shores were slaughtered for their shells and meat. Wintering manatees died as high-speed, outboard motors severed their limbs and slashed their soft skin to ribbons. Ocean pollution killed off soft coral gardens and obliterated sea grasses. Flocks of sea birds that once blackened the skies dwindled down. Signature flamingos vanished. By the mid-1940s environmentalists' concern led to significant changes. Today's legislature and replenishment programs offer protection for sensitive areas of the ecosystem. In Florida Bay the US Fish and Wildlife Service regulates access to 26 areas of critical concern to wildlife, especially birds and threatened or endangered species. Most areas are small mangrove islands. Some are totally restricted; others allow boats to approach by paddle or push pole only.

On the ocean reefs, replenishment reserves protect and enhance the spawning, nursery and permanent resident areas of fish and other marine life. Some areas restrict fishing, but allow diving; others are "no-take" areas. Prime environs of concern are shallow, heavily used reefs where conflicts occur between divers, fishermen, and different user groups. Special-use areas exist for education, science, restoration, monitoring or research. Currently, Conch Reef (off Tavernier), Looe Key (off Big Pine Key), and Pelican Shoals and Tennessee Reef (off

Long Key), are continually evaluated with update cycles that modify or eliminate areas as appropriate.

Jet Skis and WaveRunners, which disturb nesting birds and other wildlife, have been outlawed in Biscayne National Park, Everglades National Park, Dry Tortugas National Park and areas of the Florida Keys National Sanctuary. Studies by the National Park Service and the US Fish & Wildlife Service have indicated that users of Jet Skis and Waverunners tend to disturb the wildlife, particularly nesting bird colonies. Most other types of boating activities do not significantly disturb wildlife.

Before diving, fishing, snorkeling, kayaking or boating on your own, check with local shops and operators for a list of restricted areas. For additional information, events, or sanctuary regulations, write to the **Florida Keys National Marine Sanctuary**, Main House, 5550 Overseas Hwy., Marathon FL 33050. ☎ 305-743-2437. Or visit the website at www.fknms.nos.noaa.gov/.

■ Water Management

Efficient water management is the first line of defense for Everglades wildlife.

Weather has a powerful effect on the nutrient levels in Florida Bay and Everglades marshlands. During long dry periods, water runoff carrying nutrients and pesticides from dairy and sugar cane farms drains into the canals and wetlands – beginning at Lake Okeechobee then detouring hundreds of miles through residential areas, before reaching the Everglades wilderness areas. The chemically treated water eventually reaches Florida Bay and the Gulf of Mexico.

During these periods of drought, phosphorus dumped into Lake Okeechobee can raise levels of nitrates and phosphates to 20 times higher than the low amounts once found in the sanctuaries. Beneficial algae and oxygen-producing aquatic plants – the spawning ground for fish – are choked out by cattails, which thrive in the phosphate-rich water. On the other hand, periods of heavy rainfall greatly lower the nitrate and phosphate levels and help balance the chemical makeup.

■ Algae Blooms

In the ocean and salt-water bays, Florida Bay in particular, an over-abundance of nutrients produces algae blooms, which choke out living corals, sponges and turtle grasses. This has a profound effect on the entire ecosystem, as sponges are the main habitat for juvenile spiny lob-

Dolphins off Grassy Key (© Jon Huber).

sters and seagrasses are the primary nursery ground for pink shrimp. Algae blooms have also caused seagrass to die off on the Atlantic Ocean side of the Keys near the coral reefs.

At times the algae bloom has covered more than 400 square miles. Sea urchins, which once kept the algae in check, mysteriously died off in 1983. A demand for seafood has caused a large decline in algae-eating fish from over-harvesting.

■ Recovery Programs

Laws have been passed to return the entire waterflow of south Florida to a more natural state. The Dairy Rule of 1987 requires that runoff from pastures be directed into holding ponds. The Surface Water Improvement and Management Act requires pollution reduction and environmental controls by all water management districts. Proposals that huge tracts of farmland be used for pollution filtration are under consideration.

■ Parks Play an Important Role

Giving park and marine sanctuary status to larger areas of the region has helped to protect the environment, fund research studies, and educate the public through the issuance of literature, ranger-led tours and other activities.

■ The Manatee

The West Indian manatee, a large gray-brown, herbivorous, aquatic mammal found in Florida's shallow coastal waters, canals, rivers and springs, has become a highly endangered species. Population studies indicate that there may be as few as 1,200 manatees left in Florida waters. Many are killed or severely injured by power boats. Habitat destruction puts these docile creatures in jeopardy. Manatees are protected by the Marine Mammal Protection Act of 1972, the Endangered Species Act of 1973 and the Florida Manatee Sanctuary Act of 1978. It is illegal to harass, harm, pursue, hunt, shoot, wound, kill, annoy or molest manatees.

To report manatee deaths, injuries, harassment or radio-tagged manatees, call the Florida Marine Patrol at ☎ 800-DIAL-FMP.

■ The Beached-Animal Rescue & Rehabilitation Program

After the Marine Mammal Protection Act of 1972 and the Endangered Species Act of 1973 were passed, marine specialists at Sea World of Florida were approached to aid in the rescue of beached or stranded marine mammals. In cooperation with the Department of the Interior, the National Marine Fisheries Service, the Florida Department of Natural Resources and the Florida Marine Patrol, Sea World developed the Beached Animal Rescue and Rehabilitation Program in 1973. Since that time, animal care specialists have responded to hundreds of calls to aid sick, injured or orphaned manatees, dolphins, whales, otters, sea turtles and a variety of birds.

Sea World bears all costs of the rescue program, including those for research, transportation and rehabilitation. As a result of research conducted by their animal husbandry staff in aviculture, animal care and aquarium departments, valuable baseline data is being established and shared with scientists worldwide. Food preferences, responses to antibiotic therapy, the safest transportation equipment and the swiftest rescue techniques have been documented by the staff. This data is invaluable in the effort to protect marine mammals from extinction. Sea World is the larger of the two facilities in the state that are authorized to rescue, care for and release manatees.

Mangroves, Ten Thousand Islands (© Jon Huber).

Environments

■ Seabird Sanctuary

The **Florida Keys Wild Bird Rehabilitation Center** in Tavernier offers visitors a close encounter with recuperating pelicans, spoonbills, hawks, herons, owls and ospreys . Many of the injured and orphaned birds can be treated and returned to the wild to live on their own. Executive Director Laura Quinn and center volunteers are licensed by the Florida Fish and Game commission and are members of the National Wildlife Rehabilitators Association. The rehabilitators work in conjunction with local veterinary clinics to aid birds with eye, neck, chest, wing and leg injuries.

The center's educational efforts include information on handling injured birds and techniques for removing fishing lures and hooks. (See *EcoTips*, pages 108-109 and 111, for details.)

■ Dolphin Sanctuaries

Injured or ailing dolphins and those stressed out from performing in circuses and attractions are finding rest and retirement care at the

Grassy Key Research Center, part of the Theatre of the Sea, Islamorada, and at holding pens which are being set up in the Keys.

■ Reef Relief

Many factors, both natural and resulting from human intrusion, contribute to the destruction of a coral reef. Some relief has been gained by the mooring buoy system, one of the most effective programs to reduce anchor damage and to provide boaters with a convenient means of securing their boats in the sanctuary. The buoys are available on a first-come, first-served basis for everyone.

■ Turtle Hospital

Richie Moretti and partner Tina Brown operate the first turtle hospital in what used to be an exotic dance lounge, next to the Hidden Harbor Motel in Marathon (☎ 800-362-3495).

The turtle hospital has complete surgical facilities, including a sterilized operating room, pre- and post-operative care and a research room. An apartment for a live-in veterinarian is situated above the hospital.

The endangered green turtle, *chelonia mydas*, named for its greenish color, can weigh up to 330 pounds and is characterized by a pair of scales on the front of its head, a white or yellowish bottom shell and paddle-shaped flippers with one claw.

Roughly half the green sea turtle population is suffering from the plague *fibropapilloma*, a mysterious disfiguring disease that causes tumors to grow internally and on the fleshy parts of the turtle's eyes, mouth, neck, flippers, jaw and tail. The tumors get so big that they blind the turtle. The sick turtles eventually starve or drown.

Currently, researchers associate the tumors with a type of herpes virus. Moretti and Brown are working with University of Florida veterinarian Elliot Jacobson to pinpoint the cause and find a cure for *fibropapilloma*.

Jacobson's research and travel to and from Marathon are supported in part by the Save the Turtles organization. Moretti has converted one of his motel swimming pools into a saltwater holding area for ailing turtles. Guests at Hidden Harbor can observe the ongoing research.

■ Eco-Tips

Help our finned and web-footed friends stay healthy by practicing good diving, snorkeling and boating habits. The following tips developed by leading ocean environmentalists provide a good start.

Protect Key Deer

Though they are hard to resist, do not offer treats to the pint-sized Key deer in the lower Keys. Feeding lures them onto the roadway where many have been struck by cars, or into residential areas, where they may be killed or harrassed by family dogs.

Dispose of Trash Properly

Each year more than 100,000 marine animals die from eating or becoming entangled in plastic debris. Sea turtles, whales, dolphins, manatees, fish and sea birds mistake plastic bags and balloons for jellyfish. Swallowing a plastic bag or balloon has caused many of these animals a slow and painful death by blocking their digestive tracts, thus starving them to death.

Sea birds' bills and heads have gotten twisted up in the plastic rings from six-packs of beer and soda cans.

You can help prevent these mishaps by disposing of all your trash properly and discouraging others from throwing trash overboard.

Never release a helium-filled balloon into the air. Pick up any discarded fishing line you see around docks and marinas. Plastic six-pack rings should be cut up before placement in the trash or recycling bin.

Hit the Beach

Fourteen billion pounds of garbage are dumped in the world's oceans each year, most of it in the Northern Hemisphere. Volunteers for the Center for Marine Conservation have collected nearly 900 tons of beach trash. In one cleanup, 8,000 plastic bags were found along the shores of North Carolina.

If you want to find out about beach cleanups, contact the **Center for Marine Conservation**, 1725 De Sales St. NW, Suite 600, Washington, DC 20036, ☎ 202-429-5609, www.cmc-ocean.org.

Environments

Practice Good Buoyancy Control

Learn to adjust weights and vest or jacket inflation to maintain neutral buoyancy. This enables you to hang in place without kicking up the bottom or surrounding corals, critters and fellow divers.

Avoid Dangle Damage

Dangling consoles, gauges, cameras, and other assorted dive gear and instruments wreak havoc when they bang into delicate corals and tiny invertebrates, often crushing or battering tiny critters to death. Avoid slamming gear into your subsea surroundings. (Courtesy of Paul Sieswerda, Collection Manager, New York Aquarium.)

Keep Your Hands to Yourself

Mother Nature protects fishes' bodies from bacterial invasion with a layer of invisible slime. Even gently touching a fish disturbs the slime layer and produces an area similar to a burn on human skin. The fish may seem fine when it swims away, but two days later it will suffer skin infections where touched. If you are in a marine sanctuary that allows hand-feeding of fish, avoid the temptation to pet or handle them. (Courtesy of Paul Sieswerda.)

Watch Your Bubbles

Long stays under ledges or in any area where your exhaust bubbles can't rise to the surface can create air pockets that may engulf overhead sea anemones and stationary invertebrates. Being trapped in your air will cause them to dry out and die. Use discretion. (Courtesy of Paul Sieswerda.)

Keep Sea Snacks All-Natural

Feeding fish is frowned upon in all but a few marine sanctuaries. Hand-feeding lessens the animals' instinctive reaction to flee, and certain foods eaten by humans can be unhealthy and often fatal to fish. In areas such as Honduras and Mexico, where spear fishing is a way of life for the local population, the grouper or turtle that befriends snack-carrying, vacationing divers will be speared first.

In areas where fish feeding is acceptable, be sure to feed only foods that a fish or turtle would naturally eat. Frozen squid or freeze-dried shrimp or flakes are acceptable choices. Fishin' Chips makes waterproof cardboard dispensers that hold pop-out pills. The pills are an all-natural fish food that stay dry until use, don't cloud the water and are available at many dive shops; ☎ 800-522-4269 for sales locations. Be sure to recycle the packaging!

Desilt Sponges & Corals

To breathe and eat, sponges must be able to suck in water containing oxygen and nutrients. Wave action cleanses them of most natural silting, but they have no mechanism to rid themselves of silt kicked up by divers and snorkelers.

If you see a silt-covered sponge or coral, give it a hand by fanning the surrounding water to "blow" off the residue. (Courtesy of Dee Scarr, Touch the Sea, Bonaire.)

Bailout a Crab

Plastic materials are often smoother than some ocean animals' feet were meant to walk on. Plastic buckets lying mouth-up on the sea floor trap hermit crabs, who crawl in, then can't get out. They eat the bottom ring of algae, then slowly starve to death.

When you see a new bucket or container on the sea floor, simply bring it back up to the surface and dispose of it properly. If the bucket is coral-encrusted on the outside, leave it, but put a pile of debris or coral rubble inside to form an exit ramp for wandering crabs. If no rubble is at hand, cut an escape hole in the bottom or side with your dive knife or shears. Take care not to handle any coral directly or you may get a nasty infection and damage the coral. (Courtesy of Dee Scarr.)

Boaters Obey Restricted Access Signs

Boaters should stay a minimum distance of 100 yards from bird roosting, nesting and feeding areas. If your presence appears to be flushing birds from their activities, you are too close and should move farther away.

Approach Seagrass Beds Gently

Seagrass beds provide nursery areas, feeding habitat and shelter for a wide variety of marine animals. Alert and knowledgeable boaters can help protect this precious resource.

Continued accidental groundings and turbidity from boat wakes can destroy seagrass beds. Recovery may take as long as 10 years.

Environments

Use current navigation charts and make sure you have adequate water depth to avoid scraping the flats. Color changes in the water indicate differences in depth and bottom types. Shallow seagrass beds, hard-bottom, patch reefs and sand shoals in near-shore areas will appear beige, brown or light green. Deeper adjacent waters are darker green. Polarized sunglasses greatly enhance your ability to detect subtle differences in water color.

History

On Easter Sunday, May 15, 1513, adventurer Ponce de Leon and fellow Spanish chronicler Antonio de Herrera first sighted a chain of islands just north of the Bahamas.

From the explorer's ships, the Keys resembled men huddled over in pain. Thus, to this line of islands and rock islets they gave the name of *Los Martires* because the rocks as they rose to view appeared like men who were suffering; the name remained fitting because of the many lives that have been lost there since. The surrounding area was given the Spanish name for Easter – *Pascuas Florida*.

The Keys were wild and hostile during the 1500s. Indians, who fished, shelled and hunted the area, fought off any Europeans who approached the shore. Overall, the area was undesirable for anything but a stopover for fresh turtle meat. The Spaniards owned Florida until 1763, when they traded it to the British for Havana; however, by 1783 it was back under Spanish rule. In 1818, under President Thomas Jefferson's leadership, the US bought Florida for five million dollars.

■ The Indians

The Calusa and Tekesta Indians first populated the southern Everglades and the Keys. To the north were the Seminoles and Miccosukees. Word of Bahamian natives being carried from their homeland and forced into slavery by the white man prepared the Calusas to defend their freedom. Early attempts by the Spaniards to settle in the Keys were met with the sting of arrows. In 1521, a band of Calusas in primitive canoes attacked approaching Spaniards. Among those struck down was Ponce de Leon when an arrow pierced his suit of armor. He later died in Havana. Wars between the Indians and the white man raged for centuries. Many of the original Indian tribes died from white man's diseases; some were taken into slavery by the Spaniards and moved to Cuba and other areas of the Caribbean.

Many runaway black slaves sought refuge in the Everglades and were taken in by the Indians. This, along with border disputes, fueled the Indian battles with the US. By 1817, US troops led by Andrew Jackson forced most of the Indians to reservations in the West. But one tribe, the Seminoles, never surrendered to US forces. Indian attacks on the Keys continued into the mid 1880s.

Descendants of the Seminoles and the Miccosukees still populate the Everglades region and still display some measure of mistrust toward outsiders. Both tribes migrated from Georgian Creek tribes during the early 1700s in search of better fishing, hunting and farm lands. They found all three in the Everglades.

Shallow off-shore oyster beds provided the Indians with an easy food source. The cast-off shells grew into huge mounds which today attract interest as archaeological finds and are protected in Everglades National Park as historic preserves. Mound researchers have uncovered ancient tools, pottery, animal and human bones.

On the other hand, Chokoloskee Island, a huge shell mound in the northwest Everglades region, has been paved over and made into an RV camp.

■ Pirates

In the years following Ponce de Leon's first sighting, many Spanish and British vessels cruising the Florida straits became targets of piracy – first by the Indians, later by notorious figures like Henry Morgan, Blackbeard, Gasparilla, Black Caesar, and Lafitte. The pirates' small boats easily out-maneuvered and outran the huge pursuing Navy frigates. By 1821, attacks on US shipping became common and continued until 1823, when the US government dispatched Commodore David Porter, who swiftly replaced the large frigates with small schooners and one old ferry boat. Once they were able to negotiate the shallows, Porter's men put a fast end to piracy.

■ Forts

After Florida became part of the United States in 1821, military officials recognized the strategic importance of the Dry Tortugas. The nation that occupied the islands would control navigation in the Gulf.

Fort Jefferson – the "Gibraltar of the Gulf" – was built on Garden
Key in the mid-1800s and lies among a cluster of seven coral islands
that form the Dry Tortugas National Park. The fort walls measure
eight ft thick and 50 ft high. The three gun tiers are designed for 450
guns.

The fort was never fired upon, but during the Civil War it served as a
military prison for captured deserters. For almost 10 years after the
fighting stopped, it remained a prison. Among the prisoners sent here
in 1865 were four of the so-called "Lincoln conspirators" – Michael
O'Loughlin, Sammuel Arnold, Edward Spangler, and Dr. Samuel
Mudd – who had been tried and convicted of complicity in the assassination of Abraham Lincoln. The most famous of these was Dr. Mudd, a
Maryland physician who, knowing nothing of Lincoln's murder, had
set the broken leg of the fugitive assassin, John Wilkes Booth. Sen-
tenced to life imprisonment, Mudd was pardoned in 1869 for helping to
fight the 1867 yellow fever epidemic that struck the fort, felling 270 of
the 300-man garrison and resulting in 38 fatalities.

The cell occupied by Dr. Mudd during his years of confinement can still
be seen at the fort today.

It took 21 years of hard labor, hurricanes and yellow fever epidemics –
from 1854 to 1866 – for the trapezoid-shaped **Ford Zachary Taylor**
on Key West to be built. During the Civil War, the Union controlled the
fort on the island with strong local support. Fort Taylor was the home
base for a successful blockade of Confederate ships, and some histori-
ans say the blockade cut a year off the War between the States. Two
more Key West forts, the **East** and **West Martello Towers**, were authorized by Congress in 1844 to protect Fort Taylor from enemy attack,
but neither was ever completed. Fort Taylor is believed to hold the largest number of Civil War artifacts in the nation and has become a major
archaeological treasure.

History

■ Wrecking & Sponging

The absence of lighthouses and reliable charts made early ocean travel
hazardous in the shallow waters surrounding the Florida Keys. During storms many ships crashed on the reefs and became prey to wreckers, who often killed all aboard for the possibility of treasure.

By the 1830s, law and order prevailed and a more civilized type of salvaging came into play. Upon sighting floundering ships, the wreckers sailed out and saved the passengers and cargo in return for 25% of the haul. Wrecking became Key West's most profitable industry, though some say the ships were still deliberately lured onto the shoals. Non-farming settlers in Key West and at Islamorada became wreckers and Key West became the wealthiest city in the infant United States Republic from the bounty of that profitable industry. By 1886, the availability of improved charts, the advent of steam-powered ships, and the construction of lighthouses and lighted marker towers on the reefs put an end to the wrecking business. Carysfort Light, off Key Largo, was the first of the navigational beacons.

Sponge farming and exporting soon replaced the Key West wrecking industry. By the turn of the century, Key West grossed $750,000 yearly in sponge sales. Sponging continued till 1904 when over-harvesting depleted the supply. Greek spongers were blamed. Unlike Keys spongers, who harvested by reaching down with long hooked poles, the Greeks dove down to the sponge beds wearing weighted metal boots and diving helmets, enabling them to gather more sponges. Local workers claimed the Greek's heavy boots were destroying the sponge seeds and ruining the gardens. The industry moved to Tarpon Springs, where it thrived until 1938, when a blight dried up Florida's days as a major sponge producer.

■ Farming & Shark Skins

In 1822 Key West became the Keys' first permanent settlement. Spaniards who first set foot on the island found it littered with piles of bones and thus named it Island of Bones or Cayo Hueso – a name that later became Anglicized as Key West.

Early settlers farmed productive groves of Key limes, tamarind and breadfruit. In the lower Keys, pineapple farms flourished, producing up to one million crates a year. Besides fresh fruit sales, a Keys processing factory shipped canned pineapple to most of Eastern North America. As air transportation and refrigeration improved, Hawaiian plantations eventually took over the pineapple market.

Cigar maker Raul Castro (right) offers his wares at the Southern Cross Club, Key West (© Jon Huber).

In later years, a thriving shark factory was established on Big Pine Key amidst the abandoned farms. It employed workers to catch sharks and skin the hides, which were then salted down and sent north to a factory in New Jersey. There they were processed into a tough leather called shagreen, an abrasive skin used by cabinet makers for sandpaper.

■ Plume Hunting

In the 1870s, those in the forefront of women's fashion dictated the use of huge feathers in their hats. Plume hunting grew to enormous proportions in the Everglades. Greedy hunters ravaged the nesting grounds of egrets and herons, killing thousands of birds for the millinery trade. Desperate to stop the slaughter, the Audubon Society sent game wardens to protect the rookeries. Finally, the public took notice when newspapers covered the death of Guy Bradley, a game warden murdered by plume hunters. By 1890, the bird population was badly depleted, but national publicity about the murder raised public concern and brought an end to plume hunting.

■ Cigars

During the mid 1800s, Cuban cigar makers established factories in Key West. By 1880, 166 cigar factories produced over 100 million cigars per year. But once again, Key West's golden days were numbered. Continuing labor disputes forced the cigar industry to Tampa. The year 1880 also marked the beginning of talk about draining the Everglades for farmland.

■ The Spanish-American War

Key West took on historic importance when its harbor served as a port for warships during the Spanish-American War. Though Tampa was the principal base for military activity, the Key West Navy Yard, just 90 miles from Havana, became a jumping-off point for hospital and supply ships. At a special memorial in the Key West cemetery rest the bodies of those who died when the US battleship *Maine* was sunk in Havana's Harbor in 1898, the event that touched off the Spanish-American War.

■ Flagler's Railroad

In 1903, railroad tycoon Henry Flagler built his impossible "railroad that went to sea," on which wealthy visitors traveled to vacation in the Florida Keys. The railroad extended service from Homestead to Key West and to Cuba by sea-going ferries that carried the rail cars across the Gulf. On Labor Day in 1935, a nameless hurricane ravaged the Keys with 200-mph winds and an 18-ft tidal surge. It ripped out the huge caissons that the railroad builders had constructed to connect the islands. Though most of the bridges held up, the rail beds on the lowlands were destroyed. They were never rebuilt. Sections of the old railroad bridges remain and can be seen in the lower Keys.

■ Pan Am

During the 1920s, aviation started to take over where the rail and ferry left off, and America's fascination with air travel blossomed. Pan Am, the pioneer of the air, opened a magnificent art deco seaplane base in Miami at Dinner Key for their "Flying Clipper Ship" on January 9, 1929. The Postal Service, eager for mail service between Key West and Cuba, awarded a contract to Pan Am, whose owners had already obtained a contract from Cuba for mail from Havana to Key West. Pan Am owners Juan Trippe and John Hambleton convinced Cuba's dicta-

The Maine *Monument, Key West (© Jon Huber)*

tor Gerardo Machado to give them exclusive rights to take off and land on Cuban soil, thus forcing competitors to pursue other interests. The mail was to be flown in a Fokker tri-motor plane, but it could not be delivered when a storm flooded Key West's landing field. Instead, pilot Cy Caldwell flew the first air mail from Key West to Cuba in a Fairchild FC-2 float plane, *La Nina*. Pan Am opened a small office in Key West (now Kelly's Restaurant) to service flights bound for Havana.

In 1928 the price of a Havana-to-Key West ticket was $50 one-way. The 90-mile crossing took 1¼ hours.

■ Depression Years

Aviation bolstered travel to Cuba and the Caribbean during the '30s, but did little for the Keys. As the nation faced war and the Great Depression, the Keys faced a bleak future. The city of Key West went bankrupt.

It was then, with Federal aid, that Keys officials decided they still had something to offer – the sea, sun and a good winter climate. In the somewhat beaten-down, shabby gentility of the 1930s, the idea of a highway to replace the railroad was born. The famed Florida Keys Overseas Hwy. (US 1) opened in 1938. Three years later, World War II dashed all the prospects of tourist gold.

The US Navy came to the rescue again to build a submarine base in Key West. Shrimp were discovered – the Keys' now vital pink gold – and, following the war, the tourists finally began to stream in.

■ The Tamiami Trail

Most of the western Everglades region remained largely unexplored until 1915, when construction of the Tamiami Trail began. Workmen were plagued by mosquitoes and snakes. Many deaths resulted from snakebites and related fungus infections. Armed guards were eventually hired to shoot the snakes. A good portion of the roadbed was built on wet mud, which often caused the heavy machinery to sink or fall over. Completion seemed impossible. Work crews endured despite the hardships, and the 120-mile road linking Miami to Tampa was dedicated on April 26, 1928. With the completion of the Tamiami Trail and, in 1938, the first overseas highway from the mainland to Key West, commercialization of the area began. Tourism and land development have since boomed.

Outdoor Adventures

Aerial Tours

If light plane tours are a new addition to your adventure list, be sure to book an early-morning flight on a day with calm winds. Rising columns of air that cause light aircraft to bounce are more prevalent as afternoon sun heats the ground. Winds, if gusting, may also cause a bumpy ride. Be sure to bring binoculars and a camera.

Most sightseeing tours skirt the Atlantic side of the islands, where intriguing panoramas of sun, sand and sea await. As you climb, the view stretches to an azure horizon dotted with sparkling white dive- and fishing boats. Dolphin sightings are frequent and on clear days you can easily pick out individual snorkelers and swimmers.

If you choose to go sightseeing over the Everglades wilderness, you'll enjoy breathtaking views of vast marshlands and the varied plant communities that thrive there.

Crossing the Everglades at low altitude, you may spot the silhouette of a manatee or a huge alligator beneath the water's surface. West of Everglades City, in the Ten Thousand Island region, narrow waterways twist and turn into a mosaic of exotic shapes.

Private light-plane sightseeing tours to any point in the Keys are offered by **Grant Air**, based at Marathon Airport. Half-hour flights in Cessna 172s or 177s (four-seat, high-wing aircraft) start at $99 for three passengers. Custom tours can be arranged. No reservations needed; just follow the signs at the airport. ☎ 305-743-1995.

■ By Seaplane

Foremost in out-island tour popularity are half-day seaplane excursions to **Fort Jefferson** in the Dry Tortugas. Located 70 miles west of Key West, the fort is the most inaccessible National Monument in the Western Hemisphere. The islands, off the beaten path, were named for

*Fort Jefferson, now a National Monument, can be visited by boat
or charter seaplane from Key West.*

their lack of fresh water and once-abundant turtle population. Today, prime attractions are the spectacular snorkeling found on the surrounding coral reefs and a chance to explore the historic, hexagonal, brick fort where Dr. Samuel Mudd was imprisoned for his alleged part in the assassination of President Lincoln.

On the flight out you'll spot numerous shipwrecks and the treasure site of Spanish galleons, **Atocha** and **Margarita**. When the sea is calm, the clear waters of the Gulf magnify an outline of the wrecks. Flights can be booked through **Sea Planes of Key West** at Key West International Airport. Half-day trips start at $159 per person, full-day ,$275. Overnight round-trip for campers, $299 (subject to change with fuel prices). Rate includes use of snorkeling gear, soft drinks and drinking water. Flights are aboard stable, float-equipped, high-wing, four- and seven-seat aircraft. The floats also have retractable wheels, which allow them to take off from the land airport then set down in the water at Garden Key. ☎ 305-294-0709.

Garden Key has restrooms, but no food or beverage service. You must bring everything with you. Passengers are advised to pack their own snacks and cold beverages.

The flight time ranges from 30 to 40 minutes.

About Fort Jefferson

Situated on Garden Key, the immense 50-ft-high fort was once considered a strategic point for controlling navigation through the Gulf. Construction of the brick and stone fort was started in 1846, and, although work continued for almost 30 years, little was done after 1866. Updated weaponry introduced during the war, particularly the rifled cannon, had made the fort obsolete.

Moreover, in 1864 engineers discovered that the fort's foundations rested not upon a solid coral reef as originally thought, but upon sand and coral boulders washed up by the sea. As the huge structure settled, the eight-foot-thick walls began to crack. Though never a target of military action, the fort served as a prison for Civil War deserters and periodically as an anchorage for the American naval fleet. The Army abandoned the fort in 1874 following a damaging hurricane and an outbreak of yellow fever. In 1935, President Franklin D. Roosevelt rescued the fort from oblivion and proclaimed the area a national monument.

■ By Open Cockpit

For a romantic tour of Old Key West, hop into the front seat of an open-cockpit biplane. Bring a friend; it seats two. The pilot rides in the back. Helmets and goggles are supplied.

Fred Cabanas, chief pilot and owner of **Island Aeroplane Tours** offers a wide range of scenic flights. Choose a ride over south-shore beaches and island resorts; or a view of Mallory Square and Old Town Key West; an island shipwreck excursion which takes you over Channel West of Fleming Key; or combine them all with a coral-reef tour. Fred's "See-it-All" tour starts over a visual maze of coral reefs, then heads west to Boca Grand Island (13 miles west of Key West), over Woman Key, Man Key and Ballast Key. The over-ocean flights offer excellent photo opportunities. Passengers often spot sharks, rays and migrating schools of fish. Rates vary depending on air time and are apt to fluctuate. All flights depart Key West International Airport. Island Aeroplane Tours is just off South Roosevelt Boulevard at Key West Airport. ☎ 305-294-TOUR (8687) for reservations.

■ Aerobatic Flights

If flying over the ocean in an antique biplane isn't adventure enough, tighten your leather helmet and goggles for the ultimate – an aerobatic ride in a Pitts S-2C. You've always wanted to be a stunt pilot and do a loop? Great! Strap yourself in and take a lesson. For a moment the ocean becomes the sky, and the sky the sea below. Do this before lunch.

Aerial Tours

Ultralight seaplane, Windley Key (courtesy Extreme Sports Florida Keys).

Reluctant companions can relax, knowing the aerobatic flights are single-passenger only. Instructor-pilot Fred Cabanas flies 3,500 passengers a year and holds an Air Transport rating. Also at Island Aeroplane Tours. ☎ 305-294-TOUR.

■ For the Traditionalist

Flights in a standard, high-wing, four-seat Cessna are offered by **Island City Flying Service** at Key West International Airport. While these flights may not provide quite the romance and adventure of water flying or barnstorming in an open-cockpit, the view is still splendid and the price tag a bit lower; in the front seat you can open the window and take pictures. Aim straight down to keep the wing strut out of the shot. You can also arrange for a night flight over the city. Rates start at $110 for a 40-minute flight that carries from one to three people in a high-wing Cessna 172. Flying lessons are offered too. Call for reservations at ☎ 305-296-5422; or write to Island City Flying Service, 3471 South Roosevelt Boulevard, Key West FL 33040.

■ Ultra-Light Lessons

Learn to fly a Quicksilver ultra-light on floats at **Flying Fish Flight School** in the Coconut Cove marina. An ultralight is similar to a hang

Skydiving, Key West (courtesy Sky Dive Key West).

glider, but with a motor. Ten hours of lessons are required to qualify for an ultralight license. Students learn about wind and weather, basic flight maneuvers and hazards. Landings are in the water. A 20-minute introductory flight costs $55, a one-hour lesson, $100, ultralight pilot license instruction, $1,000. Call for a reservation.

Coconut Cove is at Mile Marker 85, 84801 Overseas Hwy., Islamorada FL. ☎ 305-664-4055 or 877-YES-2-FLY. E-mail: seagliders@yahoo.com.

Before your trip, we suggest you read The "Ultralight Pilots Flight Training Manual" by Curtiss Hughes. You can order a copy from the United States Ultralight Association, PO Box 667, Frederick, MD 21705; ☎ 301-695-9100, fax 301-695-0763 or visit their website at www. usua.com.

Aerial Tours

■ Skydiving

Sky Dive Key West offers a personal "Dropzone," with spectacular views from two miles up as you plummet towards earth at 120 mph and land in a soft, grassy field.

After watching a brief training tape you join an instructor for a tandem skydive and experience the rush of jumping out of "a perfectly good airplane." The 10,000-ft jump includes a 40-second free fall. If all goes well, this is followed by a 5½-minute, steerable ram-air canopy ride. Be sure to spring for the video or still photos of your jump. Jumpers must be at least 18 years old.

Sky Dive Key West is located at Sugarloaf Airport, MM 17, Sugarloaf Key. Take US 1 to Sugarloaf Lodge and turn at the airplane. ☎ 800-YOU JUMP (800-968-5867). Visit their website at www.skydivekeywest.com. E-mail: skydivekeywest@aol.com.

Boat Tours

■ The African Queen

MM 100, Oceanside
Holiday Inn
Key Largo
☎ 305-451-4655

Half-hour cruises aboard the *African Queen* depart from the Holiday Inn docks. Powered by the original engine, the *Queen* lets off steam as the first mate sounds the fog horn and pulls away from the dock. The ride lasts from 45 minutes to an hour.

Occasionally, owner James Hendricks joins the tour and shares his photo journal, which is passed around. It includes notes to Hendricks from Katherine Hepburn, foreign dignitaries, and photos from his European, Canadian, Australian and US tours. Upon return, passengers are given honorary *African Queen* captain licenses and a postcard of her for remembrance. Hendricks, dubbed the jovial millionaire by southern journalists, is indeed aglow as he shares his prized possession with guests. He purchased the vessel in 1982 and restored her as closely as possible to her original state.

The African Queen, *Key Largo (© Jon Huber).*

The *Queen*, a coal-powered steamboat, was built in Lytham, England, in 1912 for service in Africa on the Victoria Nile and Lake Albert, where the movie was filmed in 1951. She was also used by the British East Africa Railway from 1912 to 1968 to shuttle cargo and passengers across Lake Albert on the border between the Belgian Congo and Uganda.

Stop by the **Key Largo Holiday Inn Resort** to view the *Queen* or phone the resort to reserve a seat.

■ Mangrove Tours

Caribbean Watersports
MM 97, Bayside
Westin Resort
Key Largo
☎ 305-852-4707

Caribbean Watersports at the Westin Beach Resort (MM 97) offers Enviro-Tours on your choice of a shallow-draft Zodiac inflatable or a Hobie Cat sailboat. Tours take off across Florida Bay with a flexible itinerary that varies with the winds and tides. Most float past unin-habited islands and through mangrove creeks. On any given outing you may come upon endangered species such as the Florida manatee or the American bald eagleyou may see pods of bottle-nosed dolphins or have a shark encounter with baby blacktips or bonnetheads as they skim the shallows for food. Sign up at the beach shack of the Westin Beach Resort.

Caribbean Watersports
Cheeca Lodge
MM 82, Oceanside
Islamorada
☎ 305-664-9547

Caribbean Watersports at the Cheeca Lodge features the same enviro-tours as the Westin location, plus ocean reef tours with snorkeling and parasailing. They visit Indian Key, a 12-acre island off Islamorada, and Lignumvitae Key, a 280-acre island off Islamorada's Gulf side.

■ Airboats

Originally designed for hunting, airboats are now used for sightseeing the sawgrass prairies and mangrove thickets along the Tamiami Trail and Everglades City. Sign up for an exhilarating ride at any one of the following operators:

Everglades Private Airboat Tours, ☎ 941-695-4637; **Gator Park**, ☎ 800-559-2255; **Jungle Erv's**, ☎ 941-695-2805; **Wooten's Large & Small Airboat Tours**, ☎ 941-695-2781; **Speedy Johnson's Fun Cruise**, ☎ 941-695-4448; **Coopertown Boat Tours**, ☎ 305-226-6048; **Capt. Doug's Florida Boat Tours**, ☎ 941-695-4400.

■ Everglades National Park Tours

Tours Departing Everglades City
PO Box 119
Everglades City FL 33929
☎ 941-695-3311

Scenic boat tours through the Ten Thousand Islands region are arranged at the Everglades National Park, Gulf Coast Ranger Station on Chokoloskee Causeway. The 2½-hour, ranger-guided trip has a brief stop for shelling on Kingston Key, a small island on the edge of the Gulf. Frequent sightings of porpoise, manatees, eagles, nesting ospreys, and roseate spoonbills are reported. Schedules of departure times and prices are posted at the concession office and on the bulletin board at the Gulf Coast Ranger Station. Phone for reservations and additional information.

Tours Departing Flamingo

Flamingo Marina
Main Park Entrance
40001 State Rte 9336
Florida City FL 33034
☎ 305-242-7700

Ranger-led tours through Florida Bay depart the Flamingo marina at the main park. Alligators, crocodiles, egrets, herons, ospreys, cormorants and eagles are sighted. Narrators point out different type of mangrove trees and describe their function in this environment.

Everglades Safari Tours

MM 102, Bayside
The Quay Restaurant
Key Largo

Sunset tours (1½ hours) depart daily for Bird Key and the mangroves.

■ Fort Jefferson & the Dry Tortugas

Yankee Freedom II
Land's End Marina
Key West FL 33040
☎ 305-294-7009, 800-YANKEECAT (926-5332)
www.yankeefleet.com.

Tortugas Ferry operates *Yankee Freedom II*, a luxurious 100-ft catamaran cruiser that departs Land's End Marina, Key West, for day-tours of the Dry Tortugas. The $3 million aluminum yacht averages 30 knots per hour, with travel time from Key West to the Tortugas approximately 2¼ hours.

Amenities include air-conditioned cabins, comfortable cushioned seating, large windows all around, high-tech television and VCR, spacious sundeck, a complete modern galley that serves a complimentary breakfast, and lunch at Fort Jefferson. A snack and cocktail bar are open throughout the voyage. On the main deck are three separate restrooms with freshwater showers. Day-tours offer an opportunity to explore Fort Jefferson, swim, snorkel the beautiful reefs surrounding Garden Key, birdwatch and beachcomb. Snorkeling gear may be borrowed free of charge.

The ferry leaves Key West at 8 am and returns at 5:30 pm every day, weather permitting. Current price is $95 for adults, $60 for children under 16. They offer discounts to seniors, students with ID, US military personnel, and groups. Trips are weather-dependent and will be

Boat Tours

cancelled when winds exceed 25 knots. Rates and schedules subject to change.

To reach Land's End Marina, follow US 1 south to Key West; take a right as you enter the island onto Roosevelt Ave. (this is still US 1). Continue through three traffic lights and take a right onto Palm Ave. (Garrison Bight Marina). Follow through three traffic lights and take a right onto Margaret St. Follow to the end, where you will find the Key West Seaport and the Yankee Fleet.

■ Glass-Bottom Boat Tours

Glass-bottom boat tours are entertaining and educational. They offer a long look at the living reefs that parallel the Florida Keys from Key Biscayne to Key West. Most boats have rest rooms, a snack bar and go out most days of the year.

Biscayne National Underwater Park, Inc.

9710 SW 328th St.

Homestead FL 33033

☎ 305-230-1100

E-mail: dive097@aol.com

Since 95% of the park is covered by water, the best way to explore Biscayne is to get wet or at least venture out on a boat. A park concessioner offers glass-bottom boat tours with snorkeling. Interpretive programs are conducted regularly by rangers at the Dante Fascell Visitor Center, where exhibits and films also provide an introduction to the park.

The glass-bottom boat tours a coral reef area that stretches from the southern tip of Key Biscayne to the northern tip of Key Largo. As boats pass over the shallow reefs, visitors get a look at submerged WWII aircraft wrecks inhabited by huge nurse sharks, angel fish, turtles, spiny lobsters, parrot fish and schools of grunts and sergeant majors. The boats depart Convoy Point. Be sure to phone ahead to confirm the schedule. On most days trips depart at 10 am and 1:30 pm.

The *Spirit of Pennekamp*

MM 102.5, Oceanside

John Pennekamp Coral Reef State Park

Key Largo

☎ 305-451-1621

Tours aboard the *Spirit of Pennekamp* at John Pennekamp State Park are especially good. This new air-conditioned 65-ft catamaran is "sea friendly." Its twin-hull design produces a very noticeable reduction in "rocking and rolling," characteristic of mono-hull vessels. The 2½-hour excursion brings you eight miles out to Molasses Reef, an area favored by divers for its mazes of coral canyons and variety of fish life. The boat's seating area for the above-water portion of the tour is quite high and enables you to view nesting cormorants eye-to-eye at the channel markers. It also allows for a fine aerial view of winding cuts and trails laced into the mangroves as a narrator points out nesting spots for osprey, herons, kingfishers or roseate spoonbills. After passing through the mangrove channels of South Sound Creek to your left, you can see mud flats that are a feeding area for hundreds of wading birds. The birds are attracted by the edible debris and silt that collects on the shallow bar. Once on the reef, the boat slows and you move down into the viewing salon.

As the boat slithers through the coral canyons that form the reef, you are inches away from swaying lavender seafans, walls of curious grunts, and angel fish. A fierce-looking barracuda may come up and look back at you as you pass through a profusion of bubbles. As the boat glides through mazes of antler, staghorn and brain corals, the narrator points out mating wrasses, neon parrotfish and other curious reef residents.

Crew members of the *Spirit of Pennekamp* tell us the two things passengers ask to see are sharks and turtles. Sharks are a rare sight on the Pennekamp reefs, but turtles are seen on many of the trips. Queen and French angels, barracuda, parrotfish, wrasses, grunts, and moray eels are more commonly seen. Large groups may book a private tour through John Pennekamp Park, on which you first see the reef through the viewing salon, then move to a shallow reef for snorkeling. The boat carries 149 passengers. Air-conditioned and wheelchair-accessible.

The *Key Largo Princess*
Holiday Inn Docks
MM 100, Oceanside
Key Largo
☎ 305-451-4655

Two-hour, narrated reef tours, similar to those of the *Spirit of Pennekamp* are offered aboard the *Key Largo Princess*, a 70-ft glass-bottom motor yacht. It carries 125 passengers, has a full bar and snack counter. Wheelchair-accessible. Air-conditioned salon. $18.50 for adults. $8.50 under 16.

Boat Tours

The *Discovery*
Land's End Marina
Key West
☎ 305-293-0099

Glass bottom trips aboard the *Discovery* leave from the docks at Land's End Marina three times a day. The *Discovery* is the only glass-bottom boat with a true underwater viewing room. Windows in the side of the hull allow for 45° viewing. The other boats have a glass area in the bottom. Sign up at their shop in Land's End Village or call for a reservation. The two-hour narrated tour combines the colorful waterfront history of Key West and points of interest on the Eastern Dry Rocks, Key West's main coral reef. When ocean seas are rough, the tour moves to Cottrell Reef on the Gulf. Trips cost $20 plus tax for adults. Children under seven years old can ride free on the first trip of the day (two children per adult). Children under three ride free on the second and third trip of the day. Children under 12 pay $15 on all trips. The upstairs air-conditioned salon has a snack bar that sells wine, beer, snacks and soft drinks. Wheelchair-accessible.

The *Pride of Key West*
2 Duval St.
Key West
☎ 305-296-4527

The 65-ft *Pride of Key West* catamaran departs from the foot of Duval Street at 12 pm, 2 pm and at sunset. This fairly new glass-bottom yacht carries up to 110 passengers, has a snack bar and an air-conditioned salon. The two-hour excursion includes an historic harbor tour en route to the Eastern Dry Rocks coral reef. Manual wheel chairs can board the boat without a problem, but not electric ones. It costs $20 for adults, $10 for children five-12 years old, under four free. Buy tickets at the booth on Duval Street.

Glass-bottom/snorkeling excursions off Key West are offered by **Lange's Coral Princess** fleet. Located at the end of Front Street, there are two trips daily, all gear and instruction included. ☎ 305-296-3287.

If you are prone to motion sickness, take preventive measures before leaving the dock. The slow rocking motion of the boats crossing the reefs is the cause of most mal-de-mer.

■ Tall Ships

Key West

Sail off into the sunset on one of Key West's own tall ships, the *Schooner Liberty*, the *Schooner Wolf* or the *Windjammer Appledore*.

Schooner Wolf
201 William St.
Key West
Toll free ☎ 877-296-9653; local 305-296-9653
E-mail: sailaway@schoonerwolf.com
www.schoonerwolf.com

Patterned after the blockade runners that plied the Florida Straits during the 19th century, the 74-ft *Wolf* is Coast Guard-certified for 44 passengers and offers daily day-sails, sunset and starlight cruises, snorkel trips and private charters. At press time, it was on an "invasion sail" to the Cayman Islands. The Wolf departs from the foot of Elizabeth and Greene, Key West's Historic Seaport. Check their website at www.piratesinparade.com for special events.

Liberty Fleet of Tall Ships
Hilton Resort & Marina
PO Box 1662
245 Front St.
Key West FL 33041
☎ 305-292-0332, fax 305-292-6411
E-mail: stephanie@libertyfleet.com

The 80-ft schooner *Liberty* and the 125-ft schooner *Liberty Clipper* offer a variety of day-sails, sunset sails, dinner sails, weddings and private charters. Help set the sails or sit back and relax.

Launched in 1993, the *Liberty Clipper* is a steel-hulled replica of early 1800s schooners used for carrying cargo and as fishing boats in New England. Coast Guard-licensed to carry 49 passengers, the *Liberty* tours Key West most every day. She is meticulously maintained and has been chartered by both NBC and ABC Television companies for television series.

While the schooner *Liberty* spends the whole year in Key West FL, the *Liberty Clipper* makes a two-week, 1,200-mile journey up and down the Atlantic coastline between Key West and Boston twice each year. She carries up to 25 passengers, with spacious accommodations. She visits several ports of call along the way, such as Charlotte, Norfolk,

Boat Tours

Baltimore, Annapolis and New York. Often these stops coincide with special events such as the US Sail Boat Show and the Great Chesapeake Bay Schooner Race. Passengers wishing to join the trip for a portion of the journey can be picked up or dropped off at these ports.

While aboard the *Liberty Clipper,* you can learn all aspects of sailing and navigation from an experienced crew. Celestial navigation and other special topics might be included, depending on client's wishes.

Whales, dolphins, sea turtles and sea birds are seen along the route.

■ Catamaran Sunset-Sail Cruises

Catamaran sunset-sail cruises are through **Fury Catamaran** (☎ 294-8899), **Sebago Catamarans** (☎ 294-5687), **Sunny Days Catamaran** and **Stars & Stripes Catamarans** (both ☎ 294-7877).

■ Historic Boat Tour

Subtropic Dive Center
Ocean Key Marina
Zero Duval St. or 1605 North Roosevelt Blvd.
Key West FL 33045
☎ 800-853-DIVE

This Key West Historic Harbor Tour entails a 1½-hour, fully narrated cruise around the historic seaport. Trips depart from the Ocean Key Marina at Zero Duval Street aboard Subtropic Dive Center's 50-ft power catamaran. Guides tell stories of wreckers, fishermen, the Navy and the island's first settlers.

■ Liveaboard & Bare Boat Cruising

Groups as small as six can charter a 50-ft sailing yacht for a week, complete with captain and cook, for under $1,000 per person. Trips are custom-suited to your group for diving, snorkeling or simply relaxing.

If you are an experienced sailor or boater you can charter a 30-ft or larger sail or motor yacht starting from about $1,000 for seven days.

Atlantic Coast

Treasure Harbor Marine, Inc.
200 Treasure Harbor Drive
Islamorada FL 33036
☎ 800-FLA-BOAT or 305-852-2458, fax 305-852-5743
E-mail: info@treasureharbor.com

Treasure Harbor Marine features day sailboats and live-aboards. High season prices are from $110 per day for a 19-ft day sailor to $330 per day for a 44-ft uncrewed yacht. By the week rates range from $395 to $1,700. Captains available. Lower rates apply between April 1 and November 14.

Cruzan Yacht Charters

PO Box 53
3375 Pan American Drive
Coconut Grove FL 33133
☎ 800-628-0785 or 305-858-2822, fax 305-854-0887
www.cruzan.com
E-mail: charters@cruzan.com

Cruzan Yacht Charters' Captain Danny Valls offers a large selection of sail and power bare boats from 30 ft to 50 ft for half- or full-day, weekend or weekly cruises to Biscayne National Park, the Florida Keys or Bahamas. Day and moonlight cruises may be arranged for two to 12 passengers. Sample rate for a party of six aboard a 50-ft, captained sailboat would start at $3,700, plus food, drinks and port taxes. Visa and MasterCard are accepted.

Note: Coconut Grove is in the greater Miami area, about 90 miles north of Key Largo.

Canoe & Kayak Tours

Canoe and kayak tours offer close encounters with Florida's exotic birds and fish, dolphins, manatees and alligators. Sea kayaks are favored for snorkeling and ocean outings, while canoes are the choice for backcountry creeks, streams and mangrove trails. Both types of craft permit access to shallow-water wilderness areas where other boats can't go. In fact, powerboats are prohibited on many of the mangrove trails.

Paddling tours can be short or long range, guided or self-guided and as adventurous as you want them to be. Prices start at $25 for short tours and at $100 per day for week-long expeditions. The marked trails in Florida's Keys (from Key Largo to Key West) are recommended for beginners.

If you are new to paddling, ask the canoe or kayak renter to give you a short lesson in basic paddling skills and safety. Ultimately, you must determine your own skill level and plan your own adventure accordingly. Biscayne National Aquatic Park, just south of Miami, offers easy canoeing in unpopulated waters.

Winds and tides are the most important factors in planning your paddling tour. Tides can create strong currents. First-time canoe or kayak renters should stick to short protected trails. Let someone on shore know where you are going and how long you expect to be out. Don't over-estimate your abilities or under-estimate the elements. Begin all your trips into the wind, allowing an easier trip home.

■ The Florida Keys

A three-mile wilderness canoe trail at **John Pennekamp State Park** offers calm waters and well-marked routes. Located on Key Largo at MM 102.5, this is an excellent choice for beginners. The trail, sheltered

The Complete Wilderness Waterway

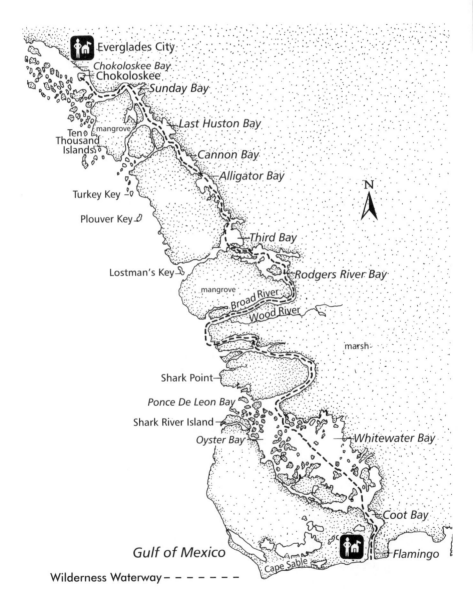

Everglades City
Chokoloskee Bay
Chokoloskee
Sunday Bay
Last Huston Bay
mangrove
Ten Thousand Islands
Cannon Bay
Alligator Bay
Turkey Key
N
Plouver Key
Third Bay
Lostman's Key
Rodgers River Bay
mangrove
Broad River
Wood River
marsh
Shark Point
Ponce De Leon Bay
Shark River Island
Oyster Bay
Whitewater Bay
Coot Bay
Gulf of Mexico
Cape Sable
Flamingo
Wilderness Waterway – – – – – – –

by dense walls of mangrove, provides a look at sea birds, an array of tropical fish and an occasional manatee. Off-limits to powerboats, it makes a tranquil setting for a morning or afternoon paddling adventure.

You may encounter some current, but it is usually very light. The park has changing facilities, rest rooms, a fast food counter, gift shop, two beaches, shaded picnic and camping areas.

Wildlife photography opportunities abound. Brown pelicans glide gracefully overhead as cormorants dive and great white herons stalk the shore for food fish. Ducks will swim right up to your craft and flying fish may surprise you by skimming the surface alongside your bow. In winter, the lovely pink roseate spoonbill may appear in the mangrove shrubs along the trail. Crystal clear water allows a good look at French and queen angelfish, barracuda, parrot fish and an occasional turtle.

Weather permitting, rentals and guided canoe trips are available. Canoes and tikis (small kayaks) rent for a low hourly rate. You must be at least 18 years old in Florida to sign for a rental. Write to **Coral Reef Park Co.**, PO Box 1560, Key Largo FL 33037. ☎ 305-451-1621.

Florida Bay Outfitters Kayak & Canoe Center (next to the Caribbean Club, Key Largo, MM 104) offers kayak and canoe rentals, camping equipment, and guided tours on Florida Bay. Free Keys chart with rental. Write to **Florida Bay Outfitters**, 104050 Overseas Hwy., Key Largo FL 33037. ☎ 305-451-3018. www.kayakfloridakeys.com

In Islamorada, **Papa Joe's Marina** (MM 79.7) offers single and double kayaks for rent on an hourly basis, seven days a week. ☎ 305-664-5505. Farther down the Keys, **Ocean Paddle South** (2244 Overseas Hwy., Marathon) gives eager kayakers several options: single or dou-

Map 1

WILDERNESS WATERWAY
Chokoloskee Bay to Sunday Bay

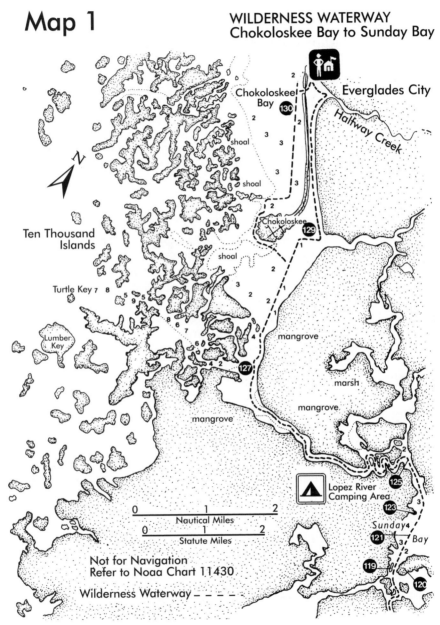

Everglades City

Chokoloskee Bay

Halfway Creek

shoal

Ten Thousand Islands

Chokoloskee

shoal

Turtle Key 7 8

Lumber Key

mangrove

marsh

mangrove

mangrove

Lopez River Camping Area

Sunday Bay

0   1   2
Nautical Miles
0   1   2
Statute Miles

Not for Navigation
Refer to Noaa Chart 11430

Wilderness Waterway – – – –

Map © Joyce Huber

ble kayaks for a 24-hour period from the store location, or by the hour and half-day from beautiful Bahia Honda State park.

Protected trails along the shallow flats of Long Key State Recreational Area (MM 67.5) wind through dense mangrove swamps, home to a huge wading-bird and marine life population. In fact, the island was once home to the Long Key Fishing Club, a mecca for the world's greatest saltwater fishermen until its destruction by a hurricane in 1935.

During the winter months, park rangers offer programs on the ecology of the area. Canoe rentals available. Write **Long Key State Recreation Area**, PO Box 776, Long Key FL 33001. ☎ 305-664-4815.

Guided wildlife tours around the mangrove islands off Key West are offered by **Mosquito Coast Kayaks**, 1107 Duval St, Key West FL. ☎ 305-294-7178. Trips start at 8:45 am and return at 3 pm. The cost is $45.

Mosquito's experienced backcountry guides lead you through the shallow mangrove channels and fringe reef areas, explaining the natural history of the area. Tour events vary; you may chase a four-foot nurse shark or a stingray through the shallows or meet up with a bald eagle. Tropical fish, sea turtles and hundreds of other species are visible below the surface, as well as shore plants, algae, sea grasses, sponge and coral communities. You can also snorkel and explore a small secluded coral reef. You'll also learn how to sail in a 15 mph wind with a large kite.

Key West kayak tours are also offered by **Adventure Charters**, 6810 Front St., Stock Island, ☎ 305-296-0362. **Safari Charter, Inc.** offers sailing, kayaking and snorkeling in the Great White Heron National Wildlife Refuge area near Key West. Guests ride in a sailboat to the Refuge, then board kayaks for local exploration. Dolphin-encounter tours are also available. Located at Banana Bay Resort & Marina, 2319 N. Roosevelt Blvd., Key West FL 33040. ☎ 888-6SAFARI or 305-296-4691. E-mail: info@safaricharters.com. www.safaricharters.com.

Island Kayak has guided backcountry tours in easy-paddling kayaks. Sign up in the booth at 2400 N. Roosevelt Blvd. ☎ 305-292-0059. E-mail: islandkayak@prodigy.net. www.islandkayakkeywest.com.

Crystal Seas Kayaking explores mangrove tunnels and winding creeks. See romantic sunsets and ospreys, herons and pelicans in their natural habitat. Experienced nature guides escort small groups. Three-hour, sunset, full-day, multi-day and custom kayak tours available. Guests are picked up at their hotel. Tours depart from Stock Island (MM 17). Everglades tours are also offered. PO Box 5406, Key West FL 33041. ☎ 305-296-3212 or toll-free 877-SEAS-877. E-mail: mail@crystalseas.com. www.crystalseas.com.

Map 2

WILDERNESS WATERWAY
Sunday Bay to Chevelier Bay

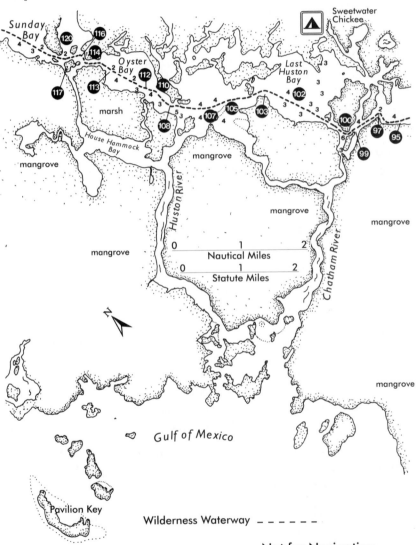

Sweetwater Chickee

Sunday Bay

Oyster Bay

Last Huston Bay

marsh

House Hammock Bay

mangrove

mangrove

mangrove

mangrove

mangrove

Huston River

Chatham River

0   1   2
Nautical Miles
0   1   2
Statute Miles

N

Gulf of Mexico

Pavilion Key

Wilderness Waterway – – – – – –

Not for Navigation
Refer to Noaa Chart 11430

Map © Joyce Huber

In the Lower Keys, **Reflections Kayak Nature Tours** promotes excursions into the Great White Heron National Wildlife Refuge and surrounding mangrove islands. Write to PO Box 430861, Big Pine Key. ☎ 305-872-2896.

Gale Force Charters at Sugarloaf Key offers wilderness kayaking tours. Passengers and kayaks are transported to the **Barracuda Islands**, a group of outlying mangrove cays. Kayaks and snorkel gear are provided. The trip lasts approximately four hours. Cost is $200 for one or two persons, $75 per person for three to six. Contact Capt. Bob and Gale Dumouchel, Sugarloaf Marina, US 1 MM 17, Sugarloaf Key FL; marina, ☎ 305-745-3135; home, ☎ 305-745-2868. E-mail: info@ galeforcecharters.com.

Crystal Seas Kayaking at Sugarloaf Marina offers advanced touring kayaks and guided day-long trips for experienced paddlers. Explore the Great White Heron Refuge while paddling through mangrove tunnels and winding creeks. Experience romantic sunsets and witness osprey, herons and pelicans in their natural habitat. Small groups. Fun, safe and personal. Complimentary transportation from Key West. Three-hour, sunset, full-day, multi-day and custom kayak tours available. ☎ 877-SEAS-877, 305-745-3135 or 305-296-3212. www.crystalseas.com. E-Mail: mail@crystalseas.com. PO Box 5406 Key West FL 33045.

Big Pine Kayak Adventures take off from the old wooden fishing bridge at MM 30. A 19-ft Carolina skiff carries guests and kayaks on a short interpretive excursion into the backcountry where you board your kayak for further exploration. These four-hour trips are as physically demanding as a one-mile walk. Half- to full-day experiences are $49 to $79 per person. Or opt for the Rent & Ride tour, which allows you to bring your own kayak. When wind conditions allow, you can be dropped off, then head back with the wind behind you. Often, you can raise your paddles and turn them flat against the wind to "sail" back.

Select from a two-hour trip to **Pelican Island**, a unique seabird habitat, backcountry tours, birding tours or ocean tours to secluded beaches where you can snorkel, picnic and beachcomb. Tours include use of a stable, lightweight one- or two-person kayak and transportation to and from the departure location. The sea kayaks are longer and wider than whitewater kayaks and rudder controls are available. A double kayak is over 18 ft long. Spray skirts are not used, allowing the occupants to remain cool and comfortable. Winter trips are centered around bird watching with professional photographer Bill Keogh. In summer, trips may include snorkeling in knee-deep water. Kayaks, which have molded seats, are easy to get in and out of. Contact Bill Keogh at ☎ 877-595-2925 or 305-872-8950. www.keyskayaktours.com.

Map 3

WILDERNESS WATERWAY
Last Huston Bay to Plate Creek Bay

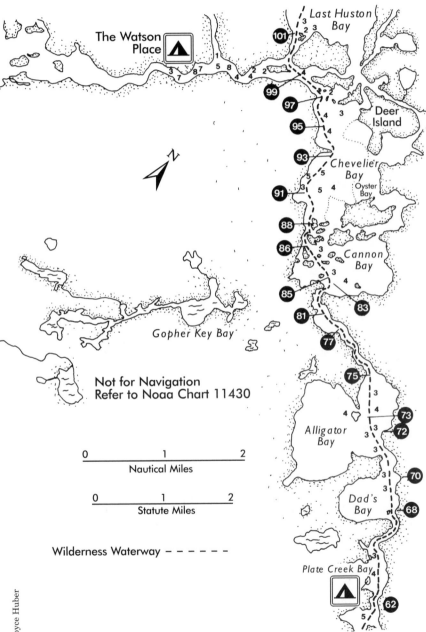

The Watson Place

Last Huston Bay

101

Deer Island

99

97

95

93

Chevelier Bay

Oyster Bay

91

88

86

Cannon Bay

85

83

81

77

Gopher Key Bay

Not for Navigation
Refer to Noaa Chart 11430

75

73

72

Alligator Bay

70

Dad's Bay

68

0   1   2
Nautical Miles

0   1   2
Statute Miles

Wilderness Waterway – – – – – –

Plate Creek Bay

62

Map © Joyce Huber

Biscayne National Underwater Park, a new area popular for canoeing, covers 181,500 acres of pristine mangrove shorelines, islands, bays and offshore coral reefs.

Shallow-water routes follow the southern shores of Biscayne Bay near park headquarters (US 1 & SW 328th St.). Canoes and kayaks are rented by the park concessionaire

Florida alligator

next to the Visitor Center. For additional information write to **Biscayne National Underwater Park**, PO Box 1270, Homestead FL 33090. ☎ 305-230-1100.

■ Everglades National Park Canoe Tours

Everglades National Park is a much more rugged environment for canoeing and kayaking than the Keys, but perfect for those who want a true wilderness adventure. Here, experienced canoe and kayak enthusiasts combine paddling with superb fly fishing and backcountry camping.

If you are new to canoe and kayak paddling, this is not the place to learn on your own. Gain experience by joining a guided-tour group. The presence of alligators, crocodiles and murky water makes swimming and wading, by intent or accident, undesirable. Seasonal low water and high mosquito levels can ruin even a short trip. Before going out on long trails you must be competent at marine navigation, and have a working knowledge of weather patterns, tides and currents in the area. The season is from early November through the end of April. Summer storms and a ferocious mosquito population take over the park from May through October.

Before embarking on any Everglades paddling tours be sure to file a float plan 24 hours in advance with the park rangers and ask for a current trail condition report. This will advise you of current water and mosquito levels. Pre-trip advisories are crucial, especially during dry winter months when water levels in some places may drop to less than an inch, leaving you in waist-deep mud.

There is an inland water route from Everglades City on the Gulf of Mexico to Flamingo on Florida Bay. Sequentially numbered markers guide you over its 99 miles. Known as the **Wilderness Waterway**, the route twists through expansive marine and estuarine areas of the park. These areas harbor almost every type of marine organism found in the Caribbean and serve as spawning grounds and nurseries for

Map 4

WILDERNESS WATERWAY
Plate Creek Bay to Third Bay

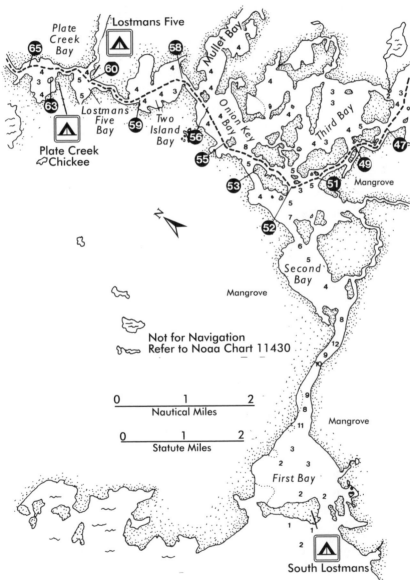

Plate Creek Bay

Lostmans Five

Mullet Bay

Onion Key Bay

Third Bay

Lostmans Five Bay

Two Island Bay

Plate Creek
Chickee

Mangrove

Mangrove

Not for Navigation
Refer to Noaa Chart 11430

Second Bay

| 0 | 1 | 2 |
Nautical Miles

| 0 | 1 | 2 |
Statute Miles

Mangrove

First Bay

South Lostmans

Map © Joyce Huber

Wilderness Waterway – – – – – – – – ·

many of them. Larger creatures such as water birds, sea turtles, many types of fish sought by fishermen, and the endangered manatee are attracted to these waters because of their abundant food supplies. The route requires a minimum of seven days by canoe and a small motor is recommended.

Primitive campsites are available along the route. Backcountry camping permits are required and may be obtained from the Everglades City or Flamingo ranger station. The permits are issued daily between 7:30 am and 4 pm. Charts 11430, 11432 and 11433 cover the area and are for sale at the main Visitor Center, Flamingo and in the Everglades City area.

Give plenty of space to power boats. In shallow areas they may not be able to come off a plane without hitting bottom. Stay to the right and turn your bow into their wake.

Canoe Camping

When canoe camping, carry at least one gallon of water per person per day. There is no freshwater in the backcountry. And be certain to bring trash bags, as you must pack all your trash out with you. Food and water must be packed in hard-shell containers. Raccoons will chew through plastic jugs and styrofoam coolers. Pets are not allowed in the backcountry or on the canoe trails. Finding dry firewood is difficult. Bring a portable stove using compressed gas or liquid fuel.

Mosquitos and sand fleas can be overwhelming, particularly after a rainstorm. You'll need an ample supply of insect repellent and a tent with fine mesh screening. We found Off - Deep Woods repellent effective, but in extreme wet periods you are better off heading away from the marsh lands completely. The bug problem cannot be overemphasized. Veteran canoe camper Joe Van Putten describes the mosquitos' arrival as follows: "You don't see them, you hear them coming. At first, I thought it was airplanes."

Ten Thousand Islands Day Trips

Trips within the Ten Thousand Island sector originate on Chokoloskee Bay at Everglades City. You can rent a canoe at the **Everglades National Park Boat Tours** office or at **North American Canoe Tours** across the street, at **Outdoor Resorts** on Chokoloskee Island, or bring your own. Put in at the canoe ramp next to the Ranger Station or next to Outdoor Resorts on Chokoloskee Island.

Map 5

WILDERNESS WATERWAY
Onion Bay to Broad River Bay

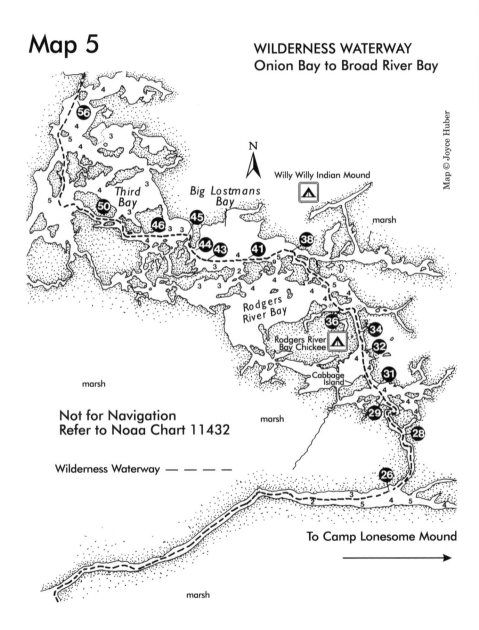

Map © Joyce Huber

Willy Willy Indian Mound

marsh

Third Bay

Big Lostmans Bay

N

Rodgers River Bay

Rodgers River Bay Chickee

Cabbage Island

marsh

marsh

Not for Navigation
Refer to Noaa Chart 11432

Wilderness Waterway — — — —

To Camp Lonesome Mound

marsh

Don't panic if you tip over. Chokoloskee Bay is shallow; it may be possible to walk to land. Be sure to have keys and valuables where they will not be lost in the water.

Time your trip so the tides help you. A falling tide flows toward the Gulf of Mexico, a rising tide flows toward the Ranger Station. If you have questions about handling a canoe, ask a ranger for assistance.

Sandfly Island Trip

Follow the marked channel south. Or circle the island in shallow water – you may have to walk your canoe across the oyster bar north of the island. Watch for strong tidal currents south of the island. The dock on Sandfly Island is two miles from the Ranger Station. There is a nature trail on Sandfly Island that features natural and cultural history. Estimated paddling time: 2½ hours (add an hour if traveling against wind and tides). Add one hour to walk the trail on the island. A marked channel leads you two miles across Chokoloskee Bay to a mangrove island.

Sandfly Island is a shell mound created by Calusa Indians, who arrived in this area over 2,000 years ago. In the early 1900s, settlers had a home, tomato farm, and even a store on the island. Today nature has reclaimed the island and few signs of human settlement remain. If you walk quietly, you may see raccoons, turtles, mangrove crabs or birds. After your walk you may want to continue exploring south of the island along Sandfly Pass.

Chokoloskee Bay Loop

Follow the marked channel west, then south; turn east and follow the north margin of the Ten Thousand Islands to the other marked channel; turn north and follow the marked channel back to the Ranger Station. This trip is mostly open water with a few small mangrove islands that are not dependable for landing, especially at high tide. Estimated paddling time: 2½ hours.

Collier Seminole State Park

Collier Seminole State Park is at Route 92 and the Tamiami Trail, about 17 miles west of Carnestown – the turnoff for Everglades City. A limited number of visitors are allowed to visit this preserve each day by canoe. A 13.5-mile canoe trip will bring you through a buttonwood and white mangrove forest, and a salt marsh, offering a look at several of the state's threatened species. These include wood storks, bald eagles, red cockaded woodpeckers, crocodiles, manatees, Florida black bears, Florida panthers and mangrove fox squirrels. Tent and RV camping. Saltwater fishing. Canoe rentals available. Write Collier Seminole State Park, Rt. 4, Box 848, Naples FL 33961. ☎ 941-394-3397.

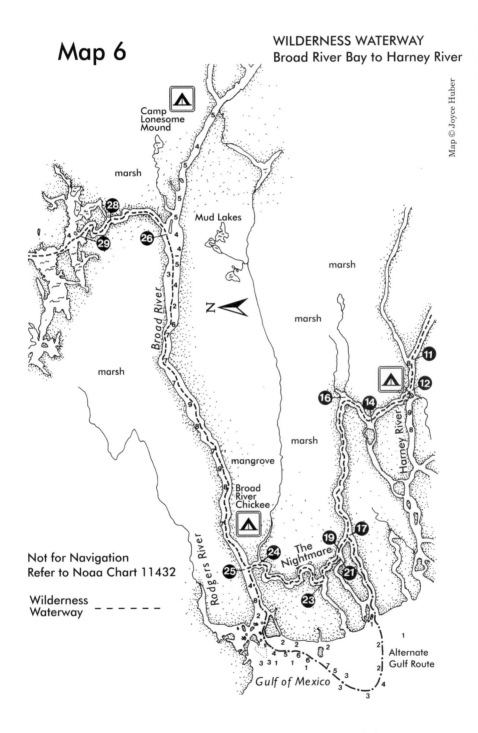

Map 6

WILDERNESS WATERWAY
Broad River Bay to Harney River

Map © Joyce Huber

Camp
Lonesome
Mound

marsh

28

29

26

Mud Lakes

marsh

marsh

Broad River

N

marsh

marsh

marsh

11

12

16

14

Harney River

mangrove

Broad
River
Chickee

17

Not for Navigation
Refer to Noaa Chart 11432

Wilderness
Waterway – – – – –

Rodgers River

24

25

19

The
Nightmare

21

23

1

Alternate
Gulf Route

Gulf of Mexico

Flamingo Area Canoe Trails

Nine Mile Pond. This scenic, 5.2-mile loop trail starts at the Nine Mile Pond parking lot and takes approximately four hours in travel time. The trail, well-marked with white plastic posts, crosses an open pond and curls through freshwater prairie, sawgrass and mangrove habitat. Watch for alligators, wading birds and an occasional snail kite. The course may be difficult to follow, but during summer months it is the preferred trail as it is relatively insect-free. During the winter dry season, portions may be impassable due to low water levels. No motors permitted.

Noble Hammock Trail begins between Nine Mile Pond and the Hells Bay trailhead on the east side of the Main Park Road. It passes through open country and small alligator ponds, through buttonwood, red mangrove and sawgrass. Its sharp corners and narrow passes require good maneuvering skills.

Historically, the trail was used for access into some of the larger hammocks for bootlegging operations and many of the old cuttings to mark the trail can still be seen. Traveling this three-mile loop takes three hours. Check for low water levels during the dry season. No motors permitted.

Hell's Bay Trail was named by old timers because it is "Hell to get into and Hell to get out of." The trailhead is halfway between Nine Mile Pond and West Lake on the west side of the Main Park Road. This sheltered route weaves through mangrove-lined creeks and ponds to a series of small bays beyond the Lard Can campsite. The trail may be difficult to follow – keep an eye out for markers. The first campsite lies approximately four miles from the starting point or within three hours travel time. The second campsite is in Hell's Bay, four miles from the first site, or 4½ hours travel time. This trail gives the best opportunity to travel through overgrown passageways of red mangrove and brackish water. Be sure to check the water levels before starting the journey. Use of motors is prohibited from the trailhead to the Lard Can campsite, but a 5½ hp motor may be used elsewhere on the trail. A Backcountry Use Permit is recommended when traveling this trail, even when not camping. See pages 255-256 for details.

West Lake Trail, an eight-mile, seven-hour Everglades tour, begins at the West Lake interpretive shelter and takes you through a series of large open lakes connected by narrow creeks lined with mangroves. Alligators and crocodiles are numerous.

Map 7

WILDERNESS WATERWAY
Harney River to Whitewater Bay

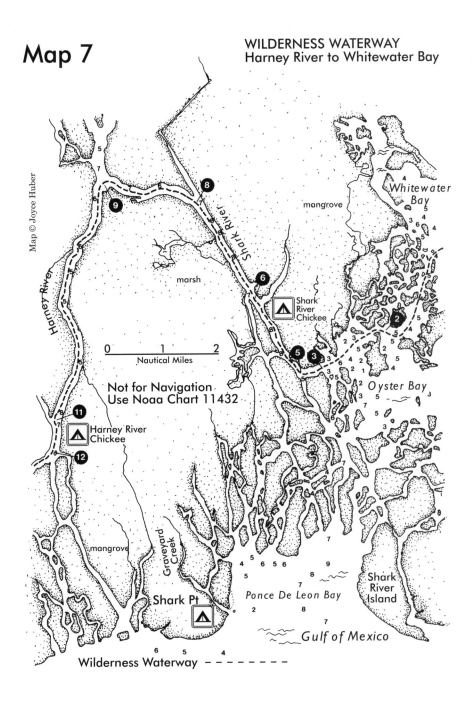

Map © Joyce Huber

Whitewater Bay

mangrove

Shark River

Harney River

marsh

Shark River Chickee

0   1   2
Nautical Miles

Not for Navigation
Use Noaa Chart 11432

Oyster Bay

Harney River Chickee

mangrove

Graveyard Creek

Shark Pt

Ponce De Leon Bay

Shark River Island

Gulf of Mexico

Wilderness Waterway – – – – – – –

Large, exposed areas along this route require extra caution on windy days. The trail meanders between thickets of red and black mangrove and buttonwood trees, then through the remains of a once-great living forest destroyed by hurricanes. Redfish and sea trout abound. A small clearing for primitive camping exists at Alligator Creek. Park rules prohibit the use of any size motor from the east end of West Lake to Garfield Bight.

Buttonwood Canal, a three-mile trail leading to Coot Bay, offers a look at alligators, crocodiles and birds. Several powerboats use this route and should be given the right of way. (See caution on page 70.)

Mud Lake Loop, connecting the Buttonwood Canal, Coot Bay, Mud Lake and the Bear Lake Canoe Trail, shelters a variety of habitats and wildlife. Motors are prohibited. Located 4.8 miles from Bear Lake trailhead, Mud Lake Loop is accessible from the Flamingo Marina through Buttonwood Canal or the Bear Lake Trailhead.

Bear Lake Canal, an 11.5-mile route, leads to Cape Sable's Camping Area, the last wilderness beach left in south Florida. To get there, you paddle along a narrow, shady canal. Accessible from the Flamingo Marina through Buttonwood Canal with a portage from the Bear Lake Trailhead. Impassable between markers 13-17 during the dry season (January through April). Motors prohibited.

Consult NOAA nautical chart 11433 for the location of shoal water (sand bars, mud banks, shallows).

Tides can create strong currents. Low tides at East Cape are at least two hours earlier than Flamingo low tides; high tides at East Cape are 1½ hours earlier than Flamingo high tides.

Canoe Trip Equipment Check List

☐ Flotation Gear. Florida law requires a Coast Guard-approved personal flotation device for each occupant.

☐ Extra paddle.

☐ Bailer.

☐ Bow and stern lines.

☐ Waterproof bags for gear.

☐ Tide chart.

☐ Water.

☐ Food (for camping or long trips).

☐ Long shirt and long pants for sun and bug protection.

☐ Wide-brimmed hat.

☐ Extra pair of shoes.

☐ Wrist watch for figuring tides and keeping track of your time.

☐ Sunglasses (polarizing are best).

☐ Sunscreen.

☐ First Aid Kit. Add insect repellent and sunscreen.

☐ Flashlight and extra batteries (in waterproof container).

☐ Compass.

☐ Charts.

For additional information write to General Park Information: **Everglades National Park**, 40001 State Road 9336, Homestead FL 33034-6733. ☎ 305-242-7700. www.nps.gov/ever.com.

Everglades Canoe Rentals

Flamingo Lodge Marina & Outpost Resort
#1 Flamingo Lodge Hwy.
Flamingo FL 33034
☎ 941-695-3101, fax 941-695-3921; camping, 800-365-CAMP (2267); reservations, ☎ 800-600-3813; www.flamingolodge.com.

Canoes and kayaks are available from the Flamingo Marina for half-day, full-day or overnight rentals. Since the Marina sits on Florida Bay and at the edge of the backcountry, you have an option of which area you would like to explore. For a nominal fee, Flamingo Lodge can transport your canoe to Noble Hammock Trail, Hell's Bay Trail, West Lake Trail and Bear Lake Trail. Canoes are available at Nine Mile Pond; arrangements must be made at the Flamingo Marina. Kayaks are available to take out only from the Flamingo Marina. Rentals are subject to weather conditions.

Most canoes hold two-three people, though some accommodate one person and others up to five. Rentals start at $27 for a half-day, $54 for a full day and $60 for overnight.

For the northwestern Ten Thousand Islands region contact: **Everglades Area Chamber of Commerce**, PO Box 130, Everglades City FL 33929; ☎ 914-695-3941.

Map 8

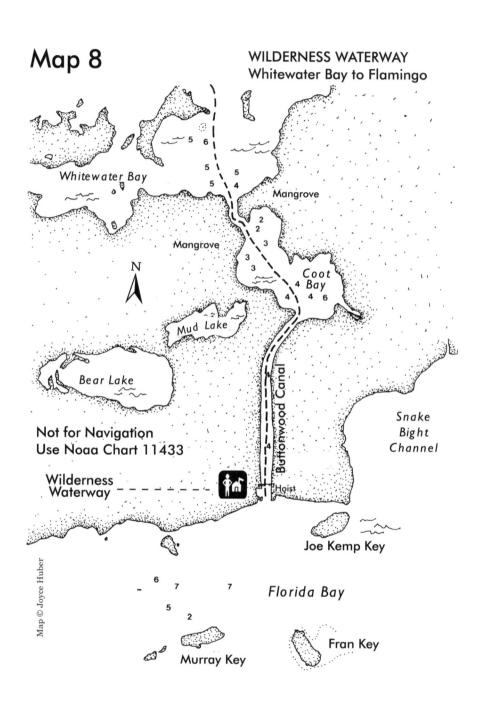

WILDERNESS WATERWAY
Whitewater Bay to Flamingo

Whitewater Bay

5 6

5   5
4
5

Mangrove

2
2
3

Mangrove

3
3

Coot
Bay
4
4   6
4

Mud Lake

N

Bear Lake

Not for Navigation
Use Noaa Chart 11433

Snake
Bight
Channel

Buttonwood Canal

Wilderness
Waterway — — — —

4

Hoist

Joe Kemp Key

Map © Joyce Huber

6
7   7   Florida Bay
5
2

Murray Key

Fran Key

 *Note that although the park is open year round, the recreational services are only open from mid-November to mid-April.*

Biscayne National Underwater Park, Inc. rents kayaks, but does not offer guided tours. PO Box 1270, Homestead FL 33030; ☎ 305-230-1100.

You can also contact **Everglades National Park Boat Tours**, PO Box 119, Everglades City FL 33929; ☎ 914-695-2591 or 800-445-7724 (Florida only).

Canoe Outfitters

Canoe outfitters offer all-inclusive guided trips, which may include pick-up from the airport, transportation between sites, tents, canoes, and meals. All you are required to bring in many cases is yourself and a change of clothing. Rates start at $100 per day. Groups are usually small, 10-12 people. Singles and couples mix. You can bring your own group or join one formed by the outfitter. You must book in advance.

The Nantahala Outdoor Center of North Carolina books two or three trips in the Everglades and Ten Thousand Islands each January and February. Prices start at $1,100 per person, including boats, food, guides and transportation from the Fort Myers airport. You bring your tent, sleeping bag and personal gear. Put together your own group of five to 10 or join others who've booked the same time period. ☎ 888-6623-1662, ext 333. www.noc.com.

North American Canoe Tours offers guided and "you-paddle" tours, which can be a half-day to a week or longer. They provide everything you need: a 17-ft all-aluminum Grumman canoe or kayak, personal flotation devices, paddles for two, a photocopy of local maps, a cooler with ice and drinking water. They also run a low-cost, 10-room bed and breakfast inn, The Ivey House, at Everglades City, ☎ 941-695-4666. Write to D. Harraden, (winter address) PO Box 5038, Everglades City FL 33929; (summer address) 65 Black Point Rd., Niantic, CT 06357; ☎ 203-739-0791

Another option for group tours only is **Mountain Workshop, Inc.** Contact Corky Clark, PO Box 625, Ridgefield, CT 06877, ☎ 203-438-3640.

Additional Reading

Two good booklets on canoeing in the Everglades are ***Boat and Canoe Camping-Everglades Backcountry & Ten Thousand Islands Region*** (64 pp paper) and ***Guide to the Wilderness Waterway of the***

Everglades National Park (64 pp paper). They are available from Florida National Parks & Monuments Association, Inc., 10 Parachute Key #51, Homestead FL 33034-6735, ☎ 305-247-1216. Phone orders accepted with Visa, MasterCard, or Discover.

Mangroves, Trees in the Seas, a beautiful photo book by Jerry, Idaz and Michael Greenberg, shows and describes the secrets of the mangrove wilderness. Available for $7.95 plus shipping from Seahawk Press, 6840 SW 92 St., Miami FL 33156.

Safety Tips

☐ Watch the time. Is half your time up? Turn around. Plan to be back before dark.

☐ Check the weather forecast and conditions before departing. If a storm threatens, head for shelter. If you cannot reach land, stay low in your canoe to avoid becoming a lightning target.

☐ Leave a float plan with someone who can take action if you don't return on time.

"Sailing" with the wind. Copyright © Bill Keogh.
Courtesy Big Pine Kayak Adventures.

Cycling Trails

Whether you want to explore for a day or a season, self-guided cycling tours are one of the best ways to discover the Everglades and the Florida Keys.

Flat terrain and well-marked trails lead you across scenic bridges, through wildlife preserves, exotic bird sanctuaries, palm-lined beaches, and historic parks. Watersports opportunities abound. A wide range of accommodations exist throughout the area, including ocean-side campgrounds.

If historic Key West is your destination, you'll find cycling an ideal way to tour the sights. Bike rentals and services are widely available. Public bike racks are everywhere.

Traffic along US 1, the main highway through the Keys, once posed a serious danger to bike riders. Today's cyclists find wider shoulders on the bridges and a well-marked bike trail for most of the 106-mile route between Key Largo and Key West. The main road and bicycling trails through Everglades National Park are well-maintained.

■ Planning Your Tour

When to Go

Visit Everglades National Park from December through March. The rest of the year brings torrential downpours and thick clouds of mosquitos. Tour the Florida Keys between December and May. Skies are predictably sunny and air temperatures range from 75° to 85° F.

Equipment

Single-speed, coaster-brake bikes are as much at home in south Florida as are high-tech, 21-speed mountain bikes. Most of the land is flat, usually just a few feet above sea level. The most uphill pedaling you'll encounter is over bridges. Rental bikes are all single-speed with baskets. Wide tires are best for the gravel and dirt trails that alternate with paved sections. For short rides in the populated areas, tools and spare equipment are usually not necessary. If you plan long-distance road riding, carry equipment sufficient to repair and inflate a tire, a spare inner-tube, some cash, sun block, a first aid kit, bug repellent and a water bottle.

Clothing & Gear

Clothing should be loose and lightweight. Cotton or Spandex cycling shorts and a loose shirt are the best choices. The new mesh cycling fabrics, available at most bike shops, wick perspiration away from your body and keep you cool. Chafing and skin irritation in the groin area can be reduced by use of a sheepskin seat cover, available in most of the bike rental shops. The climate, relaxed atmosphere and fact that the bike trails and old bridges are free of automobile traffic lead many cyclists to wear baseball caps or straw hats instead of safety helmets. Nowadays, this is an unnecessary risk.

There are many new helmets, designed for tropical wear, that will keep you cool and protect your head and face. Insure a proper fit by shopping for one before your trip. To prevent serious injury in a fall or crash, avoid pushing the helmet to the back of your head.

For mid-winter travel, pack a windbreaker. An occasional cold front during the winter months has dropped temperatures as low as 40° F, though 75° is more usual.

Dehydration & Heat Stroke

During summer and fall when midday temperatures soar beyond the comfort zone for riding, consider other activities. Plan cycling time for cooler morning or evening hours.

If you are not acclimated to hot weather riding, limit your tours to short distances and slow speeds. Avoid wearing long-sleeve jerseys and long tights, and drink plenty of cold liquids to avoid heat stroke or dehydration.

Insulated pouches such as ThermalBak or IceBak will keep drinks cool for several hours. For very short tours an insulated drink holder that clips on the handlebars may be purchased at most of the area bike shops.

Symptoms of heat exhaustion or heat stroke are weakness, headache, nausea and fainting. For treatment, seek immediate medical aid. If the person is conscious, give cold fluids and continuously wet down the skin with moist towels while en route to a hospital.

Transporting Your Bicycle

Most airlines and bus companies, as well as Amtrak, will supply a special bicycle box that enables you to carry your bike as baggage. This, in theory, insures the bike will arrive intact when you do. The box costs $12-$20. For transport, the handlebars, front wheel and pedals are removed. Or, have your local bike shop box it for you before your trip. Be sure they use bubble pack or foam to protect it. Get a clear demonstration on how to put it back together.

Check to see if your airline(s) pressurize the baggage compartment. If not, you must deflate the tires. Unpressurized compartments will cause the tires to swell and possibly burst. This may result in rim damage. (All major US carriers have pressurized baggage compartments.) Be sure to make a reservation for your bicycle. During high travel times – holidays or peak season – when the baggage compartment is loaded with standard luggage, you may be forced to ship your bike as freight.

■ Florida Keys Cycling Trails

The Florida Keys welcome cyclists. A paved bike trail runs much of the route from Key Largo to Key West. It breaks off in some spots and crosses US 1 in places. The bridges have wide shoulders and offer unmatched views of the Atlantic Ocean and Gulf-side bays. Fragrant, orange-flowered poinciana trees shade many areas of the bike path.

If you are starting from the mainland, take Card Sound Road from Homestead to Route 905 in Key Largo. This connects with and bypasses almost 30 miles of US 1. About 15 miles into Key Largo you pick up a paved bike trail on the ocean side of the highway. Greyhound will transport you and your boxed bike to any point along US 1 from their airport-vicinity terminal. Reservations: ☎ 800-231-2222; www.greyhound.com.

Finding your way around is easy; mile markers (green signs with white numbers) are posted each mile along US 1 throughout the Keys. They start with 126, just south of Florida City, and end with the zero marker at the corner of Fleming and Whitehead streets in Key West.

Key Largo & the Upper Keys

Key Largo is often the focus of a Florida Keys vacation. The bike trail begins at MM 106. Heading south, you'll pass a long stretch of trailers

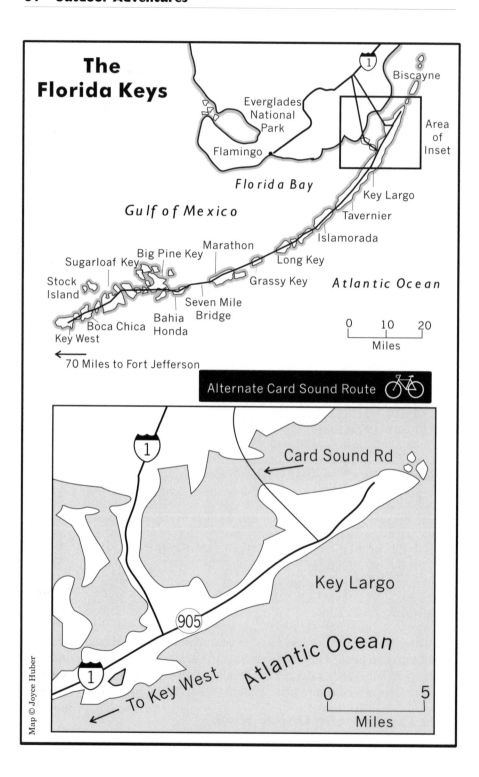

The Florida Keys

Biscayne

Everglades National Park

Flamingo

Area of Inset

Florida Bay

Key Largo

Gulf of Mexico

Tavernier

Islamorada

Marathon

Long Key

Sugarloaf Key

Big Pine Key

Stock Island

Grassy Key

Atlantic Ocean

Seven Mile Bridge

Bahia Honda

Boca Chica

Key West

0   10   20
Miles

← 70 Miles to Fort Jefferson

Alternate Card Sound Route

1

Card Sound Rd

Key Largo

905

1

To Key West

Atlantic Ocean

0   5
Miles

Map © Joyce Huber

and billboards offering diving, snorkeling and fishing. All along US 1 you can rent boats, Jet Skis or stop to relax at waterfront resorts and restaurants. Dive shops are everywhere. At the **Italian Fisherman**, a large marina, restaurant and beach complex at MM 104, you can take a swim in the bay or the pool, rent a windsurfer, sailboat or Jet Ski.

A left turn at MM 103.2 brings you to the **Key Largo Undersea Park**, the site of the first underwater hotel, **Jules' Undersea Lodge** (see pages 161 and 185). Currently operating as a research habitat, the hotel sits 30 ft below the surface. Non-divers must take a three-hour course before being allowed to enter the hotel using a hookah, a 120-ft-long breathing line with regulators attached. Surface compressors pump air through the lines into the hotel.

For a small fee you can snorkel the lagoon (use of equipment included in entrance fee), though a better choice for a snorkeling tour would be an ocean reef trip, offered each morning and afternoon at nearby John Pennekamp Coral Reef State Park for $32. To enter the park, turn left at the sign at MM 102.5. The park offers oceanside camping, picnic areas, showers, rest rooms, bike racks, a dive shop, reef trips, snack bar, aquarium, and gift shop. It has two protected swimming beaches, sailboat, powerboat and canoe rentals, glass-bottom boat rides and a nature walk.

Reservations for camping at John Pennekamp should be made in advance. For information, write to **John Pennekamp Coral Reef State Park**, PO Box 1560, Key Largo FL 33037; ☎ 305-451-1621. At MM 102 you'll pass **The Quay** on the bay side of the highway. The Quay offers a formal indoor/outdoor restaurant and an informal beachside mesquite grill, a Bayside pool, a small beach and a relaxing atmosphere. Sunset birdwatch cruises leave from The Quay dock.

Stop by the **Equipment Locker Sport & Bicycle Shop** at MM 101.4 in the Tradewinds Plaza for rental, repairs parts or accessories (☎ 305-453-0140). Continuing south, the bike path leads to the Holiday Inn docks at MM 100, where you can book a ride on the *African Queen* steamboat made famous by Humphrey Bogart and Katherine Hepburn in the 1951 film classic of the same name. At MM 99.5, just past the shopping center, the highway splits around a median. After passing the traffic light, keep to the left on the southbound side. Service, repairs, parts and rentals are possible at the **Tavernier Bicycle & Hobby Shop** (☎ 305-852-2859) at MM 92. It opens Monday through Thursday from 9:30 am to 6 pm, Friday 9:30 am to 7 pm, Saturday from 9:30 to 6 pm and Sunday from 10 am till 5 pm.

Key Largo ends at the Tavernier Creek Bridge, MM 91. The bike path stops, but you can ride on the old highway to your left. Be careful. Automobiles use this as a secondary road. On the bay side you'll find a snack bar, dive shop and boat rentals at the **Tavernier Creek Marina**. A left turn onto Burton Drive at MM 92.6 leads to **Harry Harris County Park**, a good spot for a swim and a picnic. The park opens at 8 am.

The Snake Creek Bridge, MM 87, crosses to Windley Key and Islamorada where you can sign up for a snorkel trip to explore the sunken Spanish ship, *Herrara*, or swim with dolphins at **Theatre of the Sea** (MM 85.5). Plan a long stop at **Holiday Isle,** a beach complex at MM 84 that throbs with the beat of live reggae bands amidst the sweet smell of barbecued ribs and cotton candy. Stretch out on the white sand beach, sail, sunbathe, snorkel, fish, scuba, Jet Ski, windsurf, parasail, swim or rent an inflatable island and drift off to sea. Amenities include tropical pools, rooftop and beach-side restaurants, hotels, motels and nightly entertainment.

At MM 78.5, a 24-passenger boat leaves for **Indian Key**, a historic preserve, and **Lignumvitae Key**, a state botanical site. From Islamorada (also known as Upper Matecumbe Key), ride south over Teatable Bridge and Indian Key Bridge to **Lower Matecumbe Key**. **Fiesta Key** (MM 70) features a **KOA Campground** with tent and RV sites, a game room, laundry, two Jacuzzis, and a camp store. There are motels and resorts nearby too.

For oceanside tent camping, continue another mile and a half to **Long Key State Park** at MM 67.5. The park opens at 8 am and closes at sunset year-round. Here you can swim or fish in the Atlantic and enjoy a hike on the nature trail. Watch for fast-growing tree roots that occasionally surface through the pavement along the bike trail outside the park.

The Middle Keys

The Marathon area begins the Middle Keys – from Conch Key (MM62.5) to the Seven Mile Bridge (MM 47).

Leaving Long Key Park toward Key West, you cross a 2½-mile bridge to **Conch Key** and **Grassy Key**. Salty breezes cool you as you pass the splendid ocean and bay views. Just beyond the bridge on **Duck Key** (MM 61) lies **Hawk's Cay Marina**, an oasis offering glass-bottom boat tours, boat rentals, diving, snorkeling and fishing charters. The sprawling marina/resort has 177 spacious rooms, a sandy beach, swimming lagoon and four restaurants. Bike rentals are available for daytrippers.

Next comes Grassy Key, MM 59, home base of the **Dolphin Research Center**, which offers unique educational programs, including backcountry field trips and dolphin swims. For the next few miles the bike

Seven Mile Bridge.

path winds along mangrove swamps that edge the highway. Be sure to stock up on cold beverages as there are few commercial establishments until you reach the **Wellesley Inn** (☎ 305-743-8550), MM 54, where you will find a 24-hour Denny's Restaurant offering light meals. The Wellesley is a full-service resort offering boat trips, diving and snorkeling tours.

Stop by the **Equipment Locker Sport & Cycle Shop** (MM 53) for supplies, parts or repairs. The shop is open Monday through Friday from 9 am to 6 pm, Saturday from 9 am to 5 pm and Sunday from 10 am to 3 pm. They offer repair service and rent beach cruiser bikes and kid's bikes. ☎ 305-289-1670.

The bike path passes Marathon Airport at MM 52 and on through the town of Marathon, a bustling resort community featuring sportfishing as the main attraction, along with several restaurants and motel accommodations. A left at MM 50 onto Sombrero Beach Road, followed by a two-mile ride, leads to Sombrero Beach Park's picnic areas, rest rooms and ocean, swimming beach. As you continue toward Key West, the sea turns a prettier shade of turquoise, the scenery gets better, and the smell of salt in the air grows stronger. Seagulls and pelicans perch on the bridge railings. Sweeping ocean panoramas offer dramatic photo opportunities.

The Lower Keys

MM 47 begins the Seven Mile Bridge and the Lower Keys, a natural wilderness area.

If you are touring locally and don't wish to cross all seven miles of bridge to the Lower Keys, travel along the adjacent old bridge. Be aware it is a **dead end**. Auto traffic is not permitted and you'll usually find other cyclists, especially on a weekend. If you are traveling to the lower keys and Key West, the old bridge won't get you there. It stops after a few miles. Instead travel along the shoulder of the new automobile bridge. The bike trail area before the bridge is patchy with gravel and grass. It becomes a grassy shoulder after the bridge and is more level on the Bayside.

Little Duck Key (MM 40), the first patch of land after crossing the Seven Mile Bridge , welcomes travelers with a lovely, small sand beach and shaded picnic tables. This is a fine spot to peel off some clothing and take a swim. Two more bridges pass over Missouri Key and Sunshine Key (formerly Ohio Key), a 75-acre camping island at MM 39.

The sprawling campground features 400 sites, a marina, grocery store, tennis courts, pool, and every other imaginable amenity. Write to **Sunshine Key Camping Resort**, Box 790, Sunshine Key FL 33040. ☎ 305-872-2217.

At MM 38, the trail enters **Bahia Honda State Park**. Named for its deep bay by the Spanish, the park is one of the prettiest in the Keys. It caters to 200,000 day visitors per year. Swimming sites are on the Atlantic and Gulf sides; both beaches have sandy bottoms. It also has bay- and oceanside camp sites, a nature trail, marina and dive shop.

There are three furnished duplex cabins (six units) in the park that accommodate eight people each. Linens and utensils are provided. Snacks and limited grocery items are available at the concession building. Shaded picnic tables are at the old bridge and at Sandspur Beach.

The park opens at 8 am and closes at sunset. For further information write, Bahia Honda State Recreation Area, Box 782, Big Pine Key FL 33043. ☎ 305-872-2353; www.bahiahondapark.com or www.fla-keys.com.

The Bahia Honda Bridge crosses to **Summerland Key** (MM 35), a jumping-off point to explore the offshore **Looe Key Marine Sanctuary**.

MM 33 begins **Big Pine Key**, a pine-forest island complete with free-roaming, miniature Key deer. A right turn on Key Deer Boulevard

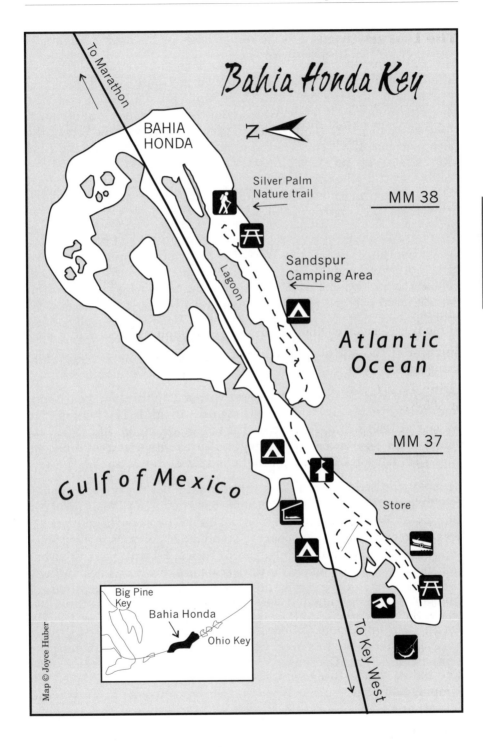

(MM 30.5) will bring you to the refuge area for the deer. This area is also a refuge for the great white heron.

After you make the turn off US 1, stay on the south side of the street where green striping marks the bike trail. Refuge headquarters lie about two miles to the left on Watson Boulevard. If you ride another 1½ miles down Key Deer Boulevard and turn left onto Big Pine Street, the path cuts into thick stands of pine and palm trees toward the Blue Hole, where several large alligators make their home. You may have trouble spotting the tiny, two-foot-tall Key deer. They come out only at dusk and early morning. Watch out too for the huge webs of the golden orb spiders in the hardwood forest.

There are 25 miles of low, wet ground, mangroves and RV parks between Big Pine Key and Key West. The bike path is intermittent with grassy or gravel shoulders. The incline in a few spots will force you to ride on the highway for a bit. Keep to the side as much as possible. You can see coral patches and distant mangrove islands from the bridges and there are spots to stop and take a swim. Avoid exploring dirt roads leading into backwoods. At MM 28.5, Bayside, Little Torch Key, **Parmer's Place Motel** (☎ 305-872-2157) rents comfortable waterfront motel rooms.

Sugarloaf Key, MM 20, has a resort with a dolphin show, boat ramp and comfortable air-conditioned rooms. At MM 17, behind the Sugarloaf Lodge, stands a vacant bat tower, a remnant of a failed attempt to lure the mosquito-hungry creatures into the area. Adjacent Sugarloaf Airport offers aerial tours and skydiving lessons.

Just past the Saddlebunch Keys, the bike path picks up on the bay side. **Big Coppitt Key** (MM 11 to 7) is home base to the Key West Naval Air Station at Boca Chica, where thundering F-16s slice the sky above. Nearer to earth, low-flying ospreys stand quiet guard over their pole-top nests. Another mile brings you to **Stock Island**, your final approach to Key West. Named for cows and pigs kept here in early days, the island is partially a service area for municipal offices and the site of the Lower Keys hospital.

A right turn onto Junior College Road, just before the Key West Bridge, will bring you to the Key West Resort Golf Course and the Tennessee Williams Fine Arts Center.

Key West

After crossing the bridge into Key West, you can turn left or right onto a paved bike trail that skirts the shoreline on both North and South Roosevelt Boulevards. Either route will lead you to the historic heart of Old Town Key West and the historic seaport. If you arrive by car, boat, ship or plane you'll find rental bikes at hotels and in town. Cycle touring is the favored way to avoid congested traffic and tour the city. Open cabs are cyclist-powered.

A right turn off the Key West Bridge brings you past a commercial strip of hotels and restaurants, Garrison Bight and the Key West Yacht Club. Farther on, North Roosevelt turns into Truman Avenue. Truman later intersects Duval Street, which leads to the historic section. The bike path ends with North Roosevelt Boulevard, but picks up again on the south side of the island at Higgs Beach. A right turn on Whitehead Street leads to Mallory Square and the center of activity.

 Be sure to obey the one-way street signs as cyclists are ticketed for going the wrong way.

A left turn at the Key West Bridge along South Roosevelt Boulevard brings you past the airport, the Salt Ponds, an ecological preserve and new condo development, Smathers Beach and Higgs Beach. The bike path stops at the south end of Higgs Beach. A right turn will lead to Truman Avenue.

The area on and around Caroline St. is shaded by huge tropical poinciana and palm trees. Stop by the Chamber of Commerce on Wall St. in the Mallory Square area for a copy of the *Solares Hill Walking and Biking Guide* that details every inch of the city. Additional bike paths throughout the city are in the planning stages.

Key West Bicycle Rentals

(most accept major credit cards)

Adventure Scooter & Bicycle Rentals features daily specials, locks, and group rates with locations all over town:

- 2900 N. Roosevelt Blvd., in the Blockbuster Video & K-Mart Shopping Center at Key Plaza. ☎ 305-293-9933.

- 3675 S. Roosevelt Blvd. at the Key Wester Resort next to the Airport. ☎ 305-293-9922.

- 3824 N. Roosevelt Blvd., at the Comfort Inn next to Key West Welcome Center. ☎ 305-292-1666.

- 601-Front St., Hyatt Key West. ☎ 305-293-9944.

- 617 Front St., at the Galleon Resort. ☎ 305-293-9955.

- 1 Duval St., Pier House. ☎ 305-293-0441.

Cycling Trails

Bike Key West provides a backpack, lock and helmet with each rental. Open Mon. through Fri., 9 am to 6 pm. Free pick-up and delivery. ☎ 305-292-9165.

The Bicycle Center offers single- and three-speed cruisers, beach cruisers, mopeds and scooters. 523 Truman Ave. ☎ 305-294-4556.

The Bike Shop specializes in expert repairs on all makes and models, with the largest selection of parts and accessories in the Keys. Free estimates. Open Mon. Through Sat., 9 am to 5:30 pm, Sun., 10 am to 5:30 pm. 1110 Truman Ave. ☎ 305-294-1073.

Conch Bike Express delivers to your hotel, condo, marina or home. All bikes have lights, a basket and lock. Open 9 am to 5 pm daily. ☎ 305-294-4318.

Moped Hospital offers bicycle, moped and scooter rentals, sales and repairs. Open 9 am to 5 pm every day except Christmas, Thanksgiving and New Years. 601 Truman Ave. ☎ 305-296-3344.

Keys Moped & Scooter Inc. sells and rents bikes and scooters. Open 9 am to 6 pm seven days except Thanksgiving, Christmas and New Years. 523 Truman Ave. ☎ 305-294-0399.

Paradise Rentals, Inc. at La Concha Holiday Inn, 430 Duval St., ☎ 293-1112, rents bikes and scooters from 9 am to 5 pm every day. Also at the Key West Sandal Factory, 105 Whitehead St. ☎ 305-292-6441.

Pirate Scooter, open seven days from 8 am to 8 pm, offers helmets and locks, free instruction and free pickup and delivery anywhere in Key West. Located at 8401 Southard St. ☎ 305-295-0000.

Tropical Bicycle & Scooter Rentals has beach cruisers, scooters and jeeps. Open seven days, 8:30 am to 5:30 pm. 1300 Duval St. ☎ 305-294-8136.

■ Cycling Everglades National Park

The main park entrance is 45 miles south on US 1 from Miami International Airport. There are no regularly scheduled bus tours or public transportation to or within the park, but Greyhound Bus will take you along US 1 to Route 9336/SW 344th St. in Florida City, which is 11 miles from the park entrance. Turn right at the first traffic light onto Palm Drive and follow the signs to the park. From there, you can cycle route 9336 – a paved road through a residential and farm area.

Greyhound buses leave three times daily from the Miami Airport-vicinity bus station located at 4111 NW 27 St., Miami FL 33142, ☎ 800-231-2222; in Key Largo, Islamorada, Ramrod Key and Big Pine, ☎ 305-296-9072- in Marathon, ☎ 800-410-5397. You can arrange for advance tickets online at www.greyhound.com.

Avoid cycling the entire distance from the airport. There is no shoulder, and traffic is fast-moving and heavy. Transporting your bike by bus or car is a safer choice.

There is an entrance fee that is good for seven days: $10 per private motorized vehicle or $5 per person entering by bicycle. At the Main Visitor Center, open daily from 8 am till 5 pm, you can view a 15-minute introductory film and displays, as well as pick up schedules of park activities. Books, postcards, insect repellent and other sundries are sold here.

Visitors are advised to bring drinking water and snacks, since these items are sometimes hard to find. With sun and insects likely to be abundant, sun screen, protective clothing and insect repellent are advised. Insects can make a visit unbearable during the summer months if you are not prepared.

Information on mosquito levels during the summer is available at ☎ 305-242-7700 (8:30 am to 4 pm EST).

The Main Park Road begins at the visitor center, wanders through the Pinelands and ends 38 miles later at Flamingo. The road is paved and well-maintained although no services are available. Several cycling trails take off from this road and a few more begin at Flamingo. Horseback riders occasionally use these trails – be cautious when passing and quietly give them the right-of-way. The north end of the park can be best explored along Shark Valley Loop.

If you are transporting your bike to the Everglades by car, you may park at the Royal Palm Visitor Center parking lot, Long Pine Key picnic area or Flamingo Outpost. If you plan to camp you will need a backcountry permit, available at the Main Visitor Center.

The only overnight visitor accommodations within the park are at Flamingo Lodge, 38 miles southwest of the Main Visitor Center.

Camping is on a first-come, first-served basis. Flamingo has 60 tent sites and 235 drive-in sites. Long Pine Key has 108 sites. During the winter, campgrounds fill every night. Plan to arrive early in the day.

Modern comfort stations and drinking water are available at both sites; cold-water showers at Flamingo only. Limited groceries and camping supplies may be purchased at the Flamingo Marina Store. Swimming in the park is discouraged. Freshwater ponds have alligators; salt water areas are shallow, with mucky bottoms. Underwater visibility is extremely poor and sharks and barracudas abound.

Shark Valley Loop

A 15-mile road that circuits the northern portion of Everglades National Park, this loop lies off US 41, the Tamiami Trail, 50 miles from the Main Visitor Center. This road edges a wide shallow waterway crowded with dense fields of sawgrass.

Alligators, otters, deer, raccoons, frogs, snakes, turtles and birds, including rare wood storks and snail kites, inhabit this watery expanse. Hardwood hammocks and other tree islands dot the landscape. The loop road, originally constructed by oil prospectors, is used for tram rides, bicycles and walking. A 65-ft observation tower along the road provides a spectacular bird's-eye view.

For your safety use extreme caution when stopping for trams. The shoulder is very steep. Be sure to come to a complete stop before dismounting and pulling to the side of the road. Watch out for snakes and alligators. Venomous pygmy rattlesnakes are common on high ground during the wet season. Also avoid touching poison ivy, poisonwood trees or the sawgrass, which can inflict nasty cuts.

Bicycles may be rented next to the ticket booth daily from 8:30 am to 3 pm. Cycling along the Tamiami Trail is not recommended – traffic is fast moving, services are few and the road shoulder is soft. The **Shark Valley Visitor Center** opens between 8:30 am and 5:15 pm. Cycling permits are required for groups of 10 or more.

The Pinelands

A network of interconnecting trails runs through the Pinelands, an unusually diverse pine forest. Under the pine canopy are about 200 types of plants, including 30 found nowhere else on Earth. Whitetail deer, opossums, raccoons and the endangered Florida panther live in the Pinelands. You can also see turtles, lizards and snakes, exotic zebra butterflies, striped grasshoppers, red-bellied woodpeckers, orchids and tree snails. The bicycle trails, a series of one-lane fire roads, are well-maintained. Avoid those marked for hiking only; they may be mucky and impassable by bike.

Mahogany Trail, located 20 miles from the Main Visitor Center and two miles from the Main Park Road, is one of the favorite walking trails and worth a side-trip to see. The raised boardwalk climbs first over swamp then into a dense jungle-like environment. In contrast to the surrounding grass prairies, here you can view red-headed woodpeckers, orchids growing in the tree tops, rare paurotis palms and towering mahogany trees, including the largest living specimen in the United States. Huge golden orb spider webs are suspended from the tree branches; colorful liguus tree snails inhabit the bark. At night, barred owls awaken to hunt. No facilities.

Golden orb spider

Cycling Trails

Flamingo Area Trails

Flamingo sits at the south end of the park, on Florida Bay. The principal jumping-off point for canoeing, fishing and boating in Everglades National Park, it is also a leader in mosquito production. Bug repellent is needed year-round. In late November we were fogged in by mosquitos at the campground, but found the trails north of Flamingo and the paved area at the marina less inhabited by these pests.

The camp store (open mid-Nov. through mid-March) rents canoes, and stocks groceries, camping supplies, bait and fuel. **Flamingo Marina and Outpost Resort** offers air-conditioned rooms, spacious cabins, camping, a pool, and gift shop. It also offers wilderness tours, fishing trips and tram tours. In season, you can rent a bicycle at the shack outside the camp store. ☎ 800-600-3813.

Snake Bight Trail, a rugged 1.6-mile route, tunnels one-way through a shaded tropical hardwood hammock. The trail starts six miles east of Flamingo from the Main Park Road. Good bird watching opportunities abound in the wooded areas from the short boardwalk at the end of the trail. Alligators frequent this spot. Bicycles are permitted on all but the boardwalk.

Rowdy Bend a 2.6-mile trail, winds along an old roadbed through buttonwood forest and open coastal prairie. The trail is often overgrown with grasses. At the end, the trail joins with the Snake Bight Trail.

West Lake Trail is half a mile round-trip. Seven miles north of Flamingo on the Main Park Road, this self-guiding boardwalk trail wanders through a forest of white mangrove (*Laguncularia racemosa*), black mangrove (*Avicennia nitida*), red mangrove (*Rhizophora mangle*), and buttonwood (*Conocarpus erectus*) trees to the edge of West Lake. Wheelchair-accessible.

Christian Point Trail is 1.8 mile one-way. One mile north of Flamingo. Cycle a rustic path beginning in dense buttonwoods full of air plants. End in open coastal prairie along the shores of Snake Bight. Good habitat for raptors.

Bear Lake Trail is 1.6 miles one-way and two miles north of Flamingo on the Bear Lake Road. Journey through a dense hardwood hammock mixed with mangroves. Excellent area for woodland birds. More than 30 different tree types. The trail ends at Bear Lake.

Eco Pond is a half-mile round-trip. Stroll around this freshwater pond at Flamingo and enjoy a wide variety of wading birds, song birds, and other wildlife. Alligators often cruise the pond. Good bird watching, especially at sunrise and sunset, from the wheelchair-accessible viewing platform at the beginning of the trail.

Guy Bradley Trail, one mile one-way, is a scenic shortcut between the campground amphitheater and the visitor center. Mingle with a variety of birds and butterflies as you amble along the shore of Florida Bay.

Bayshore Loop is a two-mile round-trip. Meander along the shore of Florida Bay and watch for remnants of a former outpost fishing village. Begin at the Coastal Prairie Trailhead at the back of loop "C" in the Flamingo Campground. Veer left at the trail junction to the bay.

Coastal Prairie Trail extends for 7½ miles one-way. Step back in time as you walk this old road once used by wild cotton pickers and fishermen. Shady buttonwoods and open expanses of succulent coastal plants await. Begin at the rear of loop "C" in the campground. A backcountry permit is required for overnight camping.

Fishing

A day of fishing anywhere is great, but in the Everglades and Florida Keys it's better! Where else can you catch bonefish from a dock, a tarpon or permit from a bridge, a marlin from a charter boat and even sea trout in a backyard canal? Here's a rundown on what to expect offshore, backcountry (the mangrove flats of Florida Bay and Ten Thousand Island region), from a party boat, a head boat, a bridge, and even onshore.

■ Offshore

Charter boats are just that. You book them for a deep-sea fishing trip and the outfitters take care of the rest. Bait, tackle and ice are usually provided, and fish are plentiful, from tail-dancing sailfish and marlin, blackfin tuna, king mackerel or reel-smoking wahoo and colorful, dolphin (the fish, not Flipper) to delicious yellowtail and mutton snapper, grouper and kingfish – each in its season.

Florida Keys captains are professional and really aim to please. They will stay out as long as the angler doesn't give up. Key West Captain Bill Wickers' favorite 'one that got away' tale is of a 700-lb marlin hooked from his boat, the *Linda D*, at 1:10 pm on 50 lb line. The fish put up a fight for the entire day and was brought to the boat at least 10 or 12 times. The angler held steady long after sunset, certain the fish would tire. At 10:30 pm the marlin let go and swam away.

Charter boats cater to parties of four to six persons with full-day rates averaging about $650, half-day around $450, for the whole boat. Everything is included except lunch, beverages and suntan lotion. Light tackle boats can accommodate one or two fishermen at substantially lower rates. Party-boat tariffs average $35 per person for a half-day, including tackle.

In Key West, where the ocean meets the Gulf, there is always a calm area to fish. On the Gulf side the boats troll for barracuda, kingfish and bonito. Oceanside catches are usually sailfish and dolphin.

Fishing Calendar

January-February

Offshore – sailfish, amberjack, kingfish. **Reef** – snapper, grouper, mackerel, barracuda. **Bay** – snapper, mackerel, cobia good on wrecks. **Flats** – bonefish, barracuda.

March-April

Offshore – sailfish, tuna, fair dolphin fish, peak season for mako shark. **Reef** – snapper, cobia, grouper, barracuda. **Bay** – good snapper, good cobia on wrecks. **Flats** – bonefish, good permit, tarpon at bridges and backcountry flats.

May-June

Offshore – dolphin fish, tuna, sailfish. **Reef** – snapper, barracuda. **Bay** – snapper. **Flats** – bonefish, permit, excellent tarpon on flats, tarpon at bridges.

July-August

Offshore – dolphin fish. **Reef** – barracuda, excellent snapper, especially at night. **Bay** – fair snapper, permit on Gulf wrecks. **Flats** – bonefish, permit.

September-October

Offshore – dolphin fish, fair to good tuna. **Reef** – fair to good snapper, excellent barracuda. **Flats** – good bonefish and redfish in October, fair to good tarpon and snook at bridges.

November-December

Offshore – sailfish, kingfish. **Reef** – snapper, good mackerel, barracuda. **Bay** – snapper, good cobia, especially on wrecks. **Flats** – bonefish, good redfish, fair to good tarpon and snook at bridges.

■ Where to Book a Charter

The Upper Keys

Gear and tackle is provided. Rates are for the whole boat. Expect to tip the captain and crew. Bring your own lunch and beverages.

Captain Bill of the **Killer White**, a 50-ft, air-conditioned, custom sports fishing boat, specializes in offshore, deep-sea cruising and reef trips for dolphin, marlin, tuna, wahoo, kingfish, sailfish, shark, grouper, and snapper. The boat has a bathroom, a refrigerator and an icemaker. Rates are $700 for eight hours; $600 for six hours; $500 for five hours. The *Killer White* is docked at the Holiday Isle Marina (MM 83.5), Islamorada FL. ☎ 800-817-0454.

DayTripper III is a customized 23-ft Seacraft open fisherman powered by 235 HP engines. Bathroom. Accommodates up to three anglers for either inshore or offshore fishing. Rates are $550 for eight hours, $400 for four hours. ☎ 800-817-0454.

DayTripper IV is a custom built 32-ft Stuart Angler with a large tuna tower, bathroom and sunshade. It carries six anglers. Captain Ron Green has 19 years of experience in the Florida Keys. He has been featured in *Florida Sportsman* magazine and was the winner of the prestigious Del Guercio Tripod and Islamorada Sailfish Tournaments.

His expert skills and knowledge of sport fishing will help you experience a fine day of fishing, whether you choose to fish the reef or go trolling offshore. Rates are $600 for eight hours, $450 for four hours. ☎ 800-817-0454.

The **Ambush,** a 34-ft custom restored Hatteras, is fast and rigged for tournament fishing. The cabin is air-conditioned, with a full galley, microwave, refrigerator, head, TV and VCR. Captain David Lowell, who has over 20 years of experience in the Islamorada waters, will customize each charter based on the requests of the anglers. *The Ambush* is docked at Worldwide Marina, behind Worldwide Sports, Bayside, Islamorada. ☎ 800-817-0454.

The Middle Keys

Marathon

The **Adios III**, a 38-ft Topaz captained by Bob Tittle, who's fished the area for 40 years, goes out for full- and half-day ocean excursions. She carries six passengers and a crew of two. Rates are $700 for a full day; $550 for a half-day. ☎ 800-817-0454.

The Lower Keys

Key West

Neptune's Fury, a 34-ft Crusader at Slip 2, Garrison Bight Marina, Key West, is available for offshore and reef fishing. Enjoy this fully equipped offshore boat, skippered by a local conch who knows these waters well. Perfect for anything from custom fishing trips to fishing tournaments. The crew is expert at finding marlin, sailfish, grouper, tuna, dolphin, barracuda, king mackerel, tarpon and wahoo. Rates are $550 for eight hours, $475 for six hours, $425 for four hours. Carries six anglers, two crew members. ☎ 800-817-0454.

OMB Deluxe, a 42-ft Post at the Garrison Bight Marina, Key West, was built for comfortable deep-sea cruising. The crew knows how to find marlin, sailfish, grouper, tuna, dolphin, barracuda, king mackerel, tarpon and wahoo. $700 for eight hours; $475 for four hours. ☎ 800-817-0454.

OMB II, a gorgeous, 40-ft Custom fishing boat at Garrison Bight Marina, Key West, offers comfortable deep-sea charter fishing. She goes out for marlin, sailfish, grouper, tuna, dolphin, barracuda, king mackerel, tarpon and wahoo. Cost is $600 for eight hours, $450 for four hours. Carries six anglers, two crew members. ☎ 800-817-0454.

Relentless Pursuit, a 40-ft Custom docked at Garrison Bight Marina, Key West, features comfort, safety and successful fishing! Skippered by an experienced local conch, the *Relentless Pursuit* tracks marlin, sailfish, grouper, tuna, dolphin, barracuda, king mackerel, tarpon and wahoo. $650 for eight hours; $450 for four hours.☎ 800-817-0454.

The Blue Runner, a 28-ft Whitewater at Garrison Marina, Key West, was built for bay fishing. Angle for permit, snapper, cobia, grouper and tarpon. Captain Steve Faraldo is experienced with the fishing areas around Key West and knows where the big ones are hiding. Full day, $550, half-day, $425. No cabin. ☎ 800-817-0454.

The *Relentless*, a beautiful 43-ft Topaz is geared for deep-sea fishing. Skippered by Captain Ricky Ferrell, *The Relentless* motors offshore for marlin, sailfish, grouper, tuna, dolphin, barracuda, king mackerel, tarpon or wahoo. Departs Garrison Bight Marina. Rates $675 for eight hours. ☎ 800-817-0454.

Too Relentless, a 25-ft Seacraft, tours the backcountry from Garrison Bight Marina, Key West. This light-tackle boat is fully equipped and designed for fishing trips to the Florida Bay (Gulf of Mexico). Captain Rush Malte will take you to where the big ones are biting. ☎ 800-817-0454.

Other Marinas Where You Can Book a Charter

Key Largo
Gilbert's Motel & Marina
MM 108
☎ 305-451-1133

Key Largo Holiday Inn Resort & Marina
MM 100, Oceanside
☎ 305-451-3661

Tavernier Creek Marina
MM 90.5
☎ 305-852-5854

Islamorada
Islamorada Yacht Basin/Lorelei
MM 82
☎ 305-664-2692, 305-664-4338

Holiday Isle Resorts & Marina
MM 84
☎ 305-664-2321

Bud N' Mary's Marina
MM 79.5
☎ 305-664-2461

Whale Harbor Dock
MM 83.5
☎ 305-664-4511

Marathon
Holiday Inn Marina
MM 54
☎ 305-451-2121

7-Mile Marina
MM 47.5 (at Seven Mile Bridge)
☎ 305-743-7712

Hawk's Cay Resort and Marina
MM 61
Duck Key
☎ 305-743-9000

Fishing

Key Colony Beach Marina
589 6th St.
Key Colony Beach
☎ 305-289-1310

Key West
Land's End Marina
201 William St.
Key West
☎ 305-296-3838

Charter Row Amberjack
Pier North Roosevelt Ave.
Garrison Bight
Key West
☎ 305-294-3093

Oceanside Marina
5950 Peninsula Ave.
Stock Island
☎ 305-294-4676

Everglades - Ten Thousand Island Area
(All mangrove fishing is from shallow-draft flats boats)

Chokoloskee Island Park
PO Box 430
Chokoloskee FL 33925
☎ 941-695-2414 for fishing guides and boats.

Captain Tony Brock
Chokoloskee FL 33925
☎ 941-695-4150

Captain Max Miller
Everglades City FL 33929
☎ 941-695-2420

■ Party Boats or Head Boats

If you're interested in rubbing elbows with lots of other fishermen, and want to share a fine fishing and people-watching experience, try a party boat or head boat. It's an inexpensive way to fish off-shore. Bait and tackle are provided. You may even make new friends and catch dinner: snapper, grouper, even dolphin and sailfish are caught off party boats. Sharks, too! Any way you go, even in your own boat or a rental, offshore is a must, a real Keys experience.

Key Largo

Sailor's Choice. Two half-day trips daily for $28 per person. Holiday Inn Docks, MM 100. ☎ 305-451-1802, 451-0041.

Islamorada

Robbies Holiday Isle Docks (South End) MM 84.5, Islamorada FL 33036. $25 for a half-day trip. Five-hour night trips cost $30 per person. ☎ 305-664-8070, (office) 305-664-4196.

Gulf Lady party fishing boat departs the Whale Harbor Marina, Islamorada. Full-day trips leave at 9:30 am and cost $55 per person. ☎ 305-664-2628/664-2461.

Ms. Tradewinds, MM 83.5, Whale Harbor Marina, goes out daily for three four-hour trips. Day-trips cost $26.95, night trips $31.95. ☎ 305-664-8341.

Captain's Lady party boat, MM 84.5 at Robbies Holiday Isle. ☎ 305-664-8498.

Captain Winner II party boat, Holiday Isle. ☎ 305-664-8070.

Catch & Release Tactics

Don't Waste Time. Quickly play and release the fish. A fish played too long may be too exhausted to recover.

Handle Fish Gently. Don't grip fish by the eyes or gills; use a firm grasp but don't squeeze too tightly. Never squeeze a fish around its middle.

Unhook Carefully. Never rip the hook out. Grab the bend of the hook and turn fly upside down so the point of the hook is pointing down toward the water. Squeeze down barbs on hook with pliers. When deeply hooked, a fish's chance of survival is much better if the leader is cut and the hook is left in place.

Revive Exhausted Fish. Revive the fish by holding it upright in the water (heading upstream in streams) and moving it back and forth to force water through its gills. When the fish revives and begins to swim normally, let it go to survive and challenge another angler.

Reproduced with permission from Orvis News.

Technique for reviving a tarpon from a boat. Hold fish upright and move forward and backward to force water through mouth and gills.

Technique for reviving a tarpon in the water is the same. Gently move the fish back and forth to move water through mouth and gills.

Key West

Capt. John's *Greyhound V*. Amberjack Pier/City Marina, Palm Ave. & N. Roosevelt. Offers day-trips for $35. ☎ 305-296-5139.

Gulfstream III, at the Garrison City Marina; day-trips, $38 per person, with gear and bait. ☎ 305-296-8494.

■ Backcountry Fishing

Florida Bay, Ten Thousand Islands Region

Mangrove fishing, Everglades City (© Jon Huber).

Backcountry is exactly what it says – out back in the wild beautiful Florida Bay, Everglades National Park, Great White Heron National Wildlife Refuge or around the uninhabited keys of the Gulf of Mexico and Ten Thousand Island region.

White pelicans, egrets, or cormorants make a beautiful backdrop for fishing these mostly flat waters. Folks who don't like offshore usually love the backcountry. Sea trout, redfish, jacks, tarpon, and snook are just some of the fish you can catch out there, where man's footprints are rare and nature's hand is heavy. In Everglades City, along Route 29 or the Tamiami Trail, you can fish the roadside canals almost anywhere you find a parking space. Watch for gators crossing the road.

■ Bridge & Shore Fishing

If you have no intention of boating, due to time restrictions, fear of sea sickness, you have small children or are sunburn-prone, fishing from shore or a bridge is for you. Snapper, grouper, sheepshead, permit and even tarpon can be and are caught from the Keys bridges. There are more than two dozen bridges that accommodate fishermen and sight-seers. You can watch pelicans, egrets, seagulls and osprey feed and preen their feathers only feet away. Here, too, the people are friendly and the sights are varied. It can be really exciting, especially when a fisherman hooks up with the 'silver king,' and the tarpon zooms parallel to the bridge. Everyone moves very quickly, as a hundred pounds or more of shimmering beauty and strength tests the angler. All who witness get to see a battle with a sporting giant of the fish clan, the tarpon. Fishing from shore, or wading with lures or bait, you can catch the spectacular bonefish or hook a barracuda. For the neophyte, a toothy and tough 'cuda is fun, but not difficult to entice. Whatever your fishing pleasure, you won't be disappointed in the Everglades or Florida Keys.

A much-applauded new trend that many Floridian fishermen are practicing is a catch-and-release policy for trophy fish that were previously killed for wall mounting.

"It insures some good fishing for our grandchildren," remarked one charter captain. Many Keys marinas feature lifelike replicas of favorite gamefish so anglers need not kill to go home with a photo of their catch. The International Gamefish Release and Enhancement Foundation, Inc. is a non-profit organization with the principal goal of encouraging releases. The group's credo says it all: "It takes a good fisherman to catch a fish, but it takes a great fisherman to release it."

■ Fly Fishing

The Florida Keys Fly Fishing School provides fly fishermen of all skill levels with an opportunity to learn or improve their saltwater fly fishing skills and techniques. The school specializes in catching the tropical flats species such as tarpon, bonefish, snook, permit, redfish and mutton snapper by sight fishing with fly rods on the flats. The classes are usually held at Cheeca Lodge in Islamorada. They do not include actual fishing, but cover casting, sighting fish, fly selection, fly

Fishing

Hammerhead shark.

tying, fly presentation, tackle specification and selection, leaders, knots, fighting fish, wind problems, flats etiquette, short and quick casting, selecting fly fishing guides and more. Films, slides, and field exercises are used to give broad coverage. Students are given plenty of personal attention. Fishing charters may be arranged after the course for an additional charge.

The instructor staff is a *Who's Who* of saltwater fly fishermen, including Stu Apte, author of *Fishing in the Florida Keys and Flamingo*, Chico Fernandez, Steve Huff, Rick Ruoff, Steve Rajeff, Flip Pallot and Sandy Moret. All of the instructors are known for their tremendous angling experience and ability and a unique desire to share with someone who seeks an ultimate angling experience. The weekend sessions provide at least one instructor for every five students. The seminars are held six weekends per year at Cheeca Lodge, beginning with a Friday evening reception and ending on Sunday afternoon. The $895 fee includes the course, breakfast and lunch for two days, and use of equipment.

For yearly schedules write Mr. Sandy Moret, Director, Florida Keys Fly Fishing School, PO Box 603, Islamorada FL 33036. ☎ 305-664-5423.

■ Flats & Back Country Fishing Guides

Capt. Hank Brown, tarpon and bonefish specialist. Director of the Florida Keys Fishing Guides Association. An encyclopedia of fishing knowledge, he manufactures "The Hank Brown Hook-Up Lures" and "Hook-Up Bucktails." ☎ 305-664-9143.

Capt. Billy Knowles. A renowned fly caster. ☎ 305-664-4259.

Capt. Craig Brewer. Born and raised in Islamorada, he knows where to find fish. ☎ 305-664-4999.

Capt. Gary Ellis offers 25 years of experience and is an excellent bonefish, tarpon, and snook guide. ☎ 305-664-8452.

Capt. Davey Wilson has been fishing the backcountry for years and specializes in bonefish. ☎ 305-664-9480.

Capt. Jim Lozar, a long-time Keys resident and an accomplished fishing guide, is well-versed in fishing the flats. ☎ 305-664-9759.

Capt. Rick Miller specializes in redfish, trout, tarpon, snook, permit, bonefish, and snapper. ☎ 305-852-7612.

Capt. Jeff Johnson offers fly, spin or artificial lure fishing. ☎ 305-852-0111.

Capt. Mario Del Toro is known for courteous service, specializing in light tackle and fly fishing for bonefish, tarpon, permit, snook and redfish. ☎ 305-664-9935.

Capt. Tony Nobregas is an experienced backcountry and flats fishing guide for light tackle and fly fishing. ☎ 305-664-9212.

Capt. Tom Demoss finds the best spots for snook, tarpon, bonefish or redfish. Light spin or fly fishing. Fly fishing instruction available. ☎ 305-852-9359.

Capt. Jeff Wright features backcountry and flats fishing for snook and tarpon. ☎ 305-664-3007.

Capt. Ralph Knowles offers experience in flats fishing for tarpon, bonefish and snook. ☎ 305-664-3572.

■ Fishing on Your Own

For visiting anglers who trailer their own small fishing craft, there are public ramps everywhere. Numerous tackle and bait shops are available throughout the area for do-it-yourself anglers. Small boaters fishing the reefs and wrecks will find abundant marine life on the shallow patch reefs on the Gulf side of the Keys and Everglades. On the ocean side there is excellent fishing on the coral reefs and shipwrecks that are inhabited by yellowtail, mangrove and mutton snapper, grouper and cobia. Mutton snapper up to 12 lbs have been caught by Key West reef fishermen.

In the small bays around Flamingo, the southern tip of Everglades National Park, especially Snake Bight, you have a chance for redfish, snapper or sea trout. All boat operators should be familiar with the nautical traffic laws. These rules prevent collisions at sea and can be obtained from any US Coast Guard Auxiliary.

Boats under power should never approach closer than 100 yards of another boat or float displaying a diver-down flag except at idle speed and with great caution. Not all nautical hazards are marked by buoys and markers. Use charts available at dive shops, marinas and marine stores. Boaters utilizing Loran-C for navigation should re-calibrate their equipment for this particular area.

Help Unhook A Pelican

Wherever you fish, a hungry pelican will show up looking for a handout. But they do not know how to avoid fish hooks or lines and often get ensnared. If you just cut the line, you are condemning the bird to entanglement and starvation. Do not be afraid if you get a pelican on your line.

REEL IN THE BIRD, GRAB ITS BILL, FOLD UP THE WINGS, AND BRING IT TO, OR CALL, THE NEAREST WILDLIFE RESCUE CENTER.

PELICAN RESCUE STEPS

I. REEL IN PELICAN HOOKED ON YOUR LINE.

Reel in your line smoothly and firmly. Be careful not to break the line. Even though the bird is struggling and flappping its wings, it only weighs about six pounds and it is really quite harmless when handled properly.

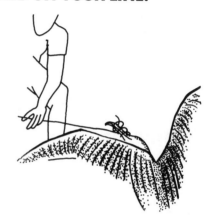

2. GRAB THE BILL.

When the bird is close to you, grab the bill. Close it and hold it securely in one hand. The inside edges of the bill are sharp but unless you rub your hand up and down the edge, a pelican bite will not hurt you.

3. FOLD UP THE WINGS.

Fold the wings into their normal closed position and hold them there. This quiets down the bird and it should stop struggling.

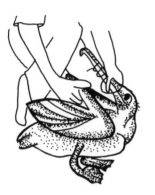

4. HOLD THE BIRD AND TRANSPORT IT TO THE NEAREST CENTER.

Turn the bird's head around so it lies along the middle of its back (that's how pelicans sleep) and the bird is easier to handle. Transport it on your lap to the nearest wildlife rescue center. KEEP A FIRM GRIP ON THE BIRD'S BILL.

5. TAKE THE BIRD TO ONE OF THE FOLLOWING RESCUE CENTERS:

UPPER KEYS

Florida Keys Wild Bird Center Key Largo, MM 93.6. ☎ 305-852-4486.

MIDDLE KEYS

Knight's Key Campground, MM 47, Marathon. ☎ 305-743-7373.

LOWER KEYS

Wildlife Rescue of the Florida Keys Indigenous Park, Whitehead St., Key West. ☎ 305-294-1441.

Note: The Wild Bird Rescue Centers receive no government funding and exist solely on donations. If you wish to make a tax-deductible donation, checks should be made out to FKWBC .

Reproduced with permission from material provided by the Florida Keys Wild Bird Center. Drawings adapted with permission from illustrations by Kelly Grinter.

Fishing

A series of mooring buoys have been placed in high-use areas within the marine parks. The buoy system was developed to reduce anchor damage to the coral and provide a convenient means of securing your boat. The buoys are available on a first-come, first-served basis for everyone.

When approaching the buoys, watch for snorkelers, divers and swimmers. Approach with the wind or current behind you and secure your boat to a pick-up line attached to the buoy.

■ Fishing Regulations

A recreational saltwater fishing license is required for Florida residents and nonresidents. The license is required for taking, attempting to take or possessing marine fish. These include finfish species, as well as marine invertebrates. Examples of finfish are hogfish, sharks, trout, mackerel, rays, catfish, eels and tarpon. Marine invertebrates include snails, whelks, clams, scallops, shrimp, crab lobster, sea stars, sea urchins and sea cucumbers. With the exception of Florida residents who are fishing from shore or a pier that has a valid pier saltwater fishing license or is fixed to the land, salt-water fishing licenses are required of all age 16 and older. Also included are all Florida residents 16 to 65 years of age who fish from a boat, float, or place they have reached by boat, float, swimming or snorkeling. Any person who is on a charter boat or with a licensed fishing guide is covered by their guide's license. Crawfish and snook stamps are required for possession of either. Lobsters (crawfish) are protected year-round in some areas of Dade and Monroe counties. Sportsman's mini-season is the last full weekend prior to August 1 (two days only).

Saltwater fishing licenses are sold at all county tax collector's offices and at many bait and tackle shops.

For updated licensing information, contact one of the Marine Patrol District offices: District 2 (Miami, Port Everglades). ☎ 305-325-3346. District 3 (Marathon). ☎ 305-289-2323

Freshwater fishing licenses are required for the freshwater fish in the canals along the Tamiami Trail and the Everglades. Licenses and regulations are available from the marina shops and most bait and tackle shops.

How to Handle Other Birds Snared By Fishhooks

Toss a towel or shirt over the bird's head and firmly grasp its bill in a closed position. Gently fold the wings into their normal position and transport the bird to the nearest wildlife rescue center (see page 109 for listings).

Covering any bird's head will help to keep the bird calm, thereby reducing its struggling efforts.

WARNING:

Before attempting to catch a heron, PUT ON A PAIR OF PROTECTIVE GLASSES. Herons defend themselves by lunging for their enemy's eyes.

Wood storks,
Corkscrew Sanctuary

Nature Hikes & Walks

State and national parks throughout the Florida Keys and Everglades provide informative walking programs – "slogs" or wet hikes though water and mud where you "taste and smell the rich odors of the swamp," beach walks to observe sea grasses, tidal pools, sponges and wading-bird habitats, woodland hikes, bird-watching, and out-island tours to examine fossilized coral or virgin tropical forests.

Many parks have raised boardwalks that climb over tidal flats, saw-grass prairies and fragrant mangrove swamps. Patient observers discover spectacular sights and sounds, from croaking frogs and alligators or pods of dolphins splashing across the horizon to soaring bald eagles, colonies of nesting wood storks or flocks of egrets gorging on fish.

Florida Keys trails are accessible throughout the year, but the best time for exploring the Everglades is Florida's dry season, mid-December through mid-April. The rest of the year brings the chance of torrential downpours that wash out many of the low-lying trails. Precipitation can exceed 50 inches a year. After a rainfall, mosquitoes, sandflies and other biting insects thicken the air.

Wildlife in the Everglades becomes more difficult to spot in summer. During winter's dry season, birds and other wildlife congregate in and around the waterholes, conveniently visible from the nature trails. These life-rich holes, cleared out of the Everglades limestone bed by the alligators, are a breeding ground for small fish, turtles and snails, which, in turn, become food for alligators, birds and mammals until the rains come.

Hammocks are isolated stands of hardwoods and other vegetation that contrasts with the surrounding plant life. These botanical showplaces, often islands of tropical hardwoods shading orchids and ferns in the middle of a sawgrass prairie, are vulnerable to floods, fires and invasions of saline waters. Hammocks form on a ridge or elevated mound of earth.

■ Florida Keys Nature Hikes

☆ *Stars denote handicap access.*

☆ **John Pennekamp State Park**, located at MM 102.5, features two nature trails. One starts at the parking lot across from the Visitor's Center and leads through a tropical hammock, home to raccoons and woodland birds. The other, an elevated mangrove trail that begins in the parking lot across from the Picnic Pavilion, offers a close encounter with an array of wading birds – herons, egrets, ducks, cormorants and coots. The park offers interpretive programs, canoe and kayak rentals, boat rentals, and ocean tours.

Lignumvitae Key, a 280-acre island on the Gulf side of Islamorada, is a virgin tropical forest accessible by charter boat. Isolated in time and space relative to the other keys, Lignumvitae Key was first settled by financier William Matheson who built a four-bedroom, coral-rock house on it in 1919, but left the rest of the island alone except for a small clearing and boat dock. The State of Florida acquired the key in 1972 and made it a protected state botanical site. Today the house serves as a visitor's center. State park rangers conduct guided tours three times daily, Thursday through Monday.

On the tour, rangers identify lignum vitae, mahogany, strangler fig, poisonwood, pigeon plum and gumbo limbo trees. Fifty people may ex-

Nature Hikes & Walks

plore the key at one time, 25 on the nature trail and 25 in the clearing. Walking shoes and mosquito repellent are recommended. Book a trip at the MM 78.5 boat ramp. ☎ 305-664-2540 .

Indian Key State Historical Site, a 12-acre island on the ocean side of Islamorada, features ruins of a wreckers' village burned down by Indians in 1840 and numerous sisal plants cultivated by famed botanist, Dr. Henry Perrine. Book a guided walking tour with the Florida Park Service at the MM 78.5 boat ramp. ☎ 305-664-2540.

☆ **Long Key State Park**, at MM 67.5, supports an abundant wading-bird population. The main trail originates on the ocean side, near the observation tower, then winds through beach areas and across a mangrove-lined lagoon. Signs along the boardwalk interpret the lagoon. Park rangers present campfire programs and lead guided walks year-round. The park opens at 8 am and closes at sunset.

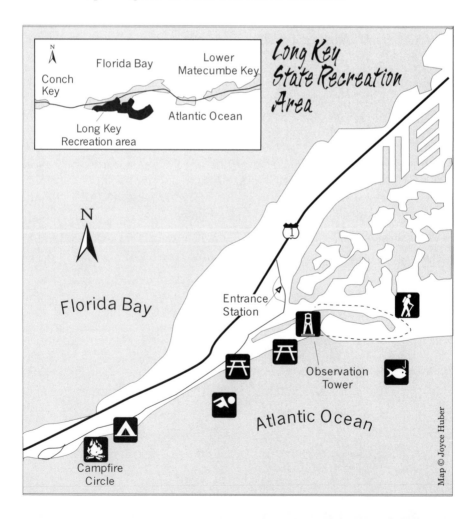

Map © Joyce Huber

Crane Point Hammock, located at MM 50, contains the last virgin thatch palm hammock in North America. Noted as an environmental and archaeological site, the 63-acre tract once sheltered early American Indians and in later history housed a Bahamian village. An early 1900s tabby concrete home built with two-foot-thick walls stands on the grounds. Pre-Colombian and prehistoric Indian artifacts have been found on the property.

Enter the sanctuary through the **Museum of Natural History of the Florida Keys**, 5550 Overseas Hwy., Marathon. It features 20 major exhibits and displays covering the

Once plentiful throughout the Keys, tiny Key deer are now confined to Big Pine Key, where they are protected by the federal government's National Key Deer Wildlife Refuge.

lives of the Keys' first settlers, as well as the area's geographic, botanical and zoologic evolution.

The trails runs through ancient coral fossils, rare hardwoods, native palms and mangroves. Crane Point Hammock and its natural history museum are open Monday thru Saturday, 9 am to 5 pm, Sunday, 12 pm to 5 pm. ☎ 305-743-9100.

Bahia Honda State Park, at MM 36.5, displays rare plants not often found on the other islands, including the satinwood tree, spiny catesbaea and dwarf morning glory. A nature trail at the far end of the park's Sandspur Beach, oceanside, follows the shore of a tidal lagoon, then twists through a coastal strand hammock and back along the beach. Bird life includes the white-crowned pigeon, great white heron, roseate spoonbill, reddish egret, osprey, brown pelican and least tern.

Guided walks are available to groups by reservation. ☎ 305-872-2353. Park Tours, and boat rentals, ☎ 305-872-1127.

The **Big Pine Key Walking Trail** starts 1½ miles north of the intersection of Key Deer Boulevard and Watson Boulevard. It winds for two-

Nature Hikes & Walks

thirds of a mile through slash pine and palms adjoining **Watson Hammock**, a unique hardwood area which is also habitat for a variety of tree cactus and a species of prickly pear not seen anywhere else in the world. The trail lies within the **Key Deer Refuge**, home of tiny deer measuring 24 to 32 inches at the shoulder and weighing 45 to 75 pounds. Fawns weigh two to four pounds with a hoof the size of a thumb nail. Rangers ask that you not feed the deer. A few alligators reside in the Blue Hole, a nearby old rock quarry.

■ Everglades Hiking Trails

Many hiking trails in Everglades National Park branch off from the Main Park Road, which begins at the Main Visitor Center and ends 38 miles later at Flamingo. These paths range from easy walks, less than a quarter-mile, to more strenuous ones of up to 14 miles. If you are hiking off the trails, let someone know your schedule and planned route before you leave. Footpaths marked by a star indicate access for the handicapped.

Watch for poisonous snakes, including coral snakes, water moccasins, diamondback and pygmy rattlers. Do not damage, remove, or disturb any plants. Like the animals, they are protected, and some are poisonous, including poison ivy, poison wood and manchineel. Pets are not allowed on the trails.

Everglades National Park Trails

Park rangers give hikes, talks, demonstrations and campfire pro-grams during the year. Activities change daily. Ask at the visitor centers for schedules.

☆ **The Anhinga Trail**, the nearest to the Main Visitors Center, offers the best opportunity to see several species of wildlife close up. It starts as a paved path, then changes to a raised boardwalk snaking through swamplands past alligators, herons and the namesake anhingas – odd black, water birds that flatten their wings against the bushes to dry. Other residents include turtles, fish, marsh rabbits and many birds – herons, egrets, and purple gallinules. Taylor Slough, a freshwater, marshy river, supplies water for this area throughout the dry winter season. This trail covers less than half a mile.

☆ **The Gumbo Limbo Trail** winds half a mile through a hammock of royal palms, gumbo limbo trees, wild coffee, and lush aerial gardens of ferns and orchids. It starts behind the Royal Palm Visitor's Center, adjacent to the Anhinga Trail.

At **Long Pine Key**, a network of interconnecting trails weave through seven miles of the Pinelands, a wooded refuge for whitetail deer, opossums, raccoons and the endangered Florida panther. Two hundred types of plants, including 30 found nowhere else on Earth, grow under the pine canopy.

☆ **Shark Valley Trail** winds 15 miles through the heart of the Everglades prairie and the headwaters for Shark River. Residents include alligators, otters, wood storks, snakes, deer, wading birds and fish. Shark Valley lies off US 41, the Tamiami Trail. A 50-ft observation tower shadows the Everglades wilderness.

☆ **The Pineland Trail** bares the shallow bed of limestone that underlies the area. Less than a half-mile long, it begins near the Main Visitor's Center. Dimples or solution holes and intricate patterns in the exposed limestone have eroded from deposits of rainwater and organic acid.

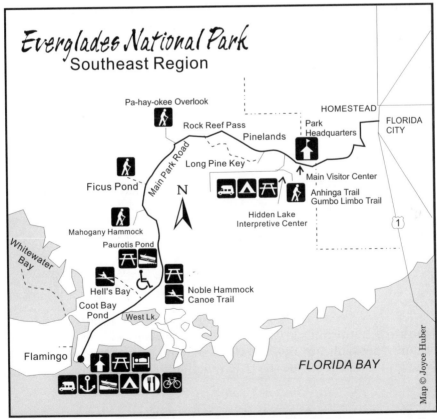

Nature Hikes & Walks

Map © Joyce Huber

The Pa-hay-okee Overlook Trail, less than a quarter-mile long, leads to an observation tower, where you can view the "river of grass," the true glades that gave the park its name. Sawgrass, Everglades beardgrass, and arrowhead shelter alligators, pygmy rattlesnakes and king snakes. Look in the treetops for red-shouldered hawks and vultures.

☆ **The Mahogany Hammock Trail**, under a half-mile, winds through a cool, fragrant, hardwood hammock of massive mahogany trees, including the largest living specimen in the United States, and paurotis palms. Look skyward for zebra butterflies, airplants, orchids and huge spiderwebs that hang from tree branches.

☆ **The West Lake Trail** curls a half-mile through mangrove thickets edging West Lake, a large, brackish nursery for fish crabs, shrimp and spiny lobsters. The trailhead starts on the south side of the main road, 31 miles from the Main Visitor's Center. Beyond West Lake, the path trails past Long Lake to Alligator Creek. Four types of mangroves, red, black, white and buttonwood, grow in this region where the glades meet saltwater.

Snake Bight Trail leads through just over 1½ miles of tropical hardwood hammock edging Snake Bight Channel. Unpaved, this densely wooded trail offers good bird and alligator watching from the short boardwalk at the path's end.

Rowdy Bend, an old road bed, twists through 2½ miles of buttonwood forest and open coastal prairie. It ends at the junction with Snake Bight Trail.

Bear Lake Trail, an excellent habitat for woodland birds, starts at the Main Park Road and leads through over 1½ miles of dense hardwood hammock to Bear Lake.

Christian Point, a short distance from the Flamingo Visitor's Center, is a rustic path of 1.8 miles that begins one mile north of Flamingo in dense buttonwood forest and ends in coastal prairie along the Snake Bight shore. A good place to see raptors.

Coastal Prairie Trail, once used by cotton pickers and fishermen, begins at the "C" Loop in the Flamingo Campground, continuing for 7½ miles one-way. Park rules require a backcountry permit for camping along this trail.

Bayshore Loop zigzags two miles along the shore of Florida Bay, beginning at Coastal Prairie Trail Head behind Loop "C" in the Flamingo Campground. Veer left at the trail junction to the bay.

Sunburn Protection

 Avoid prolonged exposure to the sun, especially during peak hours, 10 am to 3 pm. Blistering sunburns are not only painful, they may lead to skin cancer.

■ Avoid exposure when taking medicines that increase sun sensitivity.

■ Use sunblock lotion or a sunscreen with a protection factor of at least 15.

■ Wear sunglasses that block UV rays.

■ Select hats with a wide brim.

■ If your activities require prolonged exposure wear protective clothing of fabrics made to block the sun's ultraviolet rays. Very opaque fabrics are best.

Sun Precautions Inc., of Everett, Washington, offers a catalogue featuring sun-block clothing. Contact them at ☎ 800-882-7860 or on the Web at www.sunprecautions.com.

Eco Pond, a half-mile stroll around a freshwater pond, offers a viewing platform from which herons and other wading birds may be photographed.

Guy Bradley Trail, parallel to Florida Bay's shoreline, provides a scenic one-mile shortcut between the Flamingo Campground and Visitor's Center. Guy Bradley was a game warden who lost his life defending nesting birds from plume hunters in the late 1800s, when egret and heron plumes were in big demand by the millinery industry for decorating ladies' hats.

Big Cypress Trails

The Florida Trail, a well-marked footpath, runs 29 miles across the Big Cypress National Preserve swamp and pinelands linking Alligator Alley and the Tamiami Trail. Closed to all vehicles, the trail has to be considered primitive. Watch for muck soil, sharp-edged pinnacle rock and holes, poisonous plants and snakes. Two primitive campgrounds on the route offer drinking water. Check with a park ranger before attempting this hike.

For additional information contact: Big Cypress National Preserve, 33100 Tamiami Trail, Ochopee FL 34141-9710. ☎ 941-695-2000; 941-

Nature Hikes & Walks

695-4111 to reach the Oasis ranger station for information on camping, hiking, fishing and hunting. www.nps.gov

The Corkscrew Swamp Sanctuary

The Corkscrew Swamp Sanctuary sits at the northern tip of what was once the Big Cypress Swamp of Collier County in southwest Florida. The sanctuary, an 11,000-acre wilderness area, contains one of the largest stands of mature bald cypress trees in the nation. Its 2¼-mile boardwalk loop, the most scenic of the Everglades trails, traverses a

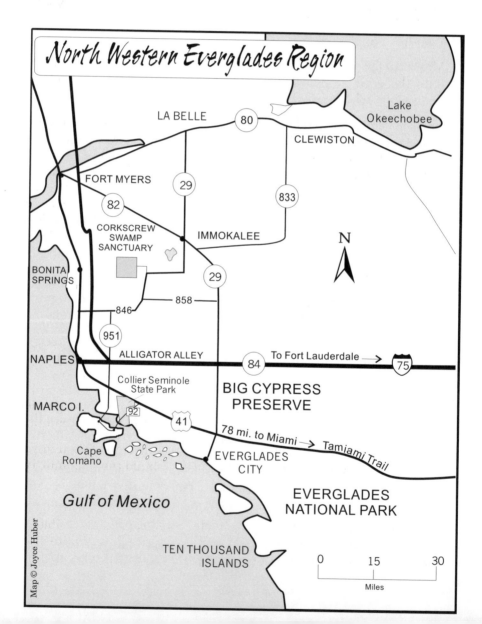

natural cathedral formed by giant bald cypress trees. Newly built to replace the old boardwalk destroyed by Hurricane Andrew in 1992, the walkway now passes through the best parts of the swamp, including nesting grounds for a woodstork colony, sweet-scented sawgrass prairies flanked by ancient forests of slash pine and saw palmetto. Wildlife abounds, with basking alligators, flocks of ibis, limpkin (a large dark brown bird that may walk jerkily along or fly off through the trees with a stiff awkward wing beat and a peculiar wail), herons, egrets, huge owls, bobcats, otters, the elusive Florida black bear and panther.

Before wandering the well-marked trail, stop at the new Blair Visitor's Center for a wonderful 14-minute sound and light presentation on the swamp.

Mosquito-larvae-eating fish (*gambouzia*) eat the mosquitos and eliminate the need for repellent. No pets. The boardwalk is wheelchair-accessible and wheelchairs are available.

The sanctuary, located between Naples and Immokalee, sits 1½ miles from County Road 846. The Sanctuary Road entrance (County Road 849) lies 14 miles from Immokalee, 21 miles from Route 41, and 15 miles from Interstate 75, Exit 17. (Do **not** take Exit 19, "Corkscrew Rd."; it won't get you there.) The Visitor's Center and Boardwalk Trail is open from 9 am to 5 pm daily. Admission is $8 for adults, $3.50 for children six-18 years old; children under six are free; college students, $5. Audubon members, $5. For information, write Corkscrew Swamp Sanctuary, 375 Sanctuary Road, Naples FL 34120. ☎ 941-348-9151. www.audubon/local/sanctuary/corkscrew.

Collier Seminole State Park

To reach Collier Seminole State Park, turn off Route 41, the Tamiami Trail (westbound), about 17 miles west of the Route 29 intersection. The 6,423-acre park, named for the late Barron Collier, a pioneer developer in Collier Country, and for the Seminole Indians, who still live nearby, offers a self-guided hiking trail that winds through 6½ miles of pine flatwood and cypress swamps. A primitive campsite is provided for overnight excursions, along with two sites for tent and RV camping.

Artifacts from the final campaigns of the Second Seminole War are displayed. One of the "walking dredges" used to build the Tamiami Trail during the 1920s is on exhibit.

There is a boat basin on the Blackwater River, which flows through the park. Canoe trail and rentals available. Handicapped-accessible. For more information, contact Collier Seminole State Park, Route 4, Box 20200, TamIami Trail East, Naples FL 34116. ☎ 941-394-3397.

Nature Hikes & Walks

The Pelican Path:
A Walking Tour of Old Key West

In Key West, you soon forget you are in the United States, as Spanish is heard drifting from porch to porch, while the conchs, the natives of English strain, tell stories in a cockney accent of anything from marlins to mermaids. Here, you forget the cares of city life. The sun is always warm, the sky is always clear and just a little way down the street is the most beautiful sea in the world, of a pure turquoise color that deepens to emerald on the horizon.

■ Key West Architecture

As the most historic city in South Florida, Key West owes much of its charm to its distinctive architecture. According to the Executive Director of the National Trust for Historic Preservation, "Some of these quaint and charming houses are to be found in no other area of the country." Their history goes back to the beginnings of Key West when the first settlers came to the island. These pioneers were from the eastern seaboard of the United States, the Bahamas, Cuba and Europe. Many of the old houses in Key West reflect this delightful mixture of

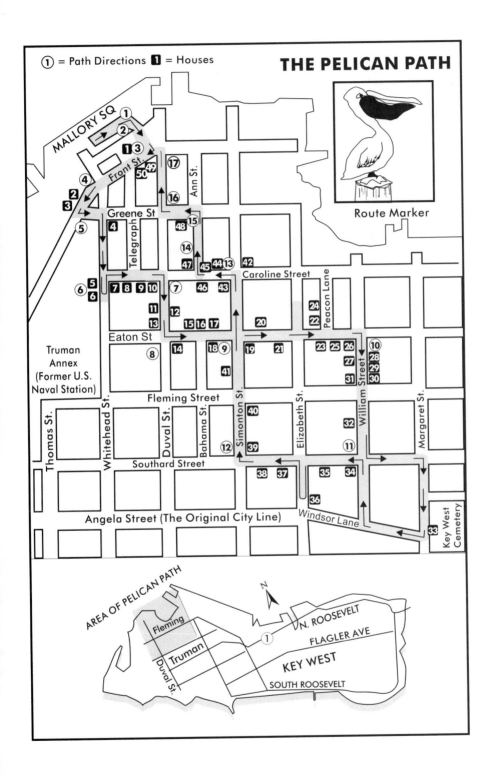

nationalities, which has created a special, almost old world atmosphere. Of these styles or types of buildings the one distinctively Key West is known as "Conch" or Bahama. Built of wood by ships' carpenters, the simple, clean lines of the buildings have the same balance and grace found in a fine sailing ship. They were built to withstand high winds and a tropical climate. Their wide porches have slender square columns that support the main roof and, in some instances, windows under the eaves open onto the porches. All the windows were protected by shutters or "blinds" that allowed light and air into the high-ceilinged rooms, yet kept out the hot tropic sun. The high peaked roofs were designed to catch the maximum amount of rain water, which was stored in great cisterns. On the small houses, hatches, similar to those found on a ship, allowed air and light into the attic bedrooms when they were open. The cupolas or "widow's walks" on many of the larger buildings were used as lookouts to scan the nearby reefs for ships that had run aground. These sturdy houses have a classic simplicity, at times relieved by lacy woodwork or delicately turned spindles on the porch rails.

Nearly all the early buildings were made of wood. Some, however, were constructed of stone quarried on the island. Two examples are on Old Mallory Square; others are the Old Stone Methodist Church and the Hemingway House. With the exception of Fort Taylor, brick was not used to any great extent until after the fire of 1886, when half the town was destroyed.

Buildings of various styles, material and periods can be seen throughout the island. Their architecture is often reminiscent of other places, but somehow there is a difference.

■ The Pelican Path

Colorful Pelican signs mark the route on this unique walking tour of Key West's historic section. Plaques on buildings of special interest are also numbered. Developed by the Old Island Restoration Foundation, it tells you about the buildings and their history.

☆ Stars are used to designate historic houses open to the public. These buildings were included in the survey conducted in 1967-1968 by the National Park Service and Old Island Restoration Foundation. Copies of the survey are available at the Monroe Country Public Library in Key West and the Library of Congress.

The Tour begins at **Hospitality House**, the headquarters of the Old Island Restoration Foundation in Old Mallory Square. Hospitality House was built after the fire of 1886 as the offices for the Southern Express Company. Later, it became the ticket office of the Mallory Steamship Company, which ran coastal steamers between New York, Charleston, Key West and Galveston. The round structures on the seaward side of the house stored cable, which was to be laid on the ocean floor for communications with Cuba and the Caribbean.

Follow the arrows on the map to keep on course.

Turn right at Pelican 1. Continue to Pelican 2 at the Mallory Square Exit. Continue on Wolfson Lane: Turn right on Front St. at Pelican 3.

1. Harbour House, 423 Front St. The first Bank of Key West, built on this site in 1885, was destroyed by fire the following year. Rebuilt shortly thereafter, the brick building was gutted again by fire in 1984. It is currently being restored. The structure is reminiscent of the architecture found in New Orleans.

Front St. was the early commercial district of Key West. Ships from all ports of the world docked here and large warehouses stored goods salvaged from the numerous shipwrecks.

Cross Whitehead St. to Clinton Place.

Clinton Place, Greene and Whitehead Sts. Within this triangle is a memorial shaft honoring the Union troops who died here during the Civil War, most of whom were victims of Yellow Fever. It was named for DeWitt Clinton, who was the Governor of New York in 1828.

2. Coast Guard Building, Front St. Built in 1856 for a Navy Coaling Station, it was later used in the Civil War as Headquarters for the East Coast Blockade Squadron. As the oldest government building, it is known as "Bldg. 1."

3. Old Customs House, Front St. This ornamental Romanesque brick building was built by the government in 1891 and was used as a Post Office, US Court House and Customs House. The state of Florida has bought the property, and the Key West Art & Historical Society is undertaking a multi-year restoration. When completed, it will be the home of the Society's historical museum.

Continue around Clinton Place, Turning right on Whitehead St.

☆ **4. Audubon House (Geiger Home)**, 205 Whitehead St. The preservation and restoration of this exceptionally fine old home was responsible for creating a city-wide interest in preserving other buildings of historical and architectural significance. The former home of Captain John H. Geiger, it is now a museum housing an extensive collection of original works by John James Audubon. Period furnishings recreate the era when the naturalist-painter visited the island in 1832. Owned and restored by the Mitchell Wolfson Family Foundation since 1960.

Whitehead St. Of the five military roads built by Commodore David Porter, only this one remains. For many years no other road transversed the full length of the island.

On your right is the **President's Gate**. This ceremonial gate, which leads to the "Little White House" museum, was opened only for Presidents and other international dignitaries.

☆ **5. Harry S. Truman Little White House Museum**, 111 Front St. Built in 1890 by the Navy as a duplex for the commandant and paymaster. Distinctive wood jalousies shade the porches on three sides. This vacation home of president Truman is now open to the public and is Florida's only presidential home site.

6. Navy Houses, 324, 326 Whitehead. There had been a shortage of suitable officers' housing at the Naval Station from the 1870s and a plan was submitted in 1898 to build Quarters C and D on the 300 block of Whitehead. They are significant as examples of early 20th-century domestic architecture designed by Navy architects to blend with the character of the surrounding private residences of Key West. In 1905, finishing touches, such as lattice work, porch screens and painting, brought the total cost to $6,000 for both houses. Extensive restoration in 1989 brought these homes back to life.

Turn Right on Caroline St.

7. Airways House, 301 Whitehead St. This building originally stood on the waterfront, where it was used as offices for Aero-Marine Airways. The first international airmail route between Key West and Havana was established on November 1, 1920. In October 1927 the route was taken over by Pan American Airways and in January of the following year six passengers made the 90-mile trip in one hour and 20 minutes.

☆**8. Captain George Cary House/Jessie Porter's heritage House Museum & Robert Frost Cottage**, 410 Caroline St. The original section of this handsome dwelling, built by Captain Carey in 1834, was torn down; however, the old chimney remains and forms a part of the present garden. The existing house was built in the mid-1850s and contains an extensive collection of furnishings, artifacts and mementos from the 1830s to the present day.

9. Judge W. Hunt Harris House, 425 Caroline St. Built toward the end of the Spanish American War, the building was utilized during that period by the Navy. Judge Harris served in the State Legislature and Senate and was, at one time, a Lieutenant Governor of Florida.

10. J.Y. Porter House, 429 Caroline St. Dr. J. Y. Porter II was born here in 1847 and died in the same room 80 years later. The Doctor's extensive research in yellow fever established our present quarantine laws. In recognition of this, he was made Florida's first Public Health Officer.

Turn right on Duval St.

☆ **11. Oldest House/Wreckers Museum**, 322 Duval St. Records and deed books indicate that this house was built on Whitehead St. in 1829, then moved to its present location in 1832. It is now owned by the State of Florida and is maintained and managed by the Old Island Restoration Foundation as an operational museum. Of special interest are the three upstairs dormer windows graduating in size and the cook house and garden in the rear.

12. Woman's Club, 319 Duval St. This beautifully proportioned house was built in 1892 by the first manager of the Inter-Ocean Telegraph Office. Since 1941 it has been the home of the Key West Woman's Club.

13. Patterson House, 336 Duval St. Built by Alexander Patterson, it was occupied by Mr. and Mrs. William Pickney and their children. The first private school was conducted here in 1842 by Mrs. Pickney's sister, Mrs. Passalogue, a French lady of rare interest and attainments. The next occupants were the Baldwins, an aristocratic British family who traced their ancestry to Lord Nelson and Sir Robert Walpole.

Turn left on Eaton St. at Pelican 8.

14. St. Paul's Church, 401 Duval. This is the oldest Episcopal church in the Diocese of South Florida. The first service was held here on Christmas Day in 1832. The present church, erected in 1916, is the fourth to be built on this site.

15. Warren House/Eaton Lodge, 511 Eaton St. The residence of the Warren family for over 80 years, this home was the office of Dr. William Richard Warren, an early island physician. It also features the tallest cistern in Key West.

16. Skelton House, 517 Eaton St.

17. Alvarez House, 523 Eaton St. These two lovely homes reflect the unique warmth and ambiance of Old Key West.

18. Otto House, 534 Eaton St. Built by Thomas Osgood Otto, Sr. and completed just before the turn of the century, it is an example of West Indian-Colonial-Victorian architecture and is one of the few remaining homes of this type on the island. The original French wallpaper was mounted on linen so that during a hurricane, if the house rocked, the paper would not crack.

Cross Simonton St. at Pelican 9.

19. Old Stone Methodist Church, 600 Eaton St. This handsome church, shaded by a giant Spanish laurel tree, was built in 1877 of stone quarried on the island. It is the oldest religious building in Key West.

☆ **20. Peter A. Williams House/Donkey Milk House**, 613 Eaton St. Built in the 1860s and occupied by the same family for over 120 years. US Marshall Williams saved his home from the Great Fire of 1886 by dynamiting along Eaton St. Winner of a 1992 Restoration Award, this unique property is open to the public as a house museum full of delightful furnishings, rare features and quality equipage.

21. George H. Curry House, 620 Eaton St. Built circa 1885, this house is the best example of Greek Revival architecture in Key West. Note the decorative brackets in the architrave and frieze. The large tree in the front is a Canary Island date palm.

Eaton St. was named for John Henry Eaton, a United States Senator and later a member of President Andrew Jackson's cabinet. His marriage to Peggy O'Neill created a scandal in Washington. Later, Jackson appointed the controversial Mr. Eaton Governor of Florida.

Continue on Eaton, crossing Elizabeth St.

22. Saunders House, 709 Eaton St. Restored in 1975, this pre-Victorian home was originally built in 1853 by Eliza and William Uriah Saunders of New Plymouth, Green Turtle Cay in the Bahamas.

23. Richard Peacon House, 712 Eaton St. Richard Peacon, owner of the town's largest grocery store, then at 800 Fleming and now known as William Fleming House, built the house between 1892 and 1899. Often called the "Octagon House," its stark symmetry makes it an architectural standout. Restored and refurbished by the late designer Angelo Donghia, the house was purchased by Calvin Klein in the 1980s for close to $1 million, then was later re-sold.

24. The Susan Peacon House, 320 Peacon Lane. Peacon Lane was formerly called Grunt Bone Alley. Built about 1848 and lived in by the Peacons for 100 years. Restored in 1972, this small conch cottage has a well-established characteristic conch garden.

25. Filer House, 724 Eaton St. Built in 1885 and considered one of the classic homes on the island, it is an outstanding example of Bahamian architecture, with Victorian influence. Note how the columns are enriched by the ornamental trim.

26. Bahama House (I), 730 Eaton St. In 1847, John Bartium and his brother-in-law Richard Roberts, of Green Turtle Cay in the Bahamas, dismantled their homes and brought them to Key West. In 1855, Bartium built the famous clipper ship *Stephen R. Mallory.* She is said to have been the only clipper ever to be built in Florida.

Turn right on William St.

27. Bahama House (II), 408 William St. This was the home of Richard Roberts, one of the early settlers of the Florida Keys. Unlike those on any other house on the island, the double verandas extend the entire length of the building. The hand-planed pine siding varies in width and has a unique beading on the lower edges.

28. Gideon Lowe House, 409 William St. The first part of the house was built in the early 1840s and the second section was added in the 1870s. It reflects an outstanding version of Classic Revival architecture.

29. Island City House, 411 William St. Built in the early 1900s, it was operated as a hotel until the late '40s. Condemned by the City, it was saved by the present owners and has been handsomely restored.

30. Russell House/Key West Bed & Breakfast, 415 William St. This lovely old house built at the turn of the century depicts the charm and grace of an earlier age.

31. Fleming Street Methodist Church, 729 Fleming St. The original church was built in 1884 by dissenting members of the mother church who objected to instrumental music. Having been destroyed by the hurricane of 1909, the present concrete structure was completed in 1912. Because many members of the congregation were seamen who wore short jackets, it became known as "the short jacket Methodist church."

Continue on William St. crossing Fleming St.

Fleming Street. Named for John W.C. Fleming, a native of England and a business partner of John Simonton. Fleming hoped to develop the salt industry here, but his death in 1832 ended the project.

32. Charles Roberts House, 512 Fleming St. Built in the late 1800s, this charming home follows every rule for pleasant island living.

Turn left on Southard St., then right on Margaret St.

The Pelican Path

33. Key West Cemetery. Reminiscent of New Orleans and Galveston graveyards, the unique above-ground vaults are described by Key West poet James Merrill as "whitewashed hope chests." You'll see the US *Maine* monument, a headstone proclaiming, "I Told You I Was Sick," chiseled poems, hand-carved angels and glass mausoleums with statuary. Traditional cornet band funeral parades still take place in the cemetery which was relocated from near the Southernmost Point on Whitehead St. after the devastating 1846 hurricane.

Turn right on Windsor Lane, then right on William St., then left on Southard St.

34. William Albury House, 730 Southard St. One of the oldest homes in Key West, it is also considered one of the most interesting. It has double porches on three sides and is crowned with a widow's walk.

35. John Albury House, 708 Southard St. Purchased from the Albury family by Cleveland Dillon in the early 1900s, the house remained in the Dillon family until the 1960s.

36. Benjamin P. Baker House, 615 Elizabeth St. Built in 1885, this house is the most elaborate example of the use of decorative gingerbread. The house displayed the strength of structures built by shipwrights when, in 1972, a tornado knocked it eight feet off its foundation. The house was picked up and put back with no structural damage.

37. John Lowe Jr. House, 620 Southard St. This residence was enlarged as the family and their fortune grew. It is typical of the mid-19th-century homes built by successful Key West merchants, with significant features that include wide porches and a widow's walk. Mr. Lowe was the owner of one of the largest sponging fleets in Florida.

38. Benjamin Curry House, 610 Southard St. The property was purchased in 1856 from Pardon Greene, who was one of the four original owners of the island. This story-and-a-half house has been the home of six generations of the Curry family.

39. William C. Lowe House, 603 Southard St. Built after 1865, the house remained in the family until 1942. It is of classic design and an outstanding example of restoration.

Turn left on Simonton St. at Pelican 12.

Simonton St. Named for an American businessman, John W. Simonton, who bought the island of Key West from the Spanish owner Juan Pablo Salas in 1821 for $2,000.

40. The Peggy Mills House and Garden, 516 Angela St. Built prior to 1889, this house was totally renovated in 1982. The gardens, created by Peggy Mills, furniture-store owner and plant lover, were started in 1930, and for 50 years Peggy never stopped adding to them. Internationally known for its varied botanical collection, the gardens also feature antique tinajones (Cuban water jugs weighing one ton empty) and winding pathways of century-old brick.

Return to Southard St. turn left, then right on Duval St. Turn right on Fleming St.

41. John Haskins Building/Marquesa Hotel, 600 Fleming St. Built prior to 1889, this structure is now a small luxury hotel, which received the 1988 First Place Winner for Historic Preservation. It has been a drugstore, car dealership and the first home of Fausto's grocery, now located in the next block.

42. William R. Kerr House, 410 Simonton St. Built in 1876 by the owner, the house shows the strong influence of Downings' Carpenter Gothic design in the roof style, verge boards and porch ornaments. Mr. Kerr, a prominent architect, built many of the important public structures on the island.

43. Richard Kemp/Cypress House, 601 Caroline St. An excellent example of Bahamian architecture in its purest form. Its simplicity of lines and styling, with fine proportions and balance, reflect the craftsmanship of ships' carpenters. The Kemp family migrated from the Bahamas to Key West shortly after the island was settled. William Kemp introduced the sponge industry to Key West and sold the first shipment of Florida sponges in New York.

Turn Left on to Caroline St.

44. Delaney House, 532 Caroline St. Built around 1889, it was owned by John J. Delaney, a merchant in the clothing business. This handsome structure has been used for various business and professional offices but has retained its original architecture.

45. George Bartlum House, 531 Caroline St. Built in the mid-1800s in three stages, it was finished in 1888. President and Mrs. Harry Truman were frequent guests in this home.

46. Bott House, 529 Caroline St. This distinctive house is one of the few brick homes in Key West.

47. George B. Patterson House, 522 Caroline St. Mr. Patterson's father, Col. Alexander Patterson, came to Key West from Connecticut in the 1820s. The design of the house reflects the Queen Anne style of architecture.

The Pelican Path

Turn right on Ann St.

☆ **48. Milton Curry House/Curry Mansion Inn**, 511 Caroline St. Built in 1905, this house is a copy of a Newport cottage which the young couple had admired. A wide, graceful porch surrounds the house on three sides. Of special interest is the elegant design and detail on the verandas and under the eaves.

49. Old City Hall, 512 Greene St. Built in 1891 on the same site as the former City Hall destroyed in the 1886 fire. This historic landmark is presently being restored by the Historic Florida Keys Preservation Board, Old Island Restoration Foundation, the City of Key West and its generous citizens.

Turn left on Greene St. Turn right on Duval St.

Duval St. has for many years been the city's main shopping and entertainment center. It was named for Florida's first Territorial Governor, William Pope Duval.

50. Florida First National Bank, Front and Duval Sts. This establishment has been in operation since 1891. The original building shows strong Spanish influence in the beautiful and intricate brickwork, as well as in the ornate balcony. On display in the lobby is part of the famous solid gold table service made by Tiffany.

Turn left on Front St.

51. Sawyer Building, 400 Front St. Erected after the fire of 1886 by a Bahamian merchant. It is one of the many structures built during this era by immigrant Irish bricklayers from Boston. The second floor was at one time used by the US District Court.

Parasailing

Parasailing combines the thrill of hang-gliding with the excitement of parachuting. It's much safer, requires no training and you don't need to jump out of an airplane or from a towering cliff. The new custom parasailing boats allow you to take off and land right on the deck.

Once you buy your ticket and climb aboard, the boat moves to an open-space, over-water area. Next, you are strapped into a life jacket and special harness. The deck hand slackens your safety line and, within seconds, you are whisked 400 ft aloft. The ride lasts about 15 minutes. As the powerboat pulls you across a panorama of coral reefs, mangrove islands and coves, you ride a column of air and see the world from a bird's-eye view. Like a kite, you are always connected to the boat by a safety line.

As long as the boat is moving, the relative wind keeps you up. When you wish to come down, the boat slows up. You settle toward earth and are reeled back aboard the boat by an electric winch. Photo and video opportunities are magnificent.

Don't worry if the boat runs out of gas and the winch motor breaks. Keep in mind that the big nylon apparatus you are hanging from is a parachute. If all fails, you will float gently down and splash into the sea.

Wear a bathing suit. When you parasail with Jim Fulper at **Holiday Isle**, getting wet is part of the fun. His custom-designed parasail boat is kept in tip-top shape, but his patrons demand an intentional dip in the sea to cool off. After 15 minutes close to Florida's sun, you'll want one too. You can sign up for a trip with Joe on the Holiday Isle beach at

Mojo's Shack (☎ 664-5390) or at the huge "parasailing" sign on the north end of the beach. Six people can go in the boat at once. Spectators ride along for a nominal fee. A special tandem-parasail set-up allows a parent to take a small child along. A new tandem harness allows for side-by-side seating. Arrangements for the handicapped are available. A new 1,000-ft flight has been recently added.

In Key Largo you can lift off at **Caribbean Watersports** on the beach at the Westin Beach Resort, MM 97, Bayside, 97000 Overseas Hwy., Key Largo FL 33037, ☎ 305-852-5553.

Caribbean Watersports at Cheeca Lodge (☎ 305-664-4651), MM 82, offers parasailing rides. Light wind and calm sea conditions are necessary.

Scuba

Spectacular coral reefs off the Florida Keys attract nearly a million sport divers each year. Patches of finger-like spur and groove reefs parallel the islands from Key Biscayne to Key West and are inhabited by over 500 varieties of fish and corals. Shallow depths, ideal for underwater video and still photography, range from just below the surface to an average maximum of 40 ft.

■ What You Need

A scuba certification card (C-card) is required to join dive boat trips or obtain air fills. Dive operators may request a look at your logbook before signing you on a trip. Without one, you may be asked to take a check-out dive. An advanced scuba certification is required for dives on the deep wrecks, *Duane* and *Bibb*.

Many dive shops offer resort courses. You take a lesson in a pool, then an introductory dive on a shallow reef with an instructor. Refresher courses are available too.

■ Gear

During winter, air and ocean temperatures average 70-75° F. Topside temperatures may drop as low as 40°-50°. Plan on wearing either a shorty or one-eighth full wetsuit. A quarter-inch wetsuit is not uncomfortable once in the water.

Wreck dive (Steven Frink / Florida Keys Tourism).

During summer, water temperatures climb to 85°, making a wetsuit unnecessary. A safe-second regulator is encouraged, but not mandatory. Standard gear – stab jackets, weight belts, weights, mask, knife, snorkel, camera and video equipment – may all be rented at most dive shops. Boaters will find small craft for rent at the marinas.

■ Weather

Good diving on the Florida Keys shallow reefs (most at depths of 45 ft or less) depends on good weather conditions. High winds that churn up surface swells also stir up the sandy bottom. You might plan a dive the morning after a storm and find visibility as low as 25 ft, yet return in the afternoon to calm seas and visibility in excess of 100 ft. October through June offer the best weather conditions. Because the reefs are fairly shallow, winds that churn up the seas may cause lowered visibility.

When storms rule out trips to the outer reefs, visit the Content Keys, a sheltered area which is almost always calm, located on the Gulf side of Marathon.

■ The Florida Keys National Marine Sanctuary

After three freighters grounded on the reefs in 1989, destroying acres of the tiny coral reef organisms, President Bush signed into law a bill designed to protect a 3,500-square-mile stretch of Florida Keys land and sea. The area known as The Florida Keys National Marine Sanctuary contains the entire strand of Keys barrier reefs on the Atlantic and

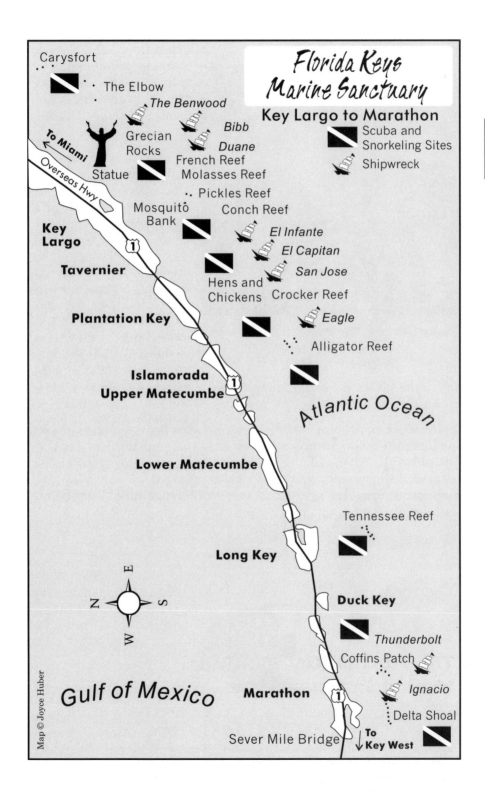

Florida Keys Marine Sanctuary

Carysfort

The Elbow

The Benwood

Grecian Rocks

Bibb

Duane

French Reef

Molasses Reef

Statue

Pickles Reef

Mosquito Bank

Conch Reef

Key Largo to Marathon

Scuba and Snorkeling Sites

Shipwreck

To Miami

Overseas Hwy

Key Largo

Tavernier

El Infante

El Capitan

San Jose

Hens and Chickens

Crocker Reef

Plantation Key

Eagle

Alligator Reef

Islamorada

Upper Matecumbe

Atlantic Ocean

Lower Matecumbe

Tennessee Reef

Long Key

Duck Key

Thunderbolt

Coffins Patch

Ignacio

Marathon

Delta Shoal

Gulf of Mexico

Sever Mile Bridge

To ↓ Key West

Map © Joyce Huber

Scuba diving in John Pennekamp Coral Reef State Park, Key Largo.

Gulf sides of the islands. Freighter traffic close to shore is prohibited, providing a safe "cushion" area between keels and corals.

The sanctuary, managed by the National Oceanographic and Atmospheric Administration, also encompasses, and dwarfs, two previous federal preserves in the Keys, the Looe Key National Marine Sanctuary and the Key Largo National Marine Sanctuary. In contrast to the new 3,500-square-mile sanctuary, the Looe Key Sanctuary is 5.32 square miles and the Key Largo sanctuary is 100 square miles. Within the sanctuary, spear fishing, wearing gloves and anchoring on the coral are prohibited.

On the ocean reefs, replenishment reserves are being set up to protect and enhance the spawning, nursery or permanent resident areas of fish and other marine life. Some areas will restrict fishing, will allow diving, but will be no-take areas. Prime areas are shallow, heavily used reefs. Check with local dive or bait shops for current information before diving on your own.

Reef Etiquette

- Do not allow your hands, knees, tank or fins to contact the coral. Just touching coral causes damage to the fragile polyps.

- Spearfishing in the sanctuary is not allowed. This is why the fish are so friendly you can almost reach out and touch them.

- Hand-feeding of fish is discouraged, especially with food unnatural to them. Besides the risk of bodily injury, such activity changes the natural behavior of the fish.

- Hook and line fishing is allowed. Applicable size, catch limits and seasons must be observed.

- Spiny lobster may be captured during the season, except in the Core Area of the Looe Key Sanctuary. Number and size regulations must be followed.

- Corals, shells, starfish and other animals cannot be removed from the Sanctuary.

- Regulations prohibiting littering and discharge of any substances except chum are strictly enforced.

- Fines are imposed for running aground or damaging coral. Historic artifacts are protected.

- The red and white dive flag must be flown while diving or snorkeling. Boats must go slowly enough to leave no wake within 100 yards of a dive flag.

■ Biscayne National Park Marine Sanctuary

Biscayne National Park Marine Sanctuary is gaining interest from those who enjoy uncrowded dive spots. This is thanks to a long struggle by Vietnam veteran and Audubon Society activist, Ed Davidson, who masterminded a successful fight to save this Northern Key Largo area from development.

Diving in Biscayne National Park is relatively new, with many virgin areas waiting to be discovered. Pristine reefs are the norm, though some of the shallow reefs were damaged during Hurricane Andrew. Major coral reef patches lie two to three miles offshore and require a boat for access. Dive and snorkeling tours take off from Convoy Point, nine mile east of Homestead. (☎ 305-230-1100).

■ John Pennekamp Coral Reef State Park

John Pennekamp Coral Reef State Park has long been the most popular diving area in Florida. John D. Pennekamp (1897-1978), editor of the *Miami Herald*, fostered the idea of reef preservation and, with fellow ecologists, raised enough money to purchase the southwest edge of Largo Sound for a headquarters site. The park, part of the Florida Keys National Marine Sanctuary, consists of 100 square miles of undersea reefs and 75 land acres as a haven not only for divers and snorkelers, but also campers, bird watchers, fishermen and sunbathers.

Before the area attained park status in 1960, corals and conch shells were harvested and bleached for souvenirs, while spear fishermen killed angelfish and anything else that moved underwater. Today, concern continues as environmentalists fight over development and accompanying ocean pollutants.

■ Scuba Tours

Dive shop signs and billboards offering reef trips line the highway throughout Key Largo. Boat trips to the best dive sites take from 15 to 30 minutes, depending on sea and wind conditions.

Scuba

The Statue, Key Largo (courtesy Stuart Newman Associates).

■ Upper Keys Dive Sites

John Pennekamp's most popular dive site and perhaps the one that symbolizes the area is **The Statue**, a nine-foot bronze replica of **Christ of the Abyss**, created by sculptor Guido Galletti for placement in the Mediterranean Sea. The statue was given to the Underwater Society of America in 1961 by industrialist Egidi Cressi.

The top of the statue is in 10 ft of water and can easily be seen from the surface. The base rests on a sandy bottom, 20 ft down, and is surrounded by huge brain corals and elkhorn formations. Stingrays and barracuda inhabit the site. A buoy marks the statue's location, but small swells make it difficult to pinpoint. If you are unfamiliar with navigating in John Pennekamp, join one of the commercial dive trips. Extreme shallows in the area provide outstanding snorkeling areas, but make running aground a threat.

More easily found is **Molasses Reef**, marked by a huge, lighted steel tower in the southeast corner of the park. Noted as the area's most popular reef dive, it carries the distinction of having had two shiploads of molasses run aground on its shallows.

The reef provides several dives, depending on where your boat is moored. Moorings M21 through M23 are for diving. M1 through M20 are shallow and better for snorkeling.

High-profile coral ridges form the perimeter of a series of coral ridges, grooves, overhangs, ledges and swim-through tunnels. In one area, divers see huge silver tarpon, walls of grunts, snappers, squirrel fish and Spanish hogfish. In another, divers swim over an ancient Spanish anchor. Visibility often exceeds 100 ft.

Be sure to check the current at Molasses Reef before entering the water, since an occasional strong flow makes the area undiveable. Depths vary from very shallow to approximately 40 ft.

Slightly northeast of Molasses stands **French Reef**, an area many consider the prettiest in John Pennekamp Park, with swim-through tunnels, caves, and ledges carpeted in pink and lavender sea fans, tube sponges, soft corals and anemones. Shallow depths range from areas where the reef pierces the surface to 45 ft.

North of French Reef lies the wreck of the ***Benwood***, a 300-ft freighter hit by a German submarine during World War II and later sunk as a navigational hazard by the Coast Guard.

Presently under guard by throngs of sergeant majors, grunts, and yellowtails, the wreck sits on a sandy bottom at 45 ft. Lobsters, huge moray eels and stingrays peek out from beneath the hull, as enormous groupers and turtles blast by. During summer, swirls of glass minnows hover over the wreck.

Despite pristine reefs and a robust fish population, a long boat ride prevents most dive operators from frequenting **Carysfort Reef**, in the northeast corner of the park.

If you are fortunate enough to catch a trip out there, expect a good display of fish and the possibility of one huge, resident barracuda, tamed by a local divemaster, swimming up to within an inch of your mask. This unique, engaging plea for a handout makes the toothy guy tough to ignore, but sanctuary officials strongly discourage fish-feeding so try to resist sharing your lunch.

Instead, explore the reef's healthy display of staghorn, elkhorn and star corals at depths varying from very shallow to 65 ft. Normally calm waters make Carysfort a good choice for novice and experienced divers, but beware the dramatic overhangs that top the walls. We discovered some the hard way – by surfacing without first looking up.

Just south of Carysfort Reef lies **The Elbow**, a crescent-shaped, spur-and-groove reef littered with the twisted remains of two steamers – the ***City of Washington*** and the ***Tonawanda***. Near the wrecks lie ballast and the frail remains of a wooden ship known as **The Civil War Wreck**. Depths average 40 ft. Visibility is usually good, with an occasional strong current. Friendly Barracuda and tame moray eels await.

■ Key Largo's Artificial Reef

In November, 1987, two vintage Coast Guard cutters were sunk off Key Largo by a team of Navy divers. The 1930s-era sister cutters *Bibb* and *Duane*, whose careers took them from the Caribbean to Cape Cod and included duties in the North Atlantic, Pacific and Mediterranean, were towed to their final resting site after cleaning and removal of potential hazards for divers.

The *Bibb* sits on her side in 125 ft of water, while the *Duane* sits upright at 130 ft. The top of the *Duane* can be viewed at 75 ft. They rest seven miles offshore and one mile south of Molasses Reef. This area is a buffer zone around the Key Largo National Marine Sanctuary. Both ships have attracted huge groupers, schooling tropicals, barracuda, eels and rays. An occasional hammerhead or nurse shark makes an appearance.

The ships, now camouflaged with a thin layer of coral, belonged to a seven-vessel "Secretary" class built by the Coast Guard in the late 1930s; their original role was to act as long-range rescue ships, according to Dr. Robert Scheina, a Coast Guard historian. "The vessels were also used to prevent poaching by Japanese fishing vessels in Alaskan Waters. And there was a third purpose – one quite familiar to today's Coast Guard. There was a problem with opium smuggling from the Orient to various outlets on the west coast of the United States. The vessels were utilized for drug interdiction back then."

With spare parts for the *Bibb* and *Duane* difficult to obtain and with excessive maintenance costs, the Coast Guard decommissioned the ships in 1985 and turned them over to the United States Maritime Administration for disposal.

South of Pennekamp Park lies **Pickles Reef**, a shallow area rich with marine life, sea fans and boulder corals. Near Pickles is **Conch Reef**, a wall dive that drops off to more than 100 ft, and the wreck of the *Eagle*, a 287-ft freighter, sunk intentionally to create an artificial reef. Residents of the wreck include parrot fish, schools of grunts, sergeant majors, moray eels and angels.

Another popular site frequented by Islamorada dive shops is **Alligator Reef**, home to walls of grunts, parrotfish and groupers, plus an occasional nurse shark. There are some nice stands of elkhorn and brain corals.

■ Middle Keys Dive Sites

Dive sites in the Middle Keys – from Long Key Bridge to the Seven Mile Bridge – are similar to, but often less crowded than, those in Key Largo. In addition to the offshore reefs and wrecks, the Marathon area has a number of sunken vessels around the new and old bridges, which serve as artificial reefs for fishing. When currents are mild, you can dive a few of these spots. They abound with fish, sponges and soft corals.

Sombrero Reef, Marathon's most popular ocean dive and snorkeling spot, offers good visibility and a wide depth range, from the shallows to 40 ft. Cracks and crevices shot through the coral canyons that comprise the reef overflow with lobster, arrow crabs, octopi, anemones, and resident fish. A huge light tower marks the area. Boaters must tie up to the mooring bouys on the reef.

Slightly north of Sombrero lies the wreck of the ***Thunderbolt***, an intentionally scuttled, 188-ft freighter lying upright in 110 ft of water, with the top of its wheelhouse at 70 ft. Resident fish include big barracuda, swarms of sergeant majors, queen and grey angelfish, blue tangs and moray eels.

Coffins Patch, just north of the *Thunderbolt*, provides good snorkeling areas with mounds of pillar, elkhorn, and brain corals at depths averaging 20 to 30 ft.

■ Diving the Lower Keys & Key West

Dive trips from the Lower Keys – Big Pine Key, Sugar Loaf Key, Summerland Key, Ramrod Key, Cudjoe Key and Torch Key – take off to reefs surrounding American Shoal and Looe Key National Marine Sanctuary.

The **Looe Key Reef**, named for the **HMS** *Looe*, a British frigate that ran aground on the shallow reefs in 1744, offers vibrant elkhorn and staghorn coral thickets, and an abundance of sponges, soft corals and fish. Constant residents include Cuban hogfish, queen parrotfish, huge barracuda, and longsnout butterfly fish. A favorite dive site of the Lower Keys, Looe Key bottoms out at 35 ft. Extreme shallow patches of seagrass and coral rubble provide a calm habitat for juvenile fish and invertebrates.

Diving off Key West includes offshore wreck dives and tours of **Cottrell Key**, **Sand Key** and the **Western Dry Marks**. Huge pelagic fish and graceful rays lure divers to this area.

Sand Key, marked by a lighthouse, lures snorkelers and novice divers to explore its fields of staghorn coral. Depths range from the surface down to 45 ft.

Cosgrove Reef, noted for its large heads of boulder and brain coral, attracts a number of large fish and rays.

Advanced divers may want to tour the **Cayman Salvage Master**, at 90 ft. This 180-ft vessel was purposely sunk to form an artificial reef.

Stargazer, the world's largest underwater sculptured reef, sits five miles off Key West between Sand Key and Rock Key. This magnificent steel wonder, completed in 1992 by artist Ann Labriola, stretches 200 ft long, 70 ft wide and stands 10 ft high – in 25 ft of water. Each of its 10 sections is perforated in the pattern of different star constellations, once used to navigate the seas. Divers and snorkelers become a living part of this mystical, artificial reef as they locate the positions of the constellations in its surface. Hard corals are beginning to grow on the structure, which shelters a small community of reef fish.

More spectacular, though, are the reefs surrounding the Marquesas Islands, 30 miles from Key West, and the Dry Tortugas National Park, 70 miles off Key West.

Seldom visited, though pristine for diving, the **Marquesa Islands**, have extreme shallows, both en route and surrounding the islands, which makes the boat trip difficult in all but the calmest seas and docking impossible for all but shallow draft cats and trimarans. Check with **Lost Reef Adventures** (☎ 305-296-9737) for trip availability.

To the west is the **Dry Tortugas National Park**, where the most fabulous diving in the Keys can be found. The Dry Tortugas are comprised of seven islands, one of which, Garden Key, is the site of 19th-century Fort Jefferson. No services are available within the park, though there is a visitors center at Fort Jefferson (☎ 305-242-7700; www.nps.gov/drto). You reach the area by charter boat or seaplane, and must carry in all of your gear and air. Check with Key West dive shops for the availability of trips. For the very adventurous, overnight camping trips can be arranged.

■ Dive Operators

The following operators provide guided reef and wreck trips. Many also can arrange complete dive and accommodation packages.

Prices include tanks and weights, unless otherwise stated (all are subject to change). Some operators will not refund unused dives, even if the operator canceled the trip. Check with the individual dive shop's policy on canceled trips before buying a package.

Upper Keys Dive Operators

Admiral Dive Center, a full-service PADI shop operating since 1985, offers dive and snorkeling trips to the best sites in Pennekamp and the National Marine Sanctuary. Referrals. Instruction. Divers and snorkelers ride on the same boats. Two-tank dives cost $50, snorkeling $30. Nitrox and Nitrox instruction available.

Owners, Captains Susan and Bill Gordon, also offer three-, five- and seven-night live-aboard dive and fishing trips aboard the 65-ft *Admiral I*, which sleeps 12 (two heads). Destinations include the Keys, Cay Sal Banks and the Bahamas. ☎ 800-346-3483 or 305-451-1114, fax 305-451-2731. E-mail: info@admiralcenter.com. www.admiralcenter.com. PO Box 0113 (MM 105, Bayside), Key Largo FL 33037.

American Diving Headquarters, the Keys' oldest dive operation, runs three fast custom dive boats. The shop visits the best sites in Pennekamp Park and the National Marine Sanctuary. Gear rentals. Snorkelers welcome. ☎ 800-634-8464, fax 305-451-9291. E-mail: amdiving@aol.com. MM 105.5, Bayside, Key Largo FL 33037.

Amy Slate's **Amoray Dive Center, Inc.**, at the Amoray Dive Resort, operates a fast dive/snorkel boat to Pennekamp and the National Marine Sanctuary. The resort, on the bay side, is conveniently located next to a cut from the bay to the ocean that leads to Pennekamp Park. Dive trips cost $54.50, snorkeling $25 without equipment. Accommodation packages are available. ☎ 800-4AMORAY or 305-451-3595, fax 305-453-9516. E-mail: amoraydive@aol.com. www.amoray.com. 104250 Overseas Hwy., MM 104, Bayside, Key Largo FL 33037.

Aqua Nut Divers at Kelly's Motel, offers dive and snorkeling tours aboard two 42-ft custom dive boats. Dive trips cost $54.50. Night dives. Nitrox. E-6 processing. Courses – NAUI, PADI, SSI and equipment rentals. ☎ 800-226-0415 or 305-451-1622, fax 305-451-4623. E-mail: kellysmo@aol.com. www florida-keys.fl.us/kellys.htm.

Captain Slate's Atlantis Dive Center has three 40-ft dive boats with showers, camera tables, new heads and decks. The shop offers dive and snorkeling tours of Pennekamp Park and the National Marine Sanctuary. Dives cost $55 with tanks and weights, $39.50 without. Snorkelers join the trips for $26.50, equipment included. Night dives. E-6 processing. Nitrox. Courses and referrals – CMAS, NASE, NAUI, PADI, SSI, YMCA. ☎ 800-331-3483, fax 305-451-9240.

Sea turtle
Copyright © Bill Keogh, Courtesy Big Pine Kayak Adventures

Herons, egrets and ibis forage for tiny snails and fish in the backcountry.
Copyright © Bill Keogh, Courtesy Big Pine Kayak Adventures

Manatee

© *Seaworld, Orlando*

Mangrove fishing, Key Largo

Copyright © *Jon Huber*

Rock Beauty
© *Jon Huber*

Bigeye, Molasses Reef, Key Largo
© *Jon Huber*

Christ of the Abyss "The Statue"
© *Jon Huber*

Dolphin Swim, Theatre of the Sea, Islamorada
© Jon Huber

Seven Mile Bridge
© Andy Newman/Keys TDC

Black Bear, Corkscrew Swamp
© Ed Carlson

Crafts, Miccosukee Indian Village
© Jon Huber

Airboat, Everglades
© Jon Huber

Kayak, Tarpon Basin, Key Largo

© *Jon Huber*

Pelican, Flamingo FL
© *Jon Huber*

Alligator, Everglades National Park
© *Jon Huber*

Wurdemann heron, Anhinga Trail, Everglades National Park
© *Jon Huber*

Osprey nest, Boca Chica
© Jon Huber

Left, tree frog. Above, nurse shark off Big Pine Key
Copyright © Bill Keogh,
Courtesy Big Pine Kayak Adventures

Canoeing the Mangrove Trails, Upper Keys
© Joyce Huber

Parasailing, Holiday Isle, Islamorada
© Jon Huber

Board sailing, Gulf of Mexico
© *Jon Huber*

Sunset, Blackwater Sound, Key Largo
© *Jon Huber*

Christian Schoemig, top, and Vincent Nuzzo at 10,000 feet
Courtesy Jose Melendez, Skydive, Key West

"The Backcountry" Mangrove Flats, Lower Keys
Copyright © Bill Keogh, Courtesy Big Pine Kayak Adventures

Key Deer
Copyright © Bill Keogh,
Courtesy Big Pine Kayak Adventures

Church, Everglades City
© Jon Huber

Old Town, Caroline Street, Key West
© Jon Huber

Duval Street at night from La Concha Roof Top
© Jon Huber

Cycling Higgs Beach, Key West
© *Jon Huber*

Pelicans, Everglades National Park
© *Jon Huber*

Conch Tour Train, Key West
Courtesy Florida Keys TDC

Key West Sunset Celebration, Mallory Square
© *Jon Huber*

Key Largo pawn shop reflects the area's seagoing spirit *© Jon Huber*

Queen angelfish color the ocean reefs throughout the Keys *© Jon Huber*

Rare roseate spoonbill inhabit the lower Keys refuges in winter *© Jon Huber*

Key Largo locals, Oliver and Jean Prew *© Jon Huber*

Glassbottom boat *Discovery* tours the Key West reefs *© Jon Huber*

Captain Slate is pictured on many Keys post-cards feeding a barracuda a piece of fish from his mouth.

Caribbean Water Sports at the Westin Beach Resort offers a variety of watersports, including scuba and snorkeling trips. Divers pay $40 for a one-tank dive, $60 for two-tanks. Snorkelers pay $30, $25 for children. Stop in at the beach shack behind the resort. ☎ 800-223-6728 or 305-852-4707, fax 305-852-5160. MM 97, Bayside, Key Largo 33037. www.caribbeanwatersports.com.

Conch Republic Divers offers dive and snorkeling trips. ☎ 800-274-3483 or 305-852-1655, fax 305-853-0031. 90311 Overseas Hwy., Tavernier FL 33070.

Ocean Divers, at the Marina Del Mar Resort, operates two 48-ft dive boats. Reef trips cost $55 for two tanks. Snorkelers, $35; with equipment, $39. Nitrox. Night dives. E-6 processing. ☎ 800-451-1113, 305-451-1113, fax 305-451-5765. www.oceandivers.com. E-mail: info@oceandivers.com. 522 Caribbean Drive, Key Largo FL 33037.

Quiescence Diving Services, Inc., on the bay, offers personalized service with no more than six divers on a boat. They visit the popular sites and some off-the-beaten track areas. Trips cost $38, $55 with tanks and weights; snorkelers pay $30, or $35 with equipment supplied. The shop operates three fast boats, has Nitrox and Nitrox training, underwater photo courses, and referrals. PADI, SSI, PDIC, NASDS, and IDA. The shop is located adjacent to the cut that leads to Pennekamp. ☎ 305-451-2440, fax 305-451-6440. E-mail: info@keylargodiving.com. www.keylargodiving.com. MM 103.5, Key Largo FL 33037.

Sea Dwellers Dive Center, Inc. operates a custom dive boat from the Holiday Inn docks and will package a dive or snorkeling vacation with the Holiday Inn Sunspree Resort. One of the oldest and most respected dive operators in Key Largo, Sea Dwellers offers scuba and snorkeling trips to the best places in Pennekamp and the National Marine Sanctuary, PADI resort courses through dive-master courses and open-water course completion dives. Custom-built dive boats are Coast Guard-inspected, comfortable and fast. The shop is well stocked with equipment, sportswear, swimsuits, souvenirs and a library of books on the Florida Keys and South Florida. Rates for a two-tank dive are $39.50, or $57.50 with tanks and weights. Snorkelers pay $25, or $33 with equipment supplied. ☎ 800-451-3640 or 305-451-3640, fax 305-451-1935. E-mail: sdwellers@aol.com. www.sea-dwellers.com.

Seafarer Dive Resort offers snorkeling and scuba tours to their resort guests. The PADI shop offers courses and referrals for most agencies. ☎ 800-599-7712 or 305-852-5349, fax 852-2265. E-mail: seafarer@ terranova.net. www.keysdirectory.com/seafarer. PO Box 185, Key Largo FL 33037.

Sharky's Dive Center operates both a scuba and a snorkeling boat from the Holiday Inn docks. Stop by their booth to sign up or ☎ 305-451-5533. For schedules, ☎ 800-935-DIVE, fax 451-0124. 106240 Overseas Hwy., Key Largo FL 33037.

Silent World Dive Center visits Pennekamp and Key Largo National Marine Sanctuary aboard custom 12- and 14-passenger boats. Divers and snorkelers visit two sites. They also offer snuba dives (see page 161), deep dives, dive and accommodations packages. Departures are at 9 am and 1 pm. Guided reef and wreck tours offered. NAUI and PADI beginner to dive-master courses. Private and group classes. Custom video of your dive available. ☎ 305-451-3252. MM 103, Bayside. PO Box 2363, Key Largo FL 33037.

Sun Divers is an all-snorkeling operation. Great for new snorkelers, their trips are $24.95 and equipment rentals are $5. Dry snorkels, designed to keep water from coming in, are available. Sign up at the Best Western Resort in Key Largo or ☎ 800-4-KEY FUN, fax 305-451-1211.

Pennekamp State Park Dive Center operates a 16-passenger dive boat and three snorkeling boats. They also offer sail-snorkel cruises aboard a catamaran. Rentals and certifications are available. ☎ 305-451-1621. For information about the park in general, ☎ 305-451-1621 or 305-451-1202.

Islamorada & Lower Key Largo Dive Operators

Bud N'Mary's Dive Center, at MM 79.8, operates a glass-bottom dive/snorkel boat. Their morning dives are for scuba only, visiting 40- to 60-ft reefs and deeper wrecks. Afternoon tours cover shallow areas for scuba, snorkeling and glass-bottom viewing. Scuba trips cost $48.50, sometimes less if more divers are on board. Snorkelers pay $25 without equipment, $35 with. They also offer fishing trips. ☎ 800-344-7352 or 305-664-2211, fax 305-664-5592.

Caribbean Water Sports at Cheeca Lodge offers scuba, snorkeling and parasailing. Two-tank dive trips with lead and tanks cost $60. Snorkelers join the dive trips for $30, equipment $6. ☎ 888-SEA REEF or 305-664-9547, fax 305-852-5160. E-mail: divecws@aol.com.

Florida Keys Dive Center runs two-tank morning and afternoon dives aboard a 36- or 42-ft dive boat. Cost for a reef or wreck tour with weights and tanks is $59. They dive the outer reefs, the *Duane*, the *Bibb* and the *Eagle*. Packages drop the per-trip cost down to $45. Hotel packages with Ocean Pointe Suite Resort (see page 219). Freshwater showers and refreshments offered after the dive. Friendly service, night dives, Nitrox training and fills. E-6 processing. Referrals. CMAS, NAUI, PADI, PDIC, SSI, YMCA. ☎ 800-433-8946 or 305-852-4599, fax 305-852-1293. 90500 Overseas Hwy., MM 90.5, Plantation Key FL 33070. E-mail: scuba@floridakeysdivectr.com. www.floridakeysdivectr.com.

Tavernier Dive Center operates two 42-ft dive boats to the ledges, reefs and wrecks. If you are staying at an affiliated hotel, the tours cost $45 (if you're not, they're $50). Snorkelers join the dive boat for $30, all equipment supplied. ☎ 800-787-9797 or 305-852-4007, fax 305-852-0869. E-mail through their website at www.tavernierdivecenter.com. MM 90.7 Overseas Hwy., Tavernier FL 33070.

Lady Cyana Divers offers ocean reef and wreck tours, all level PADI courses. Referrals for PADI, CMAS, NASDS, CMAS, NAUI, SSI, IANTD, YMCA, NASE. Two fast custom dive boats carry 19 and 28 passengers. Dive trips cost $52 with tanks and weights. Snorkelers pay $25 to join the trips, plus $10 for equipment use. Nitrox. E-6 processing. ☎ 305-664-8717. E-mail through the website at www.ladycyana.com. PO Box 1157, Mile Marker 85.9, Islamorada FL 33036.

Rainbow Reef Dive Center offers reef and wreck trips, courses and hotel packages. ☎ 800-457-4354 or 305-664-4600. www.rainbowreef-divecenter.com. 84977 Overseas Hwy., Islamorada FL 33036.

Marathon & the Middle Keys Dive Operators

Abyss Pro Dive Center, behind the Holiday Inn at MM 54, Oceanside, offers reef and wreck trips to popular sites aboard their 34-ft dive boat. Snorkelers may join if the trip is to a shallow site. Divers pay $54, including tanks and weights. Snorkelers pay $35, equipment included. ☎ 305-743-2126, fax 305-743-7081. E-mail: info@abyssdive.com. www.abyssdive.com. 13175 Overseas Hwy., Marathon FL 33050.

Captain Hook's Dive Center operates a slick 30-ft dive boat and 26-ft catamaran. They offer all levels of PADI instruction and certification for all agencies. Two-tank dive trips with tanks and weights cost $49. Snorkelers pay $35 with equipment. Friendly service. ☎ 800-CPT-HOOK or 305-743-2444, fax 305-289-1374. E-mail: cpthooks@

bellsouth.net. www.thefloridakeys.com/captainhooks. 11833 Overseas Hwy., Marathon FL 33050.

Hall's Dive Center and Career Institute offers all level of instruction, trips and referral checkouts. ☎ 800-331-4255 or 305-743-5929, fax 305-743-8168. E-mail: hallsdive@aol.com. www.hallsdiving.com. 1994 Overseas Hwy., Marathon FL 33050.

Hurricane Aqua Center & Two Conchs Dive & Charters at MM 48. This PADI shop has courses, referral check outs and trips. A two-tank dive with tanks and weights costs $59. Snorkelers join for $43, equipment included. Maximum six divers aboard their 26-ft boat. ☎ 305-743-2400, fax 305-743-2221. MM 48, 10800 Overseas Hwy., Marathon FL 33050.

Middle Keys Scuba Center visits all the sites from Sombrero Reef to Duck Key. Divers and snorkelers mix aboard their 30-ft custom dive boat. They offer NAUI and PADI certification courses and check out dives for all agencies. Photo and video rental equipment and courses. Divers pay $50 for a two-tank dive including tanks and weights. Snorkelers pay $35. ☎ 305-743-2902. E-mail: rdoileau.aol.com. www.divingdiscovery.com. 11511 Overseas Hwy., Marathon FL 33050.

The Diving Site is the only DOT hydrostatic facility in the area. This PADI shop runs resort through dive master courses, PADI referrals, dive and snorkeling trips. They operate a 40-ft custom dive boat that carries up to 24 divers and a 25 ft boat that carries four divers. Nitrox courses and fills. Morning dives are to the deeper reefs and the wreck of the *Thunderbolt*. Afternoon trips are to the shallow reefs. Two-tank dives with tanks and weights cost $52.50; snorkeling trips are $32 with equipment. ☎ 305-289-1021. 12399 Overseas Hwy., Marathon FL 33050.

Big Pine & The Lower Keys Dive Operators

Looe Key Dive Center, at the Looe Key Reef Resort (MM 27.5), takes divers and snorkelers to the best reef and wreck sites in the Looe Key Marine Sanctuary, including the wreck of the *Adolphus Busch Sr.*, aboard a fast 49-ft catamaran. Rates for a three-tank dive with tanks and weights are $67 plus tax. Snorkelers pay $25 to join the trip, adding $7 for equipment. Certification courses. MM 27.5, PO Box 509, Ramrod Key FL 33042. ☎ 800-942-5397 or 305-872-2215, fax 305-872-3786. E-mail: looekeydiv.com. www.diveflakeys.com.

Note: Because all the reefs in the Looe Key Marine Sanctuary are shallow, dive shops group divers and snorkelers on the same boat. Trips to the deeper wrecks are reserved for scuba divers.

Underseas Inc., a PADI five-star center, features reef and wreck tours for divers and snorkelers to Looe Key Marine Sanctuary aboard their 50-ft catamaran or 35-ft custom dive boat. They also have wreck dives, night dives, Nitrox and training. Still camera rentals. A two-tank dive costs $50, with weights and tanks. Snorkelers pay $25, with equipment. Universal referrals. ☎ 800-446-5663 or 305-872-2700, fax 305-872-0080. E-mail: diveuseas@aol.com.

Key West Dive Operators

Dive Key West, Inc. has a large retail shop, two fast dive boats, one 36 ft, the other 26 ft, that carry six to 12 divers. Snorkelers join the dive boats for reef dives. They visit Western Sambo, Marker I, *Joe's Tug* and the *Cayman* wreck. NAUI, NASDS, PADI and YMCA referrals. Two-tank dives cost $59, with weights and tanks. C-courses. ☎ 800-426-0707 or 305-296-3823, 305-296-0607. www.divekeywest.com. 3128 North Roosevelt Blvd., Key West FL 33040.

Lost Reef Adventures, Inc. takes divers and snorkelers aboard their 40-ft custom dive boat or their 27-ft cruiser. They visit the Sambos, Dry Rocks, Sand Key and the wrecks. PADI and NAUI instruction. Universal referrals. A two-tank dive costs $56. Snorkelers pay $30 for the trip and equipment. ☎ 800-952-2749 or 305-296-9737, fax 305-296-6660. E-mail: lostreefkw@aol.com. www.paradise.com. 261 Margaret St., Key West FL 33040.

Subtropic Dive Center, at Garrison Bight, has PADI and SSI training, Nitrox training and service, and universal referrals. They operate three boats, a 42-ft Burpee, a 28-ft dive boat, and a 48-ft catamaran used for snorkeling trips. Two-tank trips cost $55, snorkelers pay $30, with full gear included. ☎ 888-461-3483, fax 305-296-9918. E-mail: info@subtropic.com. www.subtropic.com. 1605 North Roosevelt Blvd., Key West FL 33040.

Captain Billy's Key West Diver, Inc., ☎ 305-294-7177. MM 4.5, Stock Island FL 33040

Southpoint Divers offers tours and courses. ☎ 800-891-DIVE, 305-296-6888. 714 Duval St., Key West FL 33040.

■ The Shipwreck Trail

Courtesy of the Florida Keys National Marine Sanctuary

Nine shipwreck sites in the Florida Keys National Marine Sanctuary have been designated for historic preservation as The Shipwreck Trail. Each site is identified with a spar buoy and is accessible by private boat or dive shop charter. A brief history and description of each wreck follows.

The City of Washington

History

This two-masted sailing vessel, built at Roach's Shipyard, Chester, Pennsylvania in 1887, served as a combination passenger and cargo transport between New York, Cuba, and Mexico. During 1889 she was refitted with a 2,750 hp steam engine, which dramatically increased her range and speed.

On February 15, 1898, the blast that rocked Cuba's Havana harbor and destroyed the USS *Maine* also damaged the neighboring *City of Washington* with flying debris that smashed awnings and tore up her deckhouse. Despite the imminent danger and chaos, crew members from the *City of Washington* rushed to rescue the *Maine's* survivors.

Current research supports the possibility of spontaneous combustion aboard the *Maine*, but bad relations between the US and Spain at that time made sabotage the only possibility considered. The explosion sunk the *Maine* and started the Spanish-American War.

During the war, the *City of Washington* sailed as a transport ship carrying troops. She returned to her passenger and cargo runs following the war, until retirement in 1908. Three years later she was converted into a coal-transporting barge.

On July 10, 1917, the *City of Washington* sank while being towed by the tugboat *Luchenbach #4*, after she ran aground on Elbow Reef. The *Luchenbach #4* was refloated, but the *City of Washington* broke apart and could not be salvaged.

Dive Site

Today, the *City of Washington* sits off northern Key Largo in 25 ft of water on Elbow Reef. The wreck is 325 ft long, with most of the hull's lower, bilge section intact. The bow section is badly damaged, with pieces scattered over a 140-ft radius.

Wreck features include half of a cargo hoisting gear, a segment of the forward mast, a chock from the port side of the vessel, a deck ladder.

the bilge pump assembly, the propeller shaft log running through the hull, several hull plate sections with port holes, the top rail with deck egging holes, and the stern rail assembly.

Resident marine life includes yellowtail snapper, schools of sergeant majors, moray eels, midnight parrotfish, and blue tangs.

Sea fans, plumes, branching fire coral, brain coral and star corals border the wreck.

Scuba

The Benwood

History

Built in England in 1910 for a Norwegian company, the *Benwood* operated as a merchant marine freighter carrying precious ores. She was 360 ft long with a 51-ft beam and was armed with 12 rifles, one four-inch gun, six depth charges and 36 bombs.

On April 9, 1942 the *Benwood* was on a routine voyage from Tampa, Florida, to Norfolk, Virginia, carrying a cargo of phosphate rock. Rumors of German U-boats in the area required her to travel completely blacked out, with the Keys coastal lights three miles abeam. The *Robert C. Tuttle*, also blacked out, was traveling in the same area, bound for Atreco, Texas. The two ships were on a collision course. The bow of the *Benwood* collided with the port side of the *Tuttle*. The *Tuttle* was not in immediate danger, but the *Benwood's* bow was crushed and taking on water. The captain turned her toward land and a half-hour later gave orders to abandon ship. The next day the keel was found to be broken and the ship declared a total loss. Local rumor held that the ship was hit by a German submarine.

Salvage began soon after the sinking and continued into the 1950s. She was later dynamited by the Coast Guard as a navigational hazard and continued to serve the US Army for aerial target practice after World War II.

Dive Site

The *Benwood* wreck sits between French Reef and Dixie Shoals in 25 to 45 ft of water. Normally low seas, good visibility and a close proximity to John Pennekamp Park make this one of the most popular shipwreck dives in the Keys.

The remains of the wreck are scattered across a wide area. The 25-ft-high bow of the ship is the most intact feature. The hull structure is partially intact up to the first deck. Large steel knees join the deck plate to the outer hull and sides of the vessel. These knees are massive reinforced triangles that outline the ship's hull shape despite the loss of the hull plates.

The first deck has been punctured in many places, forming a network of "nooks and crannies" perfect for fish habitat. Divers can peer through these holes into the cargo hold and see the space where ore was once carried.

During summer, swirls of glass minnows hover over the wreck. Schools of grunts, snappers and sergeant majors are year-round inhabitants. Stingrays, angels and eels are usually nearby.

Coral rubble, brain coral, fire coral and encrusting sponges cover the wreck.

The Duane

The US Coast Guard cutter *Duane* lies upright on a sandy bottom in 120 ft of water one mile south of Molasses Reef off Key Largo. After being decommissioned on August 1, 1985 as the oldest active US military vessel, the *Duane* was donated to the Keys Association of Dive Operators for use as an artificial reef. On November 27, 1987, she was towed to Molasses Reef, her hatches opened, her holds pumped full of water, and down she went to begin her final assignment.

History

The *Duane* was built in 1936 at the US Naval Yard in Philadelphia. She was a 327-ft Treasury Class cutter, one of seven such vessels, and was named for William J. Duane, Secretary of the Treasury under Andrew Jackson. She had various assignments before being sent to the Atlantic in 1941, where she eventually served with the US Atlantic Fleet. Her service included an impressive wartime and peacetime record. On April 17, 1943, she and her sister ship, the *Spencer,* sank the German U-Boat U-77. She participated in four rescues at sea, picking up a total of 346 survivors. In 1980 she was an escort vessel for thousands of Cuban refugees coming to the United States. Her last assignments included Search and Rescue work and Drug Enforcement.

Dive Site

On a clear day, the outline of *Duane's* intact hull can be seen from above. The mast and crow's nest, protruding high above the hull, lie at 60 ft, the navigating bridge at 70 ft, just forward of amidships. The superstructure deck is at 90 ft and the main deck at 100 ft. The hull structure, completely intact with the original rudders, screws, railings, ladders and ports, makes an impressive display.

Barracuda, yellowtail snapper, angelfish, wrasse, damselfish, spotted blennies, butterflyfish, trumpetfish, grunts, winged mollusk, and an occasional sea turtle inhabit the wreck.

Finger corals, watercress algae, cup coral, star coral, sea fans, and sea plumes encircle the wreck.

The Eagle

The *Eagle* lies on her starboard side in 110 ft of water three miles northeast of Alligator Reef Light. On the night of December 19, 1985, while waiting to be sunk as an artificial reef next to the *Alexander Barge*, the *Eagle* broke from her moorings. Her port anchor was dropped to prevent further drifting in the current and she was sunk at that spot.

History

The *Eagle*, then known as the Raila Dan, was launched at Werf-Gorinchem, Holland, in December 1962 as a conventional-hull freighter. She had several owners and seven name changes after her launching. On October 6, 1985, she caught fire. Two US Coast Guard cutters responded to her distress call, but the ship's superstructure was destroyed. After she was declared a total loss, the Florida Keys Artificial Reef Association purchased her for $30,000 and Joe Teitelbaum, a private citizen, donated another $20,000 to help create an artificial reef. The ship was then named the *Eagle Tire Company,* and was cleaned, gutted of all wooden parts, and all oil and fuel was removed to protect the marine life in the area.

Dive Site

The *Eagle* has a number of interesting structural features that make it a notable dive attraction. A large anchor chain exits the hawse pipe on the port bow, and continues a considerable distance before disappearing in the sand. Two large mast assemblies rest on the bottom. One is set on the forecastle; the other, amidships between cargo bays. Each has its own ladder and observation platform in place. Toward the stern there is a tandem set of cargo booms. Heat damage from the fire can be observed in the stern quarter. The deck railings at 70 ft, and her propeller and rudder at 110 ft, are still intact. In 1998, the *Eagle* was broken in two by Hurricane Georges.

Watch for grouper. snapper, cobia, amberjacks, silversides, and grunts.

Plant life in the wreck includes green algae, sponges, sea rods, sea whips, black coral, branching fire coral, and starlet coral.

The San Pedro

The *San Pedro*, a member of the 1733 Spanish treasure fleet caught by a hurricane in the Straits of Florida, sank in 18 ft of water 1¼ miles south of Indian Key. She is the oldest shipwreck on the Shipwreck Trail, with the mystique of a Spanish treasure shipwreck to draw divers and snorkelers alike.

History

The 287-ton Dutch-built vessel *San Pedro* and 21 other Spanish ships under the command of Rodrigo de Torres left Havana, Cuba, on Friday, July 13, 1733, bound for Spain. The *San Pedro* carried 16,000 pesos in Mexican silver and numerous crates of Chinese porcelain. Upon entering the straits of Florida, an oncoming hurricane was signaled by an abrupt wind change. The Spanish treasure fleet, caught off the Florida Keys, was ordered back to Havana by their captain. But it was too late. The storm intensified and scattered, sank or swamped most of the fleet.

The wreck of the *San Pedro* was found in the 1960s in Hawk Channel. At this time the site was heavily salvaged by treasure hunters. Silver coins dating between 1731 and 1733 were recovered from the pile of ballast and cannons that marked the place of her demise. Elements of the ship's rigging and hardware as well as remnants of her cargo were unearthed and removed.

Dive Site

The large pile of ballast, dense stones from European river beds, typically stacked in lower holds of sailing ships to increase their stability, marks the spot where the *San Pedro* went down. Mixed in with the ballast are red ladrillo bricks from the ship's galley. In 1989 this site became a State of Florida Underwater Archaeological Preserve. Replica cannons, an anchor from another 1733 shipwreck site, and a bronze plaque were placed on the site to enhance its interpretation.

Watch for snapper, grunts, spadefish, stingrays, parrotfish, angelfish and occasionally a barracuda and look for plants and bottom-dwelling organisms such as turtle-grass and coral.

The Adelaide Baker

In 20 ft of water, four miles south-southeast of Duck Key, lie the remains of a three-masted iron-rigged and -reinforced wooden-hull bark. The major features of this ship, locally known as the *Conrad*, but believed in fact to be the *Adelaide Baker*, are scattered over a square quarter-mile area.

History

The *Adelaide Baker*, originally called the *F.W. Carver*, was built in 1863 in Bangor, Maine. She measured 153 ft, had a beam of 35 ft and a depth of hold of 21 ft. Her double-decked hull was constructed of oak and hackmatack (tamarack or balsam poplar); two years after being built she was sheathed with copper. After being sold to the British she was renamed the *Adelaide Baker*. The wreck report documents that on January 28, 1889, she was bound for Savannah with a load of sawn timber when she wrecked on "Coffins Patches" Reef. The irregularly shaped granite ballast concentrated along the edge of the reef marks where she was first "holed," spilling ballast and lower cargo. The night of the shipwreck, wreckers in the area assisted the captain and crew to safety. There was no loss of life.

Dive Site

The *Adelaide Baker's* eroded remains are scattered along a north-northwest path 1,400 ft long. Most of the material is clustered in two areas. Cluster A is thought to be near the place where the ship went down. Large iron hold-beam knee-riders and deck-beam hanging-knees dominate this cluster. Nearby lie the lower portion of the mizzen mast and a metal water tank. Cluster B appears to have been segregated and placed there by early salvers. The iron main mast, 77 ft long, is the dominant feature here. The remains of a bilge pump, knee-riders, iron deck bit, hawse-hole frames, and miscellaneous rigging and tackle are also parts of Cluster B. Other features, separate from these clusters, are two additional mast sections, a pile of rigging, and a second water box. The widely dispersed nature of the wreck site and identifiable ship components makes it a good educational puzzle for sport divers to locate and identify shipwreck materials that are unusual among Florida shipwrecks.

Watch for these fish and invertebrates: snappers, nurse sharks, lobster, moray eels, parrotfish, goatfish, angelfish, and grouper.

Look for these bottom-dwelling organisms: mustard hill coral, branching fire coral, symmetrical brain coral, sea fans, and sponges.

The Thunderbolt

The *Thunderbolt* was intentionally sunk on March 6, 1986, as part of the Florida Keys Artificial Reef Association project. She now lies intact and upright on a sand bottom in 120 ft of water, four miles south of Marathon and Key Colony Beach.

History

The *Thunderbolt* was built, along with 15 sister ships, by Marietta Manufacturing Company at Point Pleasant, West Virginia, under contract to the US Army during World War II. The *Thunderbolt*, then named *Randolph*, was launched on June 2, 1942. These ships were built to plant and tend defensive coastal minefields for the Army's Coast Artillery Corps. However, in 1949 this function – and the *Randolph* – were transferred to the Navy. While in the Navy, this vessel was never commissioned and remained in the Naval Reserve Fleet, first in South Carolina and then in Florida. Caribbean Enterprises of Miami purchased the vessel in 1961, and later Florida Power and Light bought her for research on the electrical energy in lightning strikes – hence her new name, *Thunderbolt*. Eventually Florida Power and Light donated the vessel to the Florida Keys Artificial Reef Association.

Dive Site

The ship's hull is 189 ft long with a forecastle, which served as the cable handling area, and a cruiser stem. Prior to being sunk, the ship was stripped of all but a few major pieces of equipment. The most prominent remaining features are a horizontal cable handling reel, which lies at 80 ft and is centered on the after-end of the forecastle deck, and the remains of the ship's superstructure, including the observation deck, located at 75 ft. The aft end of the superstructure has been cut away, exposing the interior of the hull at the engineering space. The rudder and propellers, which lie at 120 ft, also remain to complement the stern section of the hull.

Watch for jack crevalle, amberjack, grouper, barracuda, cobia, sharks, tarpon, jewfish, and spiny sea urchins. Bottom-dwelling organisms include star coral, brain coral, fire coral, sea whips, sponges, hydroids, and flaming scallops.

The North America

Three ships were reported lost on Delta Shoals one mile east of Sombrero Light in the 19th century. One shipwreck that is situated immediately north of the shoal on a sand and grass flat in 14 ft of water may be the *North America*.

History

Admiralty Court Records show that a three-masted, square-rigged vessel by the name of *North America*, carrying dry goods and furniture, was lost November 25, 1842 on Delta Shoals while en route from New York to Mobile, Alabama. Local wreckers provided assistance to Captain Hall and his crew during a three-day salvage effort. Four ships were registered by the name of *North America* during this period, but the size of the remaining wreckage and Captain Hall's name in the court records suggest it may be the *North America* built in Bath, Maine in 1833. James B. Hall of New York and George S. Hall of Bath, Maine were part-owners of the *North America*, based in New York. This ship-rigged vessel had two decks, three masts, was 130 ft long and had a beam of 29 ft.

Dive Site

The vessel remains consist of a large section of wood hull filled with ballast. The wreckage measures approximately 112 ft long and 35 ft wide. Only small sections of the lower hull protrude above the sandy bottom and the majority of the structural remains are covered with ballast. The southwest extremity of the site consists of the keel and several iron drift bolts that attached the keel and keelson to the floor timbers. The majority of the remaining hull is covered by sand and only small sections of the keel can be found exposed. The ballast pile is oval-shaped and appears to be largely contained within the surviving hull structure. The longitudinal axis of the ballast pile is southwest to northeast and extends for 85 ft. Beyond the ballast, the remainder of the hull structure is covered by sand and turtle grass. The ceiling and planking are primarily attached by wooden trunnels (treenails). A few ¾-inch square copper spikes can be seen where they held the planks in position during construction, before the trunnels were installed. Cement can be found between several of the frames, where it was probably used as a temporary patch material. The remains of two barrels containing cement can be found within the confines of the ballast scatter, one near the north end and one at mid-section.

Watch for grouper, lobster, crabs, snappers, blue tangs, wrasse, damselfish, hogfish, scorpionfish, moray eels, barracudas and angelfish. Among the plants and bottom-dwelling organisms are turtle-grass, manatee-grass, anemones, sponges, fire coral, brain coral, sea whips, and sea plumes.

The Amesbury

History

The remains of a steel-hull US Naval vessel lie in 25 ft of water five miles west of Key West. This vessel was a decommissioned US Navy ship being towed by Chet Alexander Marine Salvage of Key West to a deep water location to be sunk as an artificial reef. While en route, she grounded, and before she could be refloated a storm broke up her hull. The site is locally known as Alexander's Wreck.

The *Amesbury* (DE 66) was launched and commissioned in 1943 as a destroyer escort. She was named for Lt. Stanton Amesbury, who was killed in enemy action over Casablanca in 1942, while attached to an aviation squadron in the Atlantic Area. The *Amesbury's* first assignment was duty with the Atlantic Convoy 7, followed by participation in the Normandy invasion. Returning to the United States in August, 1944, she was assigned temporary duty with the Fleet Sonar School in Key West. In 1945, she was one of the 104 destroyer escorts converted to high-speed transports at the Philadelphia Navy Yard. *Amesbury* was then assigned hull number APD-46 and equipped with a five-inch turret gun and three twin-mount 40-millimeter antiaircraft guns. Proceeding to the Pacific, she supported landings in Korea and China during 1945, carrying Underwater Demolition Team 12. The *Amesbury* returned to Florida in 1946, was decommissioned and never saw active service again. Chet Alexander Marine Salvage of Key West purchased her in 1962 for scrap.

Dive Site

The remains of the *Amesbury* consist of two sections of hull and super-structure lying 200 yards apart. The southern section contains the remains of the bow and port side. The northern section of the wreck consists of the stern and starboard side. Fifty feet behind the stem of the bow is the five-inch gun mount behind a semicircular shield. Behind that is the twin 40-millimeter Bofors-style antiaircraft gun mount on an elevated pedestal. A debris field on the east side of the hull contains pieces of the collapsed upper hull, bridge, and super-structure. The northern section of wreckage includes the stern, another Bofors gun and mount, miscellaneous debris, and heavy Welin davits used to transport and launch four Landing Craft Vehicle Personnel boats.

Watch for lobster, crabs, scorpionfish, moray eels, barracudas, angelfish, parrotfish, yellowtail snappers, damselfish, sergeant majors, southern stingrays, jewfish, black and Nassau groupers, spadefish, red snappers, cobia and pompano.

Among the bottom-dwelling organisms are starlet coral, brain coral, finger coral, mustard hill coral, cup coral, sea rods and sponges.

Snorkeling & Snuba

If you can swim, you'll love snorkeling. Florida Keys offshore reefs offer endless entertainment to anyone who can peer through a mask. There are shallow shipwrecks, such as the wreck of the *San Pedro*, an underwater archaeological preserve off Islamorada, miles of coral canyons and pinnacles, the famous statue of Christ of the Abyss in Key Largo, and every imaginable fish along the entire coast.

The best spots to snorkel are the outer reefs. Morning and afternoon boat trips are widely available. If given a choice, select the morning trips, which are less crowded, with usually calmer wind and seas.

Take a snorkeling lesson if you're new to the sport. A short pool demonstration will allow you to get comfortable using the gear before you try it in the ocean. Many hotels and dive shops offer classes.

Snuba involves breathing through a mouthpiece attached to a 20-ft air hose connected to air cylinders floating on the surface. (See Snuba of Key West and the catamaran *Fury*, page 168.)

If high winds or storms cancel ocean tours, you can still explore the bays or oceanside lagoons (dive shops will rent you the gear). We found a number of juvenile barracudas, parrot fish, filefish, angels and grunts around the bayside hotel docks and swimming lagoons. Just off the beach at John Pennekamp State Park are some old cannon and a sunken car. This artificial reef attracts numerous fish and crustaceans. An occasional manatee has been spotted there, too.

For a fee, you can snorkel over the first underwater hotel – Jules' Undersea Lodge, located in the Key Largo Undersea Park. The park is a protected lagoon open 365 days a year. Though the fish and visibility do not rival the offshore reefs, this is a good spot for beginners or when storms rule out ocean tours. To reach the lagoon, turn toward the ocean at the "Undersea Park" sign (MM 103.2). The lagoon is at the end of the road.

■ Places to Avoid

Snorkeling is unsafe in the brackish and fresh waters of the Everglades – home to alligators. There is a crocodile sanctuary on the northernmost tip of Key Largo that should be avoided. Alligators and especially crocodiles are unpredictable; despite their sluggish appearance, they are extremely dangerous.

■ Equipment

Snorkeling tours include use of a mask, snorkel and inflatable safety vest. Swim fins are almost always part of the deal and are an added benefit. They make swimming much easier and will help you keep pace with the parade of fish you'll be joining. If you plan on doing a lot of snorkeling, by all means purchase your own equipment. A mask that fits properly and a comfortable snorkel make the experience much more rewarding.

Masks and snorkels are made from rubber or silicone. The silicone is more expensive, but softer against the skin and somewhat more comfortable for prolonged use. And it lasts longer. Don't mix the two. The oils in rubber will badly discolor silicone.

If you wear eyeglasses, you may want to invest in an optically corrected mask before your trip. They start at about $95 and can be ordered from most dive shops and some optical establishments (check with your optician). You can wear contacts with a standard mask, but you will run the risk of losing them underwater.

Expect difficulty sealing your mask if you sport a beard or mustache. Water tends to wick in along the hairs. Try a bit of vaseline around the rim of your mask. It may reduce or eliminate the problem. Shaving is the best solution.

Long hair should be brushed back away from your face before you put on the mask. One thin hair becomes a very efficient siphon of water. Check for a good fit by placing the mask against your face (without the straps) and inhale. If you can't easily shake the mask off, the fit is good.

Never use ear plugs or swimming goggles for snorkeling. Pressure from even a very shallow dive can cause mask squeeze. Your nose must be included in the mask to allow you to exhale slightly and equalize the pressure as you descend. Use of ear plugs underwater can cause serious and permanent damage to your eardrums.

Before boarding the snorkel-tour boat, be sure to pick up a container of anti-fogging solution. Available in most dive shops, it will keep the glass in your mask crystal clear. Without it, your mask will quickly fog up. In a pinch, if anti-fog solution is unavailable, rub a bit of saliva around the inside of the glass and rinse lightly.

During winter the water temperature drops from 85° down to 70-75° F. Some wetwear is desirable. A shorty wetsuit or a lycra wetskin will protect you from the sun and keep you warm. Wetskins are preferred by most snorkelers since they are easier to put on than wetsuits and cost a lot less. They will protect you from sunburn too – often the biggest problem a snorkeler encounters. While snorkeling, a thin layer of water over your back keeps you feeling deceptively cool, but does nothing to block out the harmful rays of the sun. Be safe.

If you don't have a wetskin or light wetsuit, wear a long-sleeved shirt and consider long pants if you are fair-skinned.

■ Look, But Don't Touch

Everything living is protected in Florida's marine parks. Wearing gloves, touching corals and feeding fish are prohibited. Spearfishing is outlawed. Certain foods eaten by humans can be unhealthy and often fatal to fish. Touching corals may kill them or cause infection, which can spread to surrounding corals. Touching any corals may cause an allergic reaction and touching fire coral will give you a painful sting.

It is best to familiarize yourself with the marine life before you visit the reefs. Fish and coral identification books and submersible sheets can be picked up at dive shops.

Avoid wearing dangling jewelry. To a normally harmless, but somewhat toothy barracuda, it may offer the same appeal as a fishing lure.

Display a diver-down flag any time you are in the water.

■ Snorkeling Tours

Half-day tours to the underwater sanctuaries lead in popularity, but if you are after adventure you'll find numerous sail-snorkel trips that visit remote islands and shoals. New, designed-for-snorkeling, shallow-draft trimarans and catamarans visit out-islands and shallow

Common Stinging Corals and Sea Animals

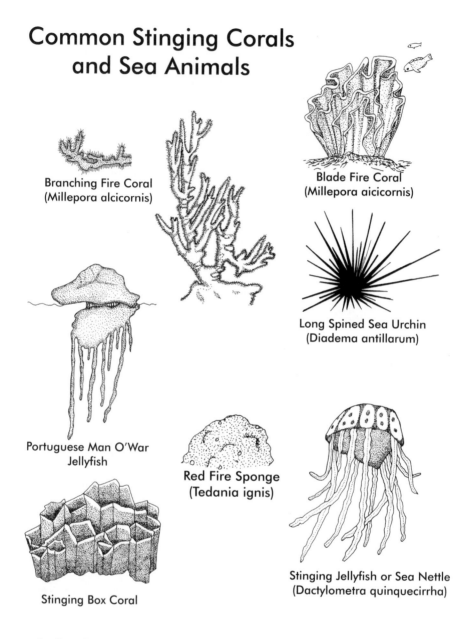

Branching Fire Coral
(Millepora alcicornis)

Blade Fire Coral
(Millepora aicicornis)

Long Spined Sea Urchin
(Diadema antillarum)

Portuguese Man O'War
Jellyfish

Red Fire Sponge
(Tedania ignis)

Stinging Box Coral

Stinging Jellyfish or Sea Nettle
(Dactylometra quinquecirrha)

reefs. Seaplane excursions to the Dry Tortugas, a magnificent chain of remote, uninhabited, coral-fringed islands (see page 168), leave from Key West.

If you're traveling with scuba-equipped companions, you'll find most dive boats allow you to join the tour for a fee. Stop in at any dive shop for trip schedules. But the best trips are aboard the snorkel boats. They park on the shallow reefs and usually visit more than one site on a trip.

Or you can spend a week on one of the live-aboard sailing yachts and tour the entire area.

Physical fitness buffs may wish to combine paddling with snorkeling tours. Both Key West Kayak and Mosquito Coast make that offer (see *Canoe & Kayak Tours* chapter, page 60, for listings).

Half-day snorkeling tours average $25, with some as high as $50. Camera and video rentals or use of special gear are extra.

■ Biscayne National Underwater Park

Biscayne National Underwater Park is the largest marine park in the United States, consisting of 181,500 acres of islands, bays and offshore coral reefs.

Snorkeling excursions are offered by **Biscayne National Underwater Park, Inc.**, PO Box 1270, Homestead FL 33030. ☎ 305-230-1100.

■ Key Largo

Southeast of the Florida Peninsula, where the Keys splash across the Gulf of Mexico and Atlantic, lies one of nature's oldest and most artfully crafted underwater gardens, the Key Largo National Marine Sanctuary.

Located in the Atlantic Ocean, the park sits three miles off Key Largo and extends eight miles out to the edge of the continental shelf. Designated a National Marine Sanctuary in 1975, it encompasses 100 square miles of submerged coral reefs. More than one million divers and snorkelers visit the sanctuary each year.

Snorkeling trips to the park are offered by the following tour operators:

- **Coral Reef Park Co.**, MM 102.5 (inside John Pennekamp State Park), ☎ 451-1621).
- **Sun Diver Station Snorkel Shacks,** MM 103, Bayside, ☎ 451-2220, or at the Best Western docks, MM 100, Oceanside, ☎ 451-9686.
- **Silent World Dive Center,** MM 103.2, ☎ 451-3252.
- **Upper Keys Dive and Sport Center,** ☎ 853-0526.
- **It's a Dive,** ☎ 453-9881.
- **Scuba-Do Charters**, MM 100, ☎ 451-3446.
- **Sharky's Inc**, MM 106 Plaza, ☎ 451-5533.

Snorkeling & Snuba

- **Divers City**, MM 104, Oceanside, ☎ 451-4554.

- **Ocean Divers**, MM 100, www.oceandives.com, ☎ 451-1113).

- **The Keys Diver**, MM 100, Bayside, ☎ 451-1177.

- *The Minnow*, MM 100, Oceanside, Holiday Inn docks, ☎ 541-7834.

- **American Diving Headquarters, Inc.** at MM 105.5, www.oceandivers.com, ☎ 451-0037. Snorkel tours usually leave at 9 am, noon and 3 pm.

■ Islamorada

Offshore from Islamorada, on the Atlantic side, are the remains of the 287-ton Dutch ship, **San Pedro**, one of Florida's oldest artificial reefs. Remains of the ship rest in a sand pocket 18 ft below the surface, offering shelter to a host of sea creatures amidst the ballast stones and coral overgrowth. Visibility can't compare with the offshore reefs, but it is an interesting dive nonetheless. Residents include gobies, damsels, moray eels and groupers.

The ship carried 16,000 pesos in Mexican silver and numerous crates of Chinese porcelain when she wrecked in 1733. For tours, contact the Long Key State Park office at ☎ 305-664-4815. Boaters use LORAN coordinates 14082.1, 43320.6. The wreck lies approximately 1¼ nautical miles south from Indian Key. Be sure to tie up to the mooring buoys to prevent anchor damage to the reef.

Islamorada dive shops visit Molasses, Alligator and Tennessee reefs – all named for ships wrecked at the site and in depths ranging from extremely shallow to about 40 ft.

Sign up for an Islamorada snorkeling trip at the **Holiday Isle Dive Center,** MM 84.9, ☎ 664-4145.

Daily reef and wreck tours are also offered at **Bud n' Mary's Dive Center**, MM 79.8, ☎ 664-2211, and **World Down Under**, MM 81.5, ☎ 664-9312.

■ Marathon - Big Pine Key

Sombrero Reef and **Looe Key National Marine Sanctuary** both offer superb reef snorkeling. Depths range from two to 35 ft.

Marathon Divers, MM 54, ☎ 289-1141, offers daily reef trips.

In **Big Pine Key**, book a tour with **Underseas Inc.** at MM 30.5, ☎ 872-2700.

Excursions to the island where *PT 109* was filmed can be arranged through **Strike Zone Charters** . On the 5½-hour trip, owners Mary & Larry Threlkeld include snorkeling gear and a fish fry on the beach. Strike Zone Charters, 29675 Overseas Hwy., Big Pine Key FL 33043, ☎ 800-654-9560 or 305-872-9863, www.strikezonecharter.com.

■ Key West

Key West offers perhaps the most diversified collection of adventure-snorkeling cruises in the islands. Sail-snorkel and snuba cruise , often including lunch and refreshments,visit secluded islands surrounded by beautiful coral reefs.

History buffs will want to book a snorkel trip on Key West's largest tall ship, the 86-ft wooden windjammer, *Appledore* (☎ 305-296-9992). Half-day reef trips depart at 10:30 am and 3:30 pm during winter. She sails to Maine for summer and fall.

The 65-ft schooner *Reef Chief* sails to off-the-beaten-track coral reefs for snorkeling, diving and fishing. The boat is roomy and comfortable. Custom charters and weddings available. ☎ 305-292-1345, E-mail: foresail@bellsouth.net. 6810 Front St., Key West FL 33040.

Sail/Snorkel Catamarans

Captain Ron Canning cruises with several local pods of dolphins and offers dolphin-watch snorkeling excursions aboard the luxury catamaran, *Patty C*, a 31-ft Gemini catamaran originally designed for coastal cruising. The boat has all the comforts of home – three bedrooms, four skylights, a bathroom, refrigerator and a shower on the stern deck. Reservations are a must. ☎ 305-294-6306. www.dolphinwatchusa.com.

Snorkeling & Snuba

On neighboring Stock Island, personalized charters can be arranged through Adventure Charters on the six-passenger trimaran, *Fanta Sea*. ☎ 305-296-0362, fax 305-296-2574. www.keywestadventures.com.

Sail-racing fans will delight in touring the out-islands aboard the *Stars & Stripes*, a huge 54-ft, 49-passenger replica of the racing catamaran famed by Dennis Conner. This ninth version was designed especially for cruising the shallow channels and reefs of Key West. For maximum comfort and enjoyment, this sailing yacht features a 29-ft beam, glass-bottom viewing, and a fully shaded lounge. The ultra shallow draft (25 inches) allows the captain to pull up to sandy beaches at Woman Key and other spots that are off-limits to many charter boats. See the *Stars & Stripes* at Land's End Marina (☎ 294-7877 or 800-634-MEOW). You can book a tour at Lost Reef Adventures, 261 Margaret St., Key West. Visit their website at www.adventurekeywest.com.

Board the *Atlantic Fury* or the sister yacht, *Pacific Fury*, one of the 65-ft, state-of-the-art catamarans for snuba (see Snuba of Key West, page 168) and snorkeling. Designed for the ultimate in sailing and snorkeling comfort, the *Fury* catamarans have a stairway into the sea, a large sundeck, shaded lounge area, freshwater showers, spacious bathrooms, top-of-the-line snorkel gear and professional instruction by the crew. Trips depart the Fury Dock at the Hilton Resort & Marina for visits to Sand Key, Rock Key, Eastern Dry Rocks and Western Sambo – all coral reef out-islands.. Trips leave at 9:30 am and 12:30 pm. Cost is $40 per person for snorkeling, $89 for snuba (discount coupons may be available on their website). For reservations, ☎ 305-294-8899, 8 am-11 pm.

During your trip, unlimited sodas and water will be served, and after snorkeling, complimentary ice cold beer and white wine. Bring sunscreen and a towel. ☎ 305-294-8899. www.furycat.com.

Snuba of Key West offers snuba instruction and tours aboard the luxurious *Fury* Catamarans. Snuba is safe family fun, and it's easy to learn. No prior diving or snorkeling experience is required and the minimum age is eight years old. After a 15-20 minute orientation during your sail out to the reef, your professionally trained snuba guide will personally take you on an underwater tour of the beautiful marine environment. Participants must be comfortable in the water. The $89 cost includes at least a full hour on the reef, all instruction and equipment, a personal guided tour, complimentary soft drinks during the trip and complimentary beer and wine after the dive. Tours leave at 9:30 am and 12:30 pm. www.furycat.com/snuba.htm

Sunny Days Sunset and Snorkel Trips feature reef snorkeling trips and champagne sunset sails aboard the *Sunny Days* and *Reef Ex-*

press. Tours depart from the corner of Greene and Elizabeth Streets, Key West. Trips of 3½ hours depart at 9 am and 1 pm. Includes gear, instruction and cold sodas. Beer and wine after snorkeling. ☎ 305-296-5556. E-mail: cattours@aol.com.

The Reef Express, a 61-ft, ultra-slick, 49-passenger power catamaran, allows for two hours of snorkeling on a three-hour trip. The trip includes sanitized snorkel gear, instruction, flotation devices and cold soft drinks. This yacht's wave-piercing design makes for a smooth ride. ☎ 305-296-5556. E-mail: cattours@aol.com.

■ Dry Tortugas National Park

The Dry Tortugas, an uninhabited island group 70 miles off Key West, sit in the midst of a pristine shallow reef tract, ideal for snorkeling, with vibrant staghorn thickets, hordes of fish and critters. On calm days, high-speed ferry, catamaran and seaplane tours depart for Garden Key, site of the Fort Jefferson Monument. Seaplane tours are half-day trips. The ferries depart Key West at 8 am and return at 7 pm. Bring a picnic lunch, cold drinks and snorkeling equipment.

Shallow, coral reef snorkeling areas (five-15 ft) are directly accessible from the beaches.

Spanish explorer Ponce de Leon discovered these island in 1513 and named them Las Tortugas, meaning the turtles, for the throngs of turtles around the islands. The latter-day name, Dry Tortugas, came about as a warning to sea travelers that the islands have no fresh water.

The great numbers of loggerhead turtles are gone, but not all. Most snorkelers spot at least one or two.

Getting There By Air

Seaplane-snorkel tours to Dry Tortugas National Park can be booked at Key West Airport. On the flight out, you'll spot the treasure site of Spanish galleons, *Atocha* and *Margarita*. When the sea is calm, the clear waters of the Gulf magnify an outline of the wrecks.

Flights can be booked through **Sea Planes of Key West** at Key West International Airport. Half-day trips start at $159 per person, or a full day for $275. Overnight round-trip for campers, $299 (subject to change depending on fuel prices). Rate includes use of snorkeling gear, soft drinks and drinking water. Flights are aboard stable, float-equipped, high-wing, four- and seven-seat aircraft. The floats also have retractable wheels, which allow them to take off from the land airport and land in the water at Garden Key in the Dry Tortugas. ☎ 305-294-0709

Garden Key has rest rooms, but no food or beverage service. You must bring everything with you. Passengers are advised to pack their own snacks and water. The flight time ranges from 30 to 40 minutes.

The **Marquesas***, equally magnificent in reef life, are approachable only in periods of exceptionally calm seas by private boat. Navigation information is available though the US Coast Guard. On the 30-mile crossing to the Marquesas, you can spot sharks and rays as they dart under the boat along the sandy bottom. Armies of tulip shells with resident hermit crabs guard the remote island beaches.*

Getting There By Boat

Tortugas Ferry operates *Yankee Freedom II*, a luxurious 100-ft aluminum catamaran cruiser that departs Land's End Marina, Key West, for day-tours of the Dry Tortugas. The $3 million yacht averages 30 knots per hour, with travel time from Key West to the Tortugas approximately 2¼ hours.

Amenities include air-conditioned cabin, comfortable cushioned seating, large windows all around, high-tech television and VCR, spacious sundeck, complete modern galley that serves a complimentary breakfast, and lunch at Fort Jefferson. A snack and cocktail bar are open all other times during the voyage. On the main deck are three separate restrooms with freshwater showers. Day tours offer an opportunity to explore Fort Jefferson, swim, snorkel the beautiful reefs surrounding Garden Key, birdwatch and beachcomb. Snorkeling gear may be borrowed free of charge.

The ferry leaves Key West at 8 am and returns at 5:30 pm in Key West every day. Current price is $95 for adults, $60 for children under 16. They offer discounts to seniors, students with ID, US military personnel, and groups. ☎ 800-634-0939. Trips are weather-dependent and will be cancelled when winds exceed 25 knots. Rates and schedules are subject to change.

To reach Land's End Marina, follow US 1 South to Key West. Take right as you enter the island onto Roosevelt Ave. (this is still US 1); continue through three traffic lights and take a right onto Palm Ave. (Garrison Bight Marina). Follow through three traffic lights and take a right onto

Margaret St. Follow to the foot of the street, where you will find the Key West Seaport and the Yankee Fleet.

Yankee Freedom II, Land's End Marina, Key West. ☎ 305-294-7009, 800-926-5332 or 800-634-0939 from outside the Keys. www.yankeefleet.com.

Launched in May 1999, the ***Fast Cat II***, an 86-ft high-speed power catamaran, carries passengers to the Dry Tortugas in a comfortable, air-conditoned salon or on the rear sundeck. The yacht's innovative wave-piercing design means a smoother, more pleasant ride. Tours depart from the corner of Greene and Elizabeth Streets, Key West. ☎ 305-296-5556. E-mail: cattours@aol.com.

Tips for Boaters

■ Be sure to display a divers flag if you are snorkeling from your own boat. Strong currents may be encountered on the outside reefs. Check before disembarking. One person should always remain on board.

■ Be aware of weather, sea conditions and your own limitations before going offshore. Sudden storms, waterspouts and weather-related, fast moving fronts are not uncommon. Nautical charts are available at marinas and boating supply outlets throughout the Keys.

■ Key Largo and Looe Key National Marine Sanctuaries provide mooring buoys to which you should attach your boat, rather than anchor. If no buoys are available, you should drop anchor only in sandy areas. The bottom in sandy areas appears white.

■ In protected areas of the Keys, destruction of coral formations through grounding or imprudent anchoring can lead to penalties and fines of up to $50,000. Fines for minor damage to coral start at $150. Give yourself plenty of room to maneuver.

■ For Key Largo National Marine Sanctuary use chart 11451 or 11462, and for Looe Key National Marine Sanctuary use chart 11442 or 11445.

Snorkeling & Snuba

Swim with the Dolphins

If you are fascinated by dolphins, an unusual encounter awaits you in any one of four Florida Keys facilities. It's a chance to interact freely with the gentle animals. Instead of simply sitting back and watching the beautiful creatures perform, you can now splash in their pool and join in their playful stunts.

You must be at least 13 years old, know how to swim and attend an orientation session with a dolphin trainer. Life jackets are available. Advance reservations are a must.

Age requirements drop to a minimum of five in some instances. Check with individual facilities. Participants must speak English. Minors must have a parent or legal guardian with them.

The in-water sessions are 30 minutes. A trainer is in charge at all times, yet once you are comfortable in the water you are encouraged to be creative and to interact by diving down with mask and snorkel.

When you first enter the water, the dolphins will "turn on" their sonar and check you over. You will hear a clicking, whistling sound. Once their get-acquainted ritual is complete, they may present a chin to be scratched, or kissed. When they roll to one side, showing their dorsal fins, it's a way of telling guests to grab hold and take an exciting ride through the water.

Don't be alarmed if one comes charging straight at you with lightning speed. They like to play "chicken" and will veer off to one side at the last moment. Of course, no one can ever predict entirely how an animal taken from the wild will behave, but these individuals are carefully screened for gentle character and the right personality.

"Our dolphins really enjoy contact with people," says Mandy Rodriguez, director of the Dolphin Research Center. "Actually, they (the dolphins) think we are providing people for their fun and enjoyment."

Located on Grassy Key near Marathon, the Dolphin Research Center maintains liaisons with university research programs and independent investigators around the world. A not-for-profit teaching and research facility, the center has received national attention when it has been called upon to accept sick or wounded dolphins found in coastal waters.

The center also accepts dolphins from other marine research facilities, where the animals sometimes suffer from overcrowded conditions. Still more dolphins, "burnt out" from years of performing in aquariums, spend their retirement at the center and achieve a complete rejuvenation living in the warm waters of the Atlantic instead of in a tank. Examination of these dolphins reveals remarkable similarities to humans beset by stressful circumstances, from simple loss of appetite to a full-blown case of bleeding ulcers. But with human attention and kindness, the animals return to good health and good spirits.

Islamorada-based **Theater of the Sea,** MM 84, offers dolphin swim programs, sea lion swims and stingray swims, along with continuous marine shows featuring sharks and other marine species. The dolphin swims ($110) feature structured interaction in the water with dolphins. Swimmers join with the dolphins as they carry out trained behaviors, such as dorsal tows and kisses in a 15-ft-deep natural saltwater lagoon. A sea lion swim ($35) involves trained behaviors with sea lions, such as foot pushes and hoop jumps in a 10-ft-deep natural saltwater lagoon. Or you can snorkel their artificial reef habitat ($75) to view tropical fish, turtles, rays and more. The lagoon is up to 12 ft deep. Theatre of the Sea (MM 84) Islamorada FL 33036. ☎ 305-664-2431. www.theatreofthesea.com.

Trainers at Theater of the Sea were instrumental in developing special exercises for spinal-cord-injured patients. Interaction with the dolphins has been useful in easing depression and in community re-integration. Patients must be alert.

Dolphins Plus Inc. keeps 12 Atlantic bottlenose dolphins and two California sea lions. Swimmers can go in the water and interact with the dolphins "up close and personal." Dolphins Plus is at the forefront of dolphin-assisted therapy, run by Island Dolphin Care, and is an active member of the Southeast Marine Mammal Stranding Network.

Dolphins Plus offers both structured and natural swims with the dolphins. For those interested in learning more about the dolphins, they offer three- and five-day classes, kids camps, or an internship program in the Education Department. Dolphins Plus works closely with Dolphin Cove, a sister Marine Mammal Research and Environmental Education Center on the bay in Key Largo. They continue the swim programs pioneered by Dolphins Plus. Dolphin Cove also offers ecotours and kayak trips. For additional information, write to Dolphins Plus, Inc., 147 Corrine Place, Key Largo 33037. ☎ 305-451-1993. E-mail: info@dolphinscove.com.

Dolphin Cove is at MM 101.9, Bayside, in Key Largo FL, ☎ 305-451-4060 or 877-365-2683. Set on a five-acre natural lagoon, it offers a wide range of marine learning programs designed for the education and enjoyment of those interested in the marine environmental systems, including swim-with-the-dolphins, guided kayak and snorkel tours, backcountry ecotours, crocodile tours, and scuba instruction.

Dolphin Research Center is a research facility and home to several Atlantic bottlenose dolphins and sea lions. Several educational programs are offered, as well as a dolphin swim. Dolphin Research Center, MM 59, Grassy Key, Marathon FL 33050. ☎ 305-289-0002. www.dolphins.org.

A new twist on swim-with-the-dolphin programs is offered by Key West's **Captain Ron Canning**, who cruises offshore with several local pods of dolphins and offers "snorkeling-with-wild-dolphins" excursions aboard the luxury catamaran, **Patty C** . ☎ 305-294-6306. Prior reservations a must.

Sightseeing & Attractions

Key Largo

The ***African Queen***, made famous by the film of that name, starring Humphrey Bogart and Katharine Hepburn, sits at the Holiday Inn docks, MM 100. Sign up at the Holiday Inn Gift shop for a half-hour ride aboard the *Queen*. ☎ 305-451-4655.

Dolphins Plus, MM 99.5, offers dolphin swims. See *Swim with the Dolphins* chapter, page 171. ☎ 305-451-1993.

Key Largo Undersea Park offers divers a tour or stay at the world's only underwater hotel, Jules' Undersea Lodge. Snorkeling tours also available. ☎ 305-451-2353. www.jul.com.

John Pennekamp Coral Reef State Park, MM 102.5, features an aquarium, nature trails, marina, public boat ramp, gift shop, dive shop, camping, swimming, soft sand beach, snorkeling, scuba and glass-bottom boat tours. ☎ 305-451-1621.

Islamorada

Theater of the Sea occupies the old Flagler Railroad excavations in Islamorada. Established in 1946, the resulting huge lagoon and marine park gives visitors a chance to shake hands or be kissed by a sea lion, touch a shark or stroke a turtle, feed a stingray or pet a dolphin. The park, located at MM 84.5, Islamorada, 74 miles south of Miami, offers continuous shows from 9:30 am to 4 pm. ☎ 305-664-2431. Write to PO Box 407, Islamorada FL 33036.

Indian Key Historical Site, MM 78.5. See *Boat Tours*, page 50. ☎ 305-664-4815.

Lignumvitae Botanical Site, MM 78.5. Guided botanical tours by boat. ☎ 305-664-4815.

***San Pedro* Underwater State Park,** off Indian Key. The site of a 1733 shipwreck. Cannon replicas, trails, coral formations and schools of tropical fish make an interesting snorkeling spot.

Marathon

Crane Point Hammock, MM 50. This 64-acre densely wooded botanical preserve contains archaeological digs and natural treasures. ☎ 305-743-9100.

Dolphin Research Center, MM 50, offers dolphin and sea lion performances, dolphin swims and educational walking tours. ☎ 305-289-0002.

Key Colony Beach Golf Course, MM 53.5. No tee times, clubs and pull carts available, reasonable fees. ☎ 305-289-1533.

The Old Seven Mile Bridge begins at MM 47. This bridge connects Marathon to the Lower Keys and is home to the Seven Mile Bridge Run and the world's longest fishing pier. A favorite cycling spot too.

Pigeon Key is a five-acre island 2.2 miles west of Marathon. Today it is operated by a non-profit local organization dedicated to preserving the history and environment of the Keys through education and research. ☎ 305-289-0025.

The Pigeon Key Foundation, a non-profit organization, has transformed this island and its buildings into a world-class educational center, a research center, a place to teach visitors about the splendor of the cultural and natural resources of the Florida Keys, and a nationally recognized concert and event location. Pigeon Key, located half-way between Key Largo and Key West, at the midpoint of the famous Old Seven-Mile Bridge, was the location of the work camp and village for the hardy souls that constructed, operated and maintained the bridge itself – a massive ribbon of steel and concrete that forever changed the history of the Florida Keys.

Lower Keys

Bahia Honda State Park, MM 37, features one of the top 10 beaches in North America. Marina, dive shop, cabins and camp sites. Terrific kayaking spot. ☎ 305-872-2353.

Bat Tower, MM 17, on Sugarloaf Key, was originally owned by an English sponge farmer named C.W. Chase. The tower property was sold to Richter C. Perky, who intended to build a fishing camp. In 1929, in an effort to eliminate the ferocious mosquito population, Perky built a tower to attract the mosquito-eating bats. Unfortunately, Mr. Perky's dreams vanished as the bats placed in his tower simply flew away. The Bat Tower now stands as a monument to one man's folly.

Within the Key Deer Refuge, at MM 30.5 on Big Pine Key, lies a sink-hole from the railroad days called the **Blue Hole**, which has an alligator observation area and a walking trail. Alligators in various sizes, freshwater fish and turtles abound. This is a natural for great photos or videos. There is an observation area and a small walking trail. One hundred yards ahead of the boardwalk lies the **Jack Watson Walking Trail**, a .66-mile trail with information on the flora and fauna of the Lower Keys.

Coupon Bight State Aquatics Preserve, MM 28.5, in Big Pine Key. This preserve separates the mainland from an oceanside peninsula. ☎ 305-872-2411.

Great White Heron National Wildlife Refuge, MM 28.5-31.5, in Big Pine Key. Home to many migratory birds in winter. Offers protection to rare and endangered species. ☎ 305-872-2239.

Key West

Audubon House and Gardens displays 18th- and 19th-century Audubon engravings and a gallery of porcelain bird sculptures. Formerly the home of Captain John H. Geiger, the house has been restored as a museum to commemorate John James Audubon's 1832 visit to Key West. At 205 Whitehead St., Key West FL 33040. ☎ 305-294-2116.

Bahama Village in the heart of Old Town features restaurants, bars, shops, public pool and playground. Home of the Goombay Festival.

The Conch Tour Train takes you on a 90-minute narrated tour of Key West. It is the fastest way to familiarize yourself with the entire

Sightseeing & Attractions

Old Town Key West

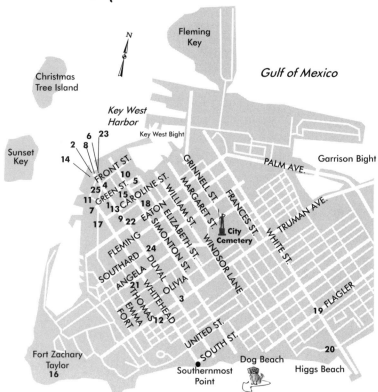

Attractions

1. Audubon House
2. Conch Tour Train
3. Hemingway House
4. Key West Cigar Factory
5. Key West Hand Print Fabrics
6. Mallory Market
7. Mel Fisher Museum
8. Old Town Trolley
9. Wrecker's Museum
10. Key Aloe
11. Key West Aquarium
12. Lighthouse Museum
13. Curry Mansion
14. Sunset Pier
15. Ship Wreck Museum
16. Fort Zachary Taylor
17. Little White House Museum
18. Donkey Milk House Museum
19. East Martellow Museum
20. West Martello Tower
21. Bahama Village
22. Red Barn Theatre
23. Waterfront Playhouse
24. Ripley's Believe It or Not Museum
25. Key West Shipwreck Historeum

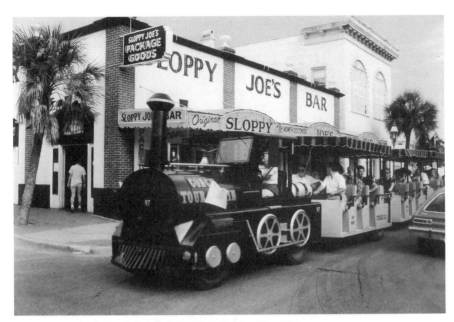

Conch Tour Train, Key West.

city. Board the train at 601 Duval St., Key West FL 33040. ☎ 305-294-5161.

Old Town Trolley Tours make 12 stops for sightseeing and shopping in Key West. Passengers may disembark for lunch and rejoin the tour later. Tours begin every 30 minutes. The station is at 1910 North Roosevelt Blvd., Key West FL 33040. ☎ 305-296-6688.

Curry Mansion, 511 Caroline St. in Old Town, displays 22 rooms of antiques, porches, verandas and a widow's walk. ☎ 305-294-5349.

Customs House, Front St. in Old Town. Considered Florida's finest example of Romanesque Revival architecture, it originally housed the Post Office, US Customs Service, US District Court, the Internal Revenue Service and the Lighthouse Service. ☎ 305-296-3913.

Donkey Milk House Museum, 613 Eaton St. Winner of a 1992 Restoration Award, this 1886 Greek Revival Home is open to the public as a house museum full of unusual furnishings and rare features. Self-guided tour. Antique shop in front parlor. Open daily 10 am-5 pm. ☎ 305-296-1866. By appointment only.

East Martello Museum and Art Gallery, 3501 S. Roosevelt Blvd., adjacent to the Key West International Airport. This Civil War fort-turned-museum displays military artifacts from the Keys. Open daily 9:30 am-5 pm. ☎ 305-296-3913.

Ernest Hemingway House was home to Ernest Hemingway and his second wife, Pauline, from 1931 to 1961. Now a registered national historic landmark, the house and gardens are where Hemingway wrote *For Whom the Bell Tolls*, *Green Hills of Africa*, *A Farewell to Arms*, *The Fifth Column* and *Snows of Kilimanjaro*. Descendants of Hemingway's cat roam the tropical grounds. Located at 907 Whitehead St.. ☎ 305-294-1575.

Fort Jefferson National Monument lies 70 miles west of Key West and may be reached by ferry or seaplane. Self-guided tours of the fort are combined with snorkeling, sightseeing, camping, and birdwatching. For boating information, call the Coast Guard Base: ☎ 305-247-6211. For flights, contact Key West Airport, ☎ 305-294-0709. For high-speed ferry service, contact Tortugas Ferry, ☎ 305-294-7009 or 800-634-0939. To reach the park directly, ☎ 305-242-6713.

Fort Zachary Taylor State Park and Beach is open from 8 am to sunset. A stronghold during the Civil War, the fort displays the largest collection of Civil War cannons in the US. It's off Duval St. Picnic grills. Spectacular sunsets. ☎ 305-292-6713.

Jessie Porter's Heritage House Museum, 410 Caroline St., offers a look at remnants of a rich and turbulent past. Antiques, treasures and odd shipwreck mementoes collected by six generations of the Porter family. After the guided tour, relax in the garden to recordings of poetry by family friend Robert Frost. ☎ 305-296-3573. Open 10 am-5 pm.

Mel Fisher's Maritime Heritage Society Museum sits opposite the Audubon House. Fascinating gold and silver jewelry and treasures from the *Atocha* are displayed. You can touch a gold bar. Gems and coins from the wreck have been fashioned into jewelry and may be purchased. Reproductions of the coins are sold too. Located at 200 Greene St., Key West FL 33040. ☎ 305-294-9936.

Higgs Beach is on S. Roosevelt Blvd. At the foot of Duval St. Children's playground, long pier, sailboat rentals, barbecue grills, picnic tables and restrooms.

The Key West Lighthouse Museum is Florida's third oldest brick lighthouse. Climb 88 steps and view the entire city from the 90-ft observation level. Great photo opportunities. Located across the street from the Hemingway House in Old Town at 938 Whitehead St., Key West FL 33040. ☎ 305-294-0012.

The Key West Aquarium, opened in 1932, was the first tourist attraction built in the Florida Keys. The exhibit includes a living reef, displays of sharks, barracudas, angel fish and a turtle pool. There is also a touch tank. A huge plastic shark outside makes a patient souvenir-photo subject. The aquarium is on the waterfront at Mallory

Square. The entrance is behind the shops. ☎ 305-296-2051. One White-head St., Key West FL 33040.

The Key West Cemetery, like the native inhabitants of this tiny, sub-tropical island, is unique. Filled with humor and history, one stone reads, "I Told You I was Sick." Carved into another headstone at a nearby grave is the self-consoling, tongue-in-cheek, message of a griev-ing widow: "At Least I Know Where He's Sleeping Tonight." At a spe-cial memorial in the cemetery rest the bodies of those who died when the USS *Maine* was sunk in Havana Harbor in 1898, touching off the Spanish-American War. The cemetery occupies 21 prime acres in the heart of the historic district. Tours available. ☎ 292-6718.

The Key West Shipwreck Historeum, at 1 Whitehead St. on Mallory Square, combines interactive theater with a tour of the his-toric Asa Tift warehouse. Fascinating, the Historeum tour combines actors, films, laser technology and the actual artifacts from the re-cently rediscovered vessel *Isaac Allerton*, which sank in 1856.

Ripley's Believe it or Not Odditorium, 527 Duval St., covers 10,000 air-conditioned square feet in the old Strand Theater. There are 1,500 exhibits, offering interactive displays and a look at the bizarre and unusual. Worth a stop! ☎ 305-293-9896.

Smather's Beach, at the end of Duval St. and S. Roosevelt Blvd., of-fers parasailing, Jet Ski rentals and picnic tables.

Turtle Kraals Museum, a former waterfront cannery site where green sea turtles were slaughtered for soup and steaks, is now a mu-seum. Visitors can learn about turtles, their preservation and Key West's turtling industry. The museum is in Key West's Historic Sea-port district at 200 Margaret St., next to the former turtle holding pens or kraals. Admission is free from 11 am to 6 pm daily, with educational tours by appointment and a turtle feeding each day at 4 pm. Headed by Tina Brown, one of the founders of Marathon's Turtle Hospital, the mu-seum features photographs and a history of Key West's turtling indus-try, a booming business in the mid-1800s. Highlights include educational information about sea turtles and the modern-day perils they face, as well as a display of turtle shells, skulls, and sea turtle products. While a young loggerhead turtle named Eddie is currently the museum's only resident, Brown hopes to use the abandoned kraals as a home for turtles with disabilities who cannot survive in the wild. For information about the Turtle Kraals Museum, ☎ 305-294-0209.

Tennessee Williams Fine Arts Center on Stock Island, 5901 West College Road, features year-round opera, dance, symphonic and cham-ber music. National touring companies perform Shakespeare and cur-rent Broadway hits. ☎ 305-296-1520.

Sightseeing & Attractions

Sunset Celebration tightrope walker, Mallory Square, Key West.

Situated in a former sea captain's home, the **Wrecker's Museum**, 322 Duval St., exhibits old documents, ship models, undersea and maritime artifacts. Open 10 am to 4 pm daily. ☎ 305-294-9502.

Writers Walk through Old Town Key West combines a one-hour walk with a literary history of the island. ☎ 305-293-9291.

Sunset Celebration. If there is a single attraction that is a must for a Key West visit, it is sunset at Mallory Square Pier. The place comes alive with entertainment. There is a tightrope walker juggling flaming clubs; dog acts; a unicyclist wriggling free of a straight jacket; two men tumbling, while a woman beats out a tune on a washboard and cymbals; plus craft vendors and food stands. You may even see the Cookie Lady, who arrives by bicycle to hawk warm brownies and cookies.

The entertainment is free, but the entertainers do pass the hat. The standard pitch is: "We welcome your dollars. We welcome your complaints. If you have any complaints, write them on a five-dollar bill and put the bill in the plate." There are no complaints, but plenty of applause, loudest when the Key West sun drops into the sea.

Alligator wrestling, Miccosukee Indian Village (© Jon Huber).

The Everglades

■ Everglades City

Eden of the Everglades, on Route 29, two miles south of Hwy. 41, offers boat tours, a unique wetlands zoo and scenic boat tours through wildlife habitats. Boats depart hourly, starting at 11 am. Turn right before Everglades City Bridge. ☎ 800-543-3367.

Jungle Erv's Everglades Information Station, on Route 29 in Everglades City, features an alligator zoo, exotic birds and a petting zoo. ☎ 941-695-2805.

■ Tamiami Trail

Wooten's Air Boat Tours and Swamp Buggy Rides, on US 41, two miles west of Ochopee, displays hundreds of alligators and live snakes. Everglades wilderness tours by airboat or swamp buggy depart every half-hour. ☎ 941-695-2781.

The Miccosukee Indian Village, MM 70, 25 miles west of Miami on the Tamiami Trail (US 41), is open daily, year-round. Miccosukee craftsmen demonstrate woodcraft, doll making, basket weaving and intricate patchwork sewing. Lively alligator wrestling and airboat rides highlight the village activities. A museum features tribal films and artifacts. ☎ 305-223-8380. PO Box 440021, Miami FL 33144.

■ Miami Area

The Monkey Jungle, off US 1 in South Dade, shelters nearly 500 primates, most running free on a 20-acre reserve. It is one of the few protected habitats for endangered primates in the United States and the only one that the general public can explore. You are caged and the monkeys run wild. To get to the park, take the Florida's Turnpike Homestead Extension (Hwy. 821) south to Cutler Ridge Blvd./SW 216 St. exit, get onto 216 St. westbound, then go west for five miles; or take US 1 south to SW 216 St., then go west on 216 for 3½ miles. ☎ 305-235-1611. 14805 S.W. 216 St., Miami FL 33170.

Miami Metrozoo is open every day from 10 am to 5:30 pm. There are more than 2,800 magnificent wild animals living in a cageless natural environment. **Paws** is a new children's petting zoo. The Zoofari Monorail takes you on an air-conditioned safari. There are elephant rides, koalas, flamingos, white tigers and a 1½-acre tropical aviary. Ticket booth closes at 4 pm. Metrozoo is about 20 minutes from Miami International Airport. From US 1, take the SW 152nd St. exit and go west three miles to the entrance. From the Turnpike extension, take the SW 152nd St. exit and drive west a quarter-mile to the Metrozoo entrance. ☎ 305-251-0403.

Miami Seaquarium is South Florida's largest marine attraction. Seals, sharks, dolphins and killer whales are the stars. Continuous shows. Magnificent aquariums. Open daily from 9 am to 6 pm. ☎ 305-361-5705. 4400 Rickenbacker Causeway, Miami FL.

Parrot Jungle and Gardens, south of Miami International Airport off US 1, offers encounters with talking birds, walks through beautiful tropical gardens, trained-bird shows in the "Parrot Bowl," where macaws and cockatoos perform feats that defy the imagination. In addition to the 1,100 parrots, there are huge alligators, giant tortoises, peacocks, exotic plants and a petting zoo. Fun for all ages. Open from 9:30 am to 6 pm. (Last ticket sold at 5 pm.) Adults, $15.95 plus tax; children ages three to 10, $10.95 plus tax. Open seven days. Wheelchairs and strollers available. ☎ 305-666-7834. 11000 SW 57 Ave., Miami FL 33156.

Restaurants & Nightlife

The Florida Keys

Seafood, always abundant in the waters of the Gulf of Mexico and Florida Keys, has dictated many local food habits and preferences. Yellowtail, red snapper, shrimp, dolphin (the fish, aka mahi mahi) and stone crab claws are prominent menu features. Conch, whether it's grilled, ground in burgers, fried in batters as fritters or raw in conch salad, is a prominent part of the local scene, along with wonderful, chewy crisp squid rings done in batter and deep-fried. Raw bars and sushi tables feature shrimp, crabs, clams and oysters, as well as fish concoctions.

The alligator, brought back from near-extinction during the 1900s, makes a nightly appearance on many menus as a house specialty, whether fried or broiled. If your tastes don't run toward exotic, avoid dishes labeled "mixed seafood grill."

Stone crab claws are quite delectable and in some minds ecologically sound, as just one claw is removed from the live crab, which is then thrown back into the sea. (The claw grows back.) Divers and snorkelers exploring the reefs spot these curious crabs brandishing one huge claw and one tiny one.

A few Cuban spots serve *lechon*, a roast of pork pungently flavored with garlic and tart sour oranges, *ropa vieja* (old clothes), a made up of left-overs, *vaca frita*, literally fried cow, and *picadillo*, a hamburger-caper-cum-raisin concoction in a savory sauce. These are usually served with boiled white or yellow rice, flavored with saffron, and black beans. Bahamas cuisine has faded from its former prominence, but you might come across fish stew served with grits or belles (pronounced bow-yowl), an adaptation of Southern hush puppies made with mashed, shelled black-eyed peas instead of ground corn meal.

Of course, no one can experience a true Keys vacation without sampling at least one slice of Key lime pie. Just any lime pie won't do, it must be made from the juice and minced rind of the piquant Key limes that flourish in the area.

Wherever your taste buds lead, you'll find the south Florida cuisine a delight.

Pricing Key	
$	Less than $25
$$	$25 to $40
$$$	$41 to $50
$$$$	More than $50

The area code for the Florida Keys area is 305

■ Key Largo

Key Largo is fast-food heaven, with popular chain restaurants everywhere. For all-day diving or fishing excursions, there are grocery stores and even gas stations that offer packaged lunches and cold beverages to go. **Miami Subs** (☎ 451-3100), MM 100, Bayside, has subs and packaged goods to go. **Tower of Pizza** (☎ 451-1461), MM 100, Oceanside, delivers fabulous New York-style pizza, sit-down service too. Or try **Dominos Pizza** (☎ 451-4951), MM 98.9, Key Largo. Another option is a pita sandwich at the **Gyros King**, MM 103.4 in Pink Plaza, Bayside, ☎ 451-4444.

Off-season, some restaurants close Mondays, Tuesdays and Wednesdays.

Bayside Grill $-$$

MM 99.5, Bayside

☎ 451-3380

Sitting on the shore of Florida Bay, behind Café Largo, the Bayside Grill tingles patrons' tastes with spicy shellfish, thick Angus steaks, chicken and fish entrées. Island drinks. Small, casual. Nice sunset views. Open daily for lunch and dinner.

Coconuts Restaurant & Lounge $$

MM 100, Oceanside

Marina del Mar Resort

☎ 453-9794

Enjoy island drinks, dancing and live entertainment at this seaside establishment. Seafood platters preside, with blackened, fried or broiled fish. Find Coconuts by turning toward the ocean onto Laguna at MM 100. It's a short drive down the road on the left. Also boat-accessible.

Crack'd Conch $

MM 105, Oceanside

(☎ 305-451-0732

A favorite eatery for conch fritters, conch stew, conch salad, fried and broiled fish, shrimp and fried alligator. Crack'd Conch also offers wine, 90 different beers and honey biscuits. Ultra-casual. Funky island decor. Open for lunch and dinner. Closed Wednesdays.

Craig's Restaurant $$

MM 90.5, Bayside

Tavernier

☎ 852-9424

Craig's "World-Famous Fish Sandwich" draws folks to this small restaurant. Tropical fish entrées, grilled chicken and Cajun specials keep them coming back. Open seven days. No reservations.

Café Largo $-$$

MM 99.5, Bayside

☎ 451-4885

Airbrushed murals depicting local scenery accent Café Largo's walls. House specialties range from hand-tossed pizzas to fresh fish, chicken, veal and pasta dishes. Fine steaks. Opens for dinner seven day from 4:30 to 11 pm. Take-out available.

Frank's Keys Café $$-$$$

MM 100.2

☎ 453-0310

White tablecloths, mango walls, French doors and soft candlelight create a romantic setting at Frank's, where Italian favorites and seafood dishes are prepared fresh. Open Thursday, Friday, Saturday and Sunday evenings from 5 pm to 10 pm.

The Fish House $-$$$

MM 102.4, Oceanside

☎ 461-HOOK (4665) or 888-451-HOOK, fax 305-451-1727

E-mail: eatfish@ddtcom.com

Terrific fresh seafood, conch-style cooking and an extensive raw bar make The Fish House a local's and visitor's favorite. Choose from an elaborate assortment of fresh fish, crab claws, steaks, chicken, fresh-caught tuna salad, thick conch and clam chowder, followed by some fine Key lime pie. It is always packed with a long waiting list after 6 pm, but worth the wait. Opens for lunch and dinner. Casual.

The Italian Fisherman $-$$

MM 104, Bayside

☎ 451-4471

Tie up your boat or drive to this casual Bayside eatery. Outdoor seating allows you to enjoy the sunsets and activities over Blackwater Sound. Lunch and dinner menus vary from pizza, sandwiches and salads to local seafood and pasta favorites. Tiki bar menu. Bring a swimsuit for a dip in the Olympic pool or some crumbs to feed the fish cruising beneath the pier. 11 am-10 pm.

Suncruz Casino Cruises

MM 100, Oceanside

☎ 451-0000

Suncruz jaunts depart the Holiday Inn docks Wednesday, Saturday and Sunday four times a day for casino gambling in international waters. Cost is $10 to board. Complimentary hors d'oeuvres. A la carte menu. Sign up in the Holiday Inn lobby.

Señor Frijoles $-$$

MM 103.9, Bayside

☎ 451-1592

Sink your teeth into sizzling fajitas, seafood nachos, Mexican pizza, Cancun chili fish, enchiladas, chicken specials or local seafood dishes.

Then wash it down with one of the bartender's renowned Margaritas, a tropical fruit drink or Mexican beer. Oh yeah, there's the sunset out back. Dock your boat alongside or park in front.

Snooks Bayside Club $$-$$$$

MM 99.9, Bayside

☎ 453-3799

Romantic, starlight seating and gourmet seafood are the specialty at Snooks Bayside Club. An array of soups and appetizers range from conch gazpacho, coconut conch chowder, stone crab claws, escargot in champagne sauce, a luscious shrimp cocktail, conch fritters, or baked brie with macadamia nuts and raspberry sauce to mussels in wine or beluga caviar. Entrée favorites are catch-of-the day, either blackened, *Tropical*, with fruit and liqueur, *Grenoblaise*, with lime and lime butter, or *Française*, with shallots, wine and butter. Garden patio or indoor dining. (Behind Largo Honda.)

Sundowners On the Bay $$

MM 104, Bayside

☎ 451-4502

Sundowners edges Blackwater Sound, with seating indoors or on the outdoor patio. Select from tasty fried fish sandwiches, burgers, cracked conch or fresh fish, chicken, pasta or steak platters. Open daily from 11 am till 10 pm.

The Quay Key Largo $-$$$$

MM 102.5, Bayside

☎ 451-0943

For a unique tropical atmosphere and superb gourmet cuisine, try the Quay Restaurant complex on Blackwater Sound. Both casual and formal seating exists, indoors or in the bayfront garden. Adjacent is the Quay Mesquite Grill, which serves excellent fried or broiled fish sandwiches. The complex also features a freshwater pool, boat docks, beach side bar and entertainment. Sunset cruises.

Other Options

Early breakfasts are served at **Howard Johnsons**, MM 102.5, ☎ 451-2032; **Harriets**, MM 95.7, ☎ 852-8689; **Holiday Inn**, MM 100; **Gilberts**, MM 107.9, ☎ 451-1133; and **Ganim's Kountry Kitchen**, MM 102, ☎ 451-3337, or MM 99.6 across from the Holiday Inn. Or turn off US 1 southbound at MM 103.5. Head toward the ocean on Transylvania Ave., until you reach **The Hideout**, a local favorite for breakfast and lunch.

■ Islamorada

Islamorada's grills sizzle with fresh seafood and the most unusual dining experiences in the Keys. You'll find the hot spot for fast food on the shores of **Holiday Isle**, MM 84, Oceanside. Food stands line this sprawling beach complex, with barbecued everything. Ice cream and pretzel vendors crowd in alongside the Keys' most dazzling display of string bikinis. Or take the elevator to the sixth-floor restaurant for a quieter view of the sea. Prices rise with the elevation.

Rip's Island Ribs N' Chicken $

MM 84, Oceanside
☎ 664-5300

Rip's, at the Holiday Isle resort, offers a nice variety of sandwiches, seafood, steaks and ribs for lunch and dinner. Enormously popular. Expect a long waiting line on weekends, especially in season.

The Lorelei $-$$

MM 82, Bayside
☎ 664-4656

Enjoy sunset views and fresh seafood at The Lorelei. Open seven days from 5-10 pm. The outdoor Cabana Bar features burgers, fish sandwiches, breakfast, lunch, dinner and a raw bar. 7 am-12 pm. Entertainment on weekends. Get here by car or by boat.

Marker 88 $$$

MM 88, Bayside
Plantation Key
☎ 305-852-9315

Chef André Mueller sets the standards for exotic fish and steak entrées at this romantic, gourmet oasis. Choose from expertly prepared Scampi Mozambique, Snapper Rangoon, Lobster Marco Polo and a host of other gourmet creations. Desserts are equally wonderful. Closed Mondays. Reservations a must.

Whale Harbor Restaurant $$

MM 83.5, Oceanside
☎ 664-4959

Three dining choices await at this harborfront restaurant – the Harbor Room's seafood buffet, the Harbor Bar & Grill raw bar and the Dockside Restaurant, which offers children's menus and daily specials. Lovely setting in the old Islamorada lighthouse, adjacent to the Islamorada docks.

Woody's Italian Gardens $

MM 82, Bayside

☎ 664-4335

Try a hand-tossed pizza or pasta at Woody's. Family dining in the early evening. Late-night food with adult entertainment every night but Monday.

The Coral Grill $-$$

MM 83.5, Bayside

☎ 664-4803

If you like buffets, head straight to the Coral Grill. They offer two dining areas – downstairs with full menu service and an all-you-can-eat soup, salad and dessert bar for under $10. The upstairs buffet features hot or cold snowcrab legs, roast prime rib, fried shrimp, grouper in butter and wine, steamed shrimp, fried fish, 40 varieties of salads and changing daily specials. Children three and under eat free. Half-price for four- to 11-year-olds. Earlybird specials from 4:30 to 6 pm. Sunday, 12 pm-9 pm; weekdays, 4:30-10 pm.

Green Turtle Inn Restaurant $$-$$$

MM 81.5, Bayside

☎ 664-9031

Opened in 1947 for both travelers to Key West and the local fishermen, the Green Turtle retains an old-time Keys' atmosphere and excellent cuisine. Wood-paneled walls are covered with celebrity photos. Dinners include conch chowder, fresh salad, choice of potato, and steaming hot rolls fresh from the restaurant bakery. Enjoy the fish of the day, jumbo shrimp, Florida lobster, stone crabs, or the prime rib special, served nightly. Alligator or conch steak are for the adventurous. Leave room for their rum pie. Open from noon daily, except Mondays

Manny & Isa's Kitchen $

MM 81.6, Oceanside

☎ 664-5019

Cuban favorites top the list at Manny & Isa's. Select from seafood served in spicy sauce, shrimp or lobster enchilada, black beans and rice, *ropa vieja*, steaks, chicken and chops. Cool down with a frosty sangria or beer. Terrific Key lime pie and island desserts. Small, casual. Open for lunch and dinner every day except Tuesday.

Jammers Grill & Pub $

MM 86.7, Oceanside

☎ 852-8786

Jammers' appetizer menu winds on and on with fiery hot and spicy wings and ribs, stuffed mushrooms, nachos, conch bites and assorted designer munchies. Meals range from chicken sandwiches, lavish burgers topped with everything you can think of, club sandwiches, cracked conch, fried fish, down to ordinary franks and cheese. The bar refreshes your taste buds with frosty tropical drinks. Open for lunch and dinner. Karaoke on Wednesdays and Saturdays. The restaurant's game room has pinball, a pool table, air hockey and video games. Children's menu.

Morada Bay $

MM 81.6, Bayside

☎ 664-0604

Island pinks and sea greens splash across the tables at Morada Bay. The menu sparkles with chic salads, burgers topped with tangy goat cheese and grilled mushrooms, fish sandwiches, fajitas, seafood platters and tempting beef and chicken kabobs, ribs and shrimp. Open daily for lunch and dinner. Playful and casual. Indoor or Bayside seating.

Pierre's $$-$$$$

MM 81.6, Bayside

☎ 664-3225

Gourmet blends of Asian and Mediterranean tastes highlight Pierre's elegant restaurant. Selections from the sea include Thai curry snapper, lotus-root-crusted yellowtail and spicy shrimp. Next to Morada Bay. Romantic and elegant candlelight setting. Open seven days for dinner.

Islamorada Fish Company $-$$

MM 81.5, Bayside

☎ 664-9271

This popular seafood market, now located in the former Green Turtle Cannery building, draws quite a crowd for lunch and dinner. The market's display cases dazzle shoppers with the thousands of pounds of fish offered. Diners sit under umbrella'd picnic tables. Fish and shellfish sandwiches and platters are worth the usual wait. Open from 11:30 am to 9 pm. The fish market is open at 8 am.

Plantation Yacht Harbor $-$$,

MM 87, Bayside
Plantation Key
☎ 852-2381
www.pyh.com

Lobster, stone crab, oysters and clams. Sunday brunch with a notable omelette and waffle bar. Breakfast, lunch and dinner served daily. Daily 11 am-9 pm. Live bands.

Squid Row $-$$

MM 81.9, Oceanside
☎ 664-9865

Squid Row offers cozy, roadside dining and is devoted to serving excellent fresh fish and hand-cut steaks. Earlybird menu and happy hours. Will cook your own legal catch. Opens at 11:30 for lunch or dinner.

Dino's of Islamorada $-$$

MM 81, Oceanside
☎ 664-0727

Dino's family restaurant delights the senses with crusty, hand-tossed, brick-oven pizza, topped with all sorts of vegetables, cheeses and spices – Pizza Cariofi touts artichokes, Sicilian olives, fontina cheese, asago cheese and mozzarella; Pizza Della Casa melds pancetta, ricotta, gruyere, smoked mozzarella and sun dried tomatoes. The restaurant's formal dining room menu dazzles by size alone. Standard Italian pastas are available along with some specials – Paglia e Fieno Primavera, with spinach and egg noodles in an array of mixed vegetables, olive oil and fragrant garlic; or Capellini con Gambretti, angel hair pasta with baby shrimp and wild mushrooms in a creamy sauce. Poultry dishes, homemade sausage, veal, steaks, chops and fresh fish and shellfish dishes are served with homemade bread and a house salad.

Steaming cups of cappuccino or espresso end the meal, with a dessert cart selection of tiramisu, fritas or Italian pastries.

Papa Joe's Landmark Restaurant $-$$

MM 79.7, Bayside
☎ 664-8109

Papa Joe's dockside eatery specializes in lobster and fresh fish, but also offers chicken and steaks. Chefs will prepare your own catch of the day. Simple surroundings. Open for lunch and dinner every day but Tuesday.

■ Long Key

Little Italy Restaurant $-$$

MM 68.5, Bayside

☎ 664-4472

Opens daily for early breakfasts and lunch and dinner. Italian specialties, fresh seafood and steaks in a cozy atmosphere. Open 6:30 am-2 pm, 5 pm-10 pm. A good stop when traveling from Miami to Key West.

■ Duck Key

Hawk's Cay Resort and Marina

MM 61, Oceanside

☎ 743-7000

Hawk's Cay Resort and Marina features **WaterEdge**, $$-$$$, for elegant dining. Seating indoors or outdoors. The chef's specialties include blackened or grilled seafood, salads, ribs and chicken. 5:30 to 10 pm.

■ Marathon

Don Pedro Restaurant $

MM 53.5, Oceanside

☎ 743-5247

Mix tasty Cuban favorites with South Florida seafood at this storefront café. Appetizers run from Jalapeno poppers (cream cheese) to Cuban tamal (seasoned ground meat in cornmeal dough) with pork, green salad and breaded crab fingers. Entrées include roasted pork (lechon asado), Cuban tamal with pork, grilled chicken cutlet, Argentinian steak, fried yellowtail (rabirrubia entera frita), stuffed shrimp and shredded beef with red sauce (ropa vieja). All entrées include yellow rice, black beans, sweet plantains and Cuban bread. Sweeten the meal with creamy flan, coconut custard or Key lime pie with café latte, colada, Cuban coffee (espresso) or iced tea. Homemade sangria is offered by the glass, half-pitcher or full pitcher. Open for dinner, Monday through Sunday.

Barracuda Grill $$

MM 49.5, Bayside

☎ 743-3314

www.barracudagrill.com

If you're dreaming of food that is basically American/Asian mixed with a pinch of Jewish, a splash of Tex-Mex and a dollop of Italian, head for the Barracuda Grill. Appetizers range from Killer Clam Chowder, Barefoot nachos with just-made chips, grilled tuna with wasabi and soy, to Tommy's Tuna Tataki with punchy soy-ginger dip, Zack's Wayout Island conch or Jack Hill's Red Hot Calamari. Entrées include blackened mahi mahi, Fred's Tenderloin Stroganoff, Mitzi's Marvelous meatloaf, mangrove snapper with veggie stir fry, Cowboy steak (a huge 22-28 oz Angus cut), grilled tenderloin of beef, with Scotch bonnet pepper jelly glaze on the side, and grilled veal rib chops or lobster. It's all sumptuous. Nice selection of wines. Open for dinner at 5:55 pm, Monday through Saturday.

Key Colony Inn $$

MM 54, Oceanside
700 West Ocean Drive
Key Colony Beach
☎ 743-0100

Italian family food lures tourists and locals to this cozy restaurant. Menu offerings range from pasta, veal and chicken dishes to tasty seafood and steaks. Full bar, outdoor or indoor seating, take-out available. Open seven days for lunch and dinner. Reservations.

Herbies

MM 50, Bayside
No credit cards

Get your fill of conch chowder, conch fritters, cracked conch sandwiches or fried fish platters at this small roadside eatery. Eat inside or on the porch. Lemonade and iced tea. Open for lunch and dinner during winter. Closed Sundays the rest of the year.

Takara $$

MM 49.5, Bayside
☎ 743-0505

Enjoy artfully prepared sushi, sashimi, crispy tempura shrimp, fish and vegetables, teriyaki steak, lobster, salmon and chicken. Open weekdays for lunch and dinner, daily for dinner during the high season.

The Stuffed Pig $

MM 49, Bayside
☎ 743-4059
No credit cards

Looking for an early BIG breakfast? Follow the smell of country ham and bacon to The Stuffed Pig. It opens at 5 am with the Pig's Breakfast sizzling on the grill. The dish includes two eggs, two pancakes, two sausages, two slices of bacon, home fries and hot biscuits or toast. Or you might prefer the fisherman's favorite – grits and grunts, which is two eggs, fried fish, potatoes and toast. Egg substitute available for those watching cholesterol levels.

Shucker's Raw Bar & Grill $$

MM 50.5, Oceanside
6900 Overseas Hwy
☎ 743-8686

One of the Keys' most popular spots, Shucker's extensive menu has a variety of sandwiches, seafood platters, chunky conch chowder, shrimp, chicken and steaks. Fine food. Full-service bar.

The Quay $$

MM 54, Bayside
☎ 289-1810

Sits on the Gulf of Mexico, with indoor and outdoor seating. Select from just about anything that swims – grilled, baked or broiled, including shrimp, alligator, frogs legs and fish. Plus pasta, chicken, steaks, chops and a host of tropical drinks. Open for lunch and dinner. Popular. Reservations recommended during the high season.

■ Lower Keys

Mangrove Mama's Restaurant $-$$

MM 20, Bayside
Sugarloaf Key

One of the Keys' best-kept secrets, Mangrove Mama's tacky little green house offers lunch, dinner or Sunday brunch. Their cracked conch is lightly battered and fried on a homemade roll. Mama's Black and Bleu Fish Sandwich melts bleu cheese over a blackened catch-of-the day fillet. Steamed shrimp, steaks, salads and chowders are all fresh and tasty.

Sunday Brunch specials include the "Momelet" – a three-egg omelet folded with red peppers, green peppers, onions, mushrooms and garlic – and eggs Benedict with grilled Canadian Bacon. Full-service bar. Seating indoors or outside.

Monte's Restaurant and Fish Market

MM25, Bayside

Summerland Key

☎ 745-3731

No Credit Cards

Enjoy fresh fish, stone-crab claws, shrimp, lobster, conch and shellfish, fried or broiled. Picnic-style dining. The dining area adjoins the fish market. Expect a wait from 5:50 pm on. Open daily for lunch and dinner. No reservations. Cash only.

Bobalu's Southern Café $

MM 10, Bayside

Big Coppitt Key

Bobalu's may be a little weather-beaten on the outside, but their Southern fried chicken, fish and greens keep the locals coming back for more. Open Tuesday through Saturday for lunch and dinner.

■ Key West

Key West splits into a three areas for dining – **Old Town** and the **Historic Seaport District**, **North Roosevelt Drive's strip malls**, and the quiet **south side**. Old Town is where you'll find Mallory Square street vendors hawking conch fritters, pretzels and iced drinks, open-air cafés, pizza joints, plush resort restaurants and elegant Victorian houses with porch dining. Establishments along the Seaport District's promenade reflect the island's ongoing upbeat and trendy renaissance. **Land's End Village**, located at the north end of the promenade, is home to landmark seafood eateries. The stripmalls along North Roosevelt Boulevard pack in fast-food chains offering everything you can think of "to go." Key West's south side has a few excellent waterfront restaurants and a smattering of storefront diners.

If deciding where to eat makes you dizzy, stop at the Old Beach Inn's oxygen bar at 227 Duval St., for a revitalizing, five-minute blast of 99.9% oxygen for $5. If you like your oxygen flavored, grab a plastic nasal cannula for $1 – the oxygen is flavored by being passed through tubes of different aromas.

A&B Lobster House $$

700 Front St.

☎ 305-294-5880

Grand views of the Key West Bight and a sumptuous menu of fresh seafood have drawn crowds to A&B's supper club since 1947. The building has undergone a total renovation, with a new casual-elegant decor. The menu features local seafood specialties, pasta and meat dishes. Enjoy baked crab and artichoke au gratin, oysters Rockefeller, grilled portabello mushrooms, oyster stew or roasted ginger mussels for an appetizer. You can have either Maine or Florida lobster if you order Surf and Turf. Other favorites are grilled yellowfin tuna; jumbo Key West pink shrimp; homemade fettucine, topped with oyster mushrooms, andouille sausage, goat cheese and cilantro; black grouper Oscar stuffed with lump crabmeat and stone crabs; sesame-seared yellowfin tuna; sesame-encrusted tuna steak; grilled salmon with mashed potatoes and fennel cucumber salad. Sit inside the air-conditioned dining room or on the porch overlooking the marina. Cocktails and after-dinner drinks are served at **Berlin's Cigar Bar**, adjacent to the dining room. Downstairs, **Alonzo's Oyster Bar** serves lunch from 11:30 am until 4 pm.

Abbondanza $

1208 Simonton St.

☎ 292-1199

Follow the aroma of sizzling garlic and butter to Abbondanza's casual Italian restaurant on Simonton Street. Bread and pastas are homemade on premises daily. Local seafood dishes. Full bar. Open for lunch and dinner seven days.

Antonia's Restaurant $$

615 Duval St.

☎ 294-6565

Stop by Antonia's for great homemade pasta, divine Italian beef and seafood dinners followed by fluffy tiramisu, torte or crème brûlée for dessert. Extensive wine list. Open daily for dinner.

Bagatelle $$-$$$

115 Duval St.

☎ 296-6609

Offering fine seafood and classy surroundings, Bagatelle features indoor or outdoor dining in a magnificent Victorian mansion. Chic. Reservations suggested during high season.

Banana Café $$-$$$

1211 Duval St.

☎ 294-7227

Dine on the Banana Cafe's front balcony or in the cool shade of the side-deck. French cuisine highlights the menu, with more than 40 different crêpes rolled around zesty concoctions of fish, vegetables, and meats. Other favorites include roast duck, beef tenderloin, rack of lamb, fish of the day, and goat flan – all accompanied with garlicky mixed salads. Save room for dessert – sherbet of the day, lavender lard custard with caramelized sugar or banana rum mousse. Reservations suggested. Entertainment on weekends. Open seven days for breakfast and lunch. Wednesdays through Sunday for dinner.

Benihana Japanese Steakhouse $$-$$$

3591 South Roosevelt Blvd.

☎ 294-6400

Up to eight guests sit around the tables inset with grills, watching the Tepan chefs flash their knives and fashion food into nightly steak and seafood dinners. Entertaining. Open seven days for dinner.

Blond Giraffe $

629 Duval St.

1209 Truman Ave.

☎ 888-432-MATE

E-mail: blondgiraffe@aol.com

Stop here for Key West's best Key lime pie. The Blond Giraffe Key Lime Pie Factory used to sell meals and Key lime pie. They became so busy with the coffee and pie orders, they dropped everything else on the menu. Right now they're working on a rum-spiked Key lime pie, but till that happens the choices are Key lime pie with coffee or Maté – an herbal coffee-alternative beverage that users claim will rejuvenate the body and slim the waistline. Sort of a dieter's antidote for that second piece of pie. At least one MD recommends Maté for arthritis, headache, obesity, fatigue, stress, allergies and hay fever, stating that it cleanses the blood, tones the nervous system, retards aging, stimulates the mind, controls the appetite, stimulates the production of cortisone and is believed to enhance the healing powers of other herbs.

Maté's magic potion contains resins, fiber, volatile oil, and tannins, plus carotene, vitamins A, C, E, B-1, B-2, B-complex, riboflavin, nicotinic acid, pantothenic acid, biotin, magnesium, calcium, iron, sodium, potassium, manganese, silicon, phosphates, sulfur, hydrochloric acid, chlorophyll, choline and inositol. In 1964, investigators from the Pasteur Institute and the Paris Scientific Society concluded that Maté contains practically all of the vitamins necessary to sustain life.

We can't guarantee that Maté will do anything, but the pie with ordinary coffee is sensational.

Blue Heaven $-$$

729 Thomas St.

☎ 296-8666

Enjoy a wild assortment of pancakes and eggs in the back yard of this Bahamas Village house, while roosters, chicks and hens peck at the grounds around you. Or try their one-time bordello suite upstairs for Caribbean seafood and vegetarian cuisine. Fun.

Café Sole $-$$

1029 Southard St. at Frances

☎ 294-0230

Set in a charming conch house and lush covered garden, Café Sole serves wonderful French-American meals with a Caribbean or Italian twist. Chef John Correa prepares bouillabaisse with fresh fish, fresh stocks, vegetables and crostini spread with garlic mayonnaise. For Poulet Geneviève, he fricassees chicken with tarragon and port wine. His creamy conch chowder has chunks of conch and fresh grilled corn. Terrific salads. Take out is available. Open from 6 pm daily except Wednesdays.

Camille's Restaurant $-$$

7032 Duval St.

☎ 296-4811

Voted "Key West's Best Breakfast & Lunch" by WKRY radio's Peoples Choice Awards for five years in a row and "The Best Dining On a Budget in Monroe County" by *South Florida Magazine*, Camille's shines on all counts. It's located on Duval Street halfway between Mallory Square and the Southernmost point.

The restaurant's famous Sunday Brunch starts at 8 am, featuring several varieties of eggs Benedict, omelets, light waffles and pancakes. Bring an appetite. Open every day for breakfast and lunch. Breakfast is served till 3 pm daily. Dinner Tuesday through Saturday. Beer and wine.

Chico's Cantina $-$$

MM 4.5, Oceanside

Stock Island

☎ 296-4714

Chico's tiny roadside Cantina serves spicy, home-style Mexican casa dias, tacos, burritos, black beans, fajitas filled with a choice of vegetables, shrimp, chicken, beef or combinations, grilled fish and tangy, fresh salsa. Beer and wine. Take out available. Open every day but Monday.

Café Blanco $$

917 Duval St.

☎ 305-296-7837

$20 minimum for credit card use

Formerly the Lighthouse Café, Café Blanco serves Italian specialties – seafood fra diavolo, lasagna ala Bolognese, pasta with meat or spicy tomato sauce. Beer and wine offered with dinner. Sit indoors or outside in the garden. Reservations.

Café des Artistes $$$-$$$$

1007 Simonton St.

☎ 305-294-7100

People come from far and near for Chef Andrew Berman's Lobster Tango Mango, made with Maine lobster flambéed in cognac with saffron butter, mango and basil. His Crevettes Vieux Carré is made with Gulf shrimp topped with a Creole shellfish sauce, candied pecans and Parmesan croutons. Other menu favorites are duck in fresh raspberry sauce, pan-roasted veal rib in wild mushroom sauce, prime sirloin in brandy green peppercorn sauce, filet mignon with béarnaise. The hors d'oeuvres include a spectacular assortment of tarts, meats and fish in puff pastry, caviar, escargots, goat cheese with salmon, and roast quail filled with foie gras and apricots. Open every day for dinner. Reservations recommended.

Chops $$-$$$

at the Holiday Inn La Concha

430 Duval St.

☎ 296-2991

Features venison chops, duck breast, rabbit, and seafood. Open 5:30-10:30 pm. The rooftop lounge at La Concha serves exotic island drinks and sunset views.

The Deli Restaurant $

531 Truman Ave.

☎ 294-1464

Open since 1950, the Deli Restaurant features conch chowder, local seafood, roast turkey, roast beef, pork, southern fried chicken and sweet pies. Breakfast and sandwiches are served all day. Closed on Tuesdays and Wednesdays.

Dennis Pharmacy $

1229 Simonton St.

☎ 294-1577

Pull a stool up to the counter at this old-fashioned pharmacy and sink your teeth into a juicy cheeseburger or a chicken-fried steak and a bowl of home made soup. Reputed to be the inspiration for Jimmy Buffett's *Cheeseburger in Paradise*, the Pharmacy's menu also offers grilled chicken, fish sandwiches, pork dishes, stews, fried shrimp and specials. Beer, wine and soft drinks are served with or without the meal. Open for breakfast, lunch, dinner and prescriptions.

Finnegan's Wake Irish Pub & Eatery $

320 Grinnell St.

☎ 293-0222

Dig into corned beef and cabbage, bangers and mash (sausages and mashed potatoes), shepherd's pie, Irish stew, potato leek soup, potato pancakes or a juicy steak, while lively Irish music chimes in the the spirit of the legendary Tim Finnegan. Cool down with a pint of Guinness. Finnegan's Wake opens daily at 11 am; the kitchen closes at 12 pm, the bar at 4 am.

Half Shell Raw Bar $-$$

1 Lands End Village

☎ 294-7496

Rub elbows with the locals at this delightful seafood restaurant on the wharf. Menu features are fish, shrimp and conch, fried or broiled to perfection. Raw oysters and clams. Friendly service. Cold beer. Try for a table on the back porch, overlooking the docks, where you'll spot six or seven huge silver tarpon waiting for a handout. Decor is funky, with license plates from across the USA and fishing stuff hanging on the wooden walls. Open for lunch and dinner. Extremely popular with good reason.

Hog's Breath Saloon $

400 Front St.

☎ 296-4222

Hog's Breath Saloon packs guests into its bustling open-air restaurant and raw bar. Nightly entertainment from sunset to 2 am.

The Original Hog's Breath Saloon was established in 1976 by Jerry Dorminy in Ft. Walton Beach. Intended as a watering hole for fishermen and sailors, it also became a big hit with military personnel in the area looking for a place to party. The saloon's slogan, "Hog's breath is better than no breath at all," is taken from Dorminy's grandmother's expression, "bad breath is better than no breath at all." A cult of Hog Heads started, who take home the tee shirt and spread the word.

The decor is a cross between a surf and tackle shop, with surf boards and fishing gear hung on the walls. Wooden tables are laminated with tropical ocean charts.

Seating is indoors or outside on a big patio. In addition to the full-service bar, Hog's Breath serves up tender fish sandwiches, peel & eat shrimp, chicken or fish dinners served with red potatoes and corn, smoked fish dip, conch chowder and assorted appetizers. There's take-out and a raw bar open till 11 pm. Open daily from 1 pm till 11 pm.

Jimmy Buffett's Margaritaville Café $

500 Duval St.

☎ 292-1435

Newly renovated, the Café serves up impressive margaritas, Cajun martinis and slews of other tropical coolers. Cheeseburgers, fish and shrimp baskets and sandwiches highlight the menu. Funky decor. Open for lunch and dinner. Live music.

Kelly's Caribbean Bar, Grill & Brewery $-$$

301 Whitehead St.

☎ 293-8484

Kelly's, owned by *Top Gun* actress Kelly McGillis, serves decent Caribbean cuisine in a tropical garden setting. Specialties of the house include penne tossed with bay scallops and red pepper creme sauce, clams caribe – littlenecks poached with island spices and garlic over a bed of angel hair pasta, grilled lobster tail, island crab cakes, jambalaya made with shrimp, chicken, pork, andouille sausage and Louisiana crawfish in a spicy tomato-herb broth, shrimp and steak dishes. Try one of their micro-brewed beers.

Original home of Pan American Airways in 1927, the interior decor features old aircraft seats and early aircraft memorabilia. Open for lunch and dinner.

La Trattoria Venezia & Virgillo's $$

524 Duval St.
Key West
☎ 296-1075

You can almost hear the gondoliers singing at this sophisticated Venetian café. Traditional chicken, lamb, and seafood with wonderful pastas beckon from the menu. Reservations suggested during high season.

Louie's Back Yard $$-$$$$

700 Waddell St.
Vernon & Waddell Streets
Key West
☎ 294-1061

Oceanfront, on the corner of Vernon and Waddell Streets, Louie's Back Yard serves extraordinary lunches and dinners in the most elegant of surroundings. Catch of the day might be served with mango salsa. Stonecrab claws are the best in Key West. Every dish is expertly prepared with the freshest seafood, vegetables and meats. Lunch regulars line up for "Hot Fry Chicken Salad," and the Conch Fritters. Conch chowder is superb.

The restaurant is housed in a huge Victorian manor house with splendid porches and the Afterdeck Oceanside Bar.

Back in the 1900s, Key West residents thrived on sponging and wrecking. A brave man with a fast boat could easily make a fortune salvaging goods from ships wrecked by the whims of wind and wave.

Captain James Randall Adams was one such wrecker. Having made his fortune, he ordered the construction of a gracious Classic Revival Home on Waddell Street – the building that is now known as Louie's Backyard. Captain Adams was fond of boasting that everything in his home, with it's unusual two-story side porch and Doric columns, was salvaged merchandise. The house stayed in the Adams family for years. It then changed owners several times before it was bought by Frances and Louie Signorelli, who opened the first Louie's Backyard – a restaurant that seated 12, had one lone waiter, and operated out of a cigar box.

The restaurant, growing quickly, soon became famous for it's fine food and relaxed oceanfront ambiance – and for Ten Speed, the legendary mutt that sauntered up to the outdoor bar most afternoons for his customary cocktail of Kahlua and cream! Frequented by the likes of Jimmy Buffet and Tom McGuane, Louie's Backyard received award after award for it's superb cuisine.

The present owners, Phil Tenney and Pat Tenney, carry on the established tradition of dining excellence. The building has been lovingly renovated and enlarged, with special attention paid to maintaining its historical integrity. In June of 1984, Louie's Backyard earned a spot in the National Register of Historic Places.

Pepe's Café $

806 Caroline St.

☎ 294-7192

Gourmet breakfast lovers flock to this landmark café. Frosted glasses of fresh orange juice, and artfully prepared French toast or egg dishes are served indoors or outside under a canopy of flowering vines. Pub-style fare, from burgers to fresh fish, great steaks and sensational desserts, are offered for lunch and dinner. The garden room includes a white picket fence with passerby peep holes at two levels – one for people and one for their pets.

Turtle Kraals Bar and Restaurant $

1 Land's End Village

☎ 294-2640

Adjacent to the Half Shell Raw Bar in Land's End Village, Turtle Kraals offers Tex Mex food made with local seafood. Entrées include shellfish burritos, tacos, fresh fish, hamburgers and a large selection of imported beers. The restaurant occupies an old turtle cannery, reminiscent of the days when turtles were brought in by the boatload from as far away as the Cayman Islands and Nicaragua.

Turtle Kraals is open daily for lunch and dinner.

Kraals is an Afrikan word meaning holding pen or enclosure. It refers to the concrete pilings that were driven into the ocean bottom to form a holding pen for the turtles until they could be shipped to the Northeast or slaughtered and made into soup in the cannery.

This former cannery site, where green sea turtles once were slaughtered for soup and steaks, is now a museum where visitors can learn about turtles and their preservation. The Turtle Kraals Museum is behind the restaurant, next to the former turtle holding pens or kraals. Admission is free to the public from 11 am to 6 pm daily, with educational tours offered by appointment and a turtle feeding each day at 4 pm. Headed by Tina Brown, one of the founders of Marathon's Turtle Hospital, the museum features photographs and a history of Key

West's turtling industry, which was a booming business in the mid-1800s. Highlights include educational information about sea turtles and the modern-day perils they face, as well as a display of turtle shells, skulls, and sea turtle products. While a young loggerhead turtle named Eddie is currently the museum's only resident, Brown hopes eventually to use the abandoned kraals as a home for turtles who are blind or missing a flipper – those with disabilities who cannot survive in the wild. For information about the Turtle Kraals Museum, ☎ 305-294-0209.

Mangia Mangia $$

900 Southard St.

☎ 294-2469

Fresh homemade pasta tops the list at Mangia Mangia (Eat Eat). Standard fettuccine and linguine dishes flank some "Floribbean" creations on the daily specials. Eat, eat indoors or outside under the poinciana and palm trees.

Martin's Café Restaurant $$

416 Applerouth Lane

☎ 296-1183

Hard to find, but worth the attempt if you like "German-Island" cuisine. Familiar German favorites – sauerbraten, red cabbage, spaetzle, wiener schnitzel – grace the menu, alongside fresh local seafood with a *deutsch* twist. Cognac and champagne Dijon sauces over yellowtail or grouper, served with a nice selection of German wines and beers. Open for dinner Tuesday through Sunday.

Applerouth Lane is off Duval between Southard and Fleming Streets. Turn south across from *Ripley's Believe It or Not Odditorium* to find this little one-way street.

Mallory Market, the center of the Historic Key West Waterfront, offers every imaginable fast food and a few you may not have thought of. One particularly good vendor sells conch fritters outside the Shipwreck Historeum, across from the Key West Aquarium.

Everglades

The area code in the Everglades area is 941

■ Everglades City

The Rod and Gun Club Resort $

200 Riverside Drive

☎ 695-2101

Once an exclusive hideaway for statesmen and movie stars, the Rod and Gun Club's restaurant is a fun stop for lunch or dinner. Bring your camera. The restaurant's screened porch/dining room overlooks the Barron River, habitat to egrets, herons and other beautiful wading birds. Cypress-wood paneling and trophy fish adorn the lobby walls as do newspaper clippings about President Nixon, Burt Reynolds and other visitors. The meals are fast-food, Everglades style – fried fish, oysters and fries in a basket.

Everglades Seafood Depot $

102 Collier Ave.

☎ 695-0075

Just before the town circle as you enter Everglades City, Everglades Seafood Depot offers fried fish platters, broiled Florida lobster tail, fresh local oysters, alligator tail, soups, salad, and stone crabs in season. Bar service. Open seven days for lunch and dinner.

The Oyster House Restaurant $

Chokoloskee Causeway, Hwy. 29

South Everglades City

☎ 695-2073

E-mail: r.a.millerjr@worldnet.att.net

This spot favored by locals features a fresh oyster bar, local seafood and carry-out service for lunch or dinner.

Everglades Corner Subway $

At the corner of Hwy. 29 and 41, by the police station

☎ 695-0099

Oar House Restaurant $

305 Collier Ave.

☎ 695-3535

You catch it and the Oar House chef will cook it. Or opt for a menu selection – stone crab claws, fried alligator cubes, steaks, frog legs, local fried oysters, soups and salads. Open daily from 6 am till 9 pm. Breakfast, lunch and dinner. Full bar next door.

■ Flamingo

Flamingo Lodge $

#1 Flamingo Lodge Hwy

☎ 695-3101, fax 695-3921

Reservations ☎ 800-600-3813

www.flamingolodge.com

Flamingo Lodge offers seafood and steaks. The only restaurant in Everglades National Park, it is located at the end of the Main Park Road. The Flamingo camp store offers snack food, packaged sandwiches, coffee and sodas. Both are closed from May to November.

Where to Stay

Note: Vacation packages offered by tour companies such as Liberty Travel/GoGo Tours may save you hundreds of dollars on a Florida Keys trip. Divers may find some good deals with their local dive shops. Many of the resorts and dive shops in the Keys offer packages or specials for groups, seniors, families with children. Check before you book on your own. Most of the larger resorts are listed on the Florida Keys website: www.fla-keys.com.

Resort and motel rates vary with the time of year, the high season being mid-December to mid-April. Check with your travel agent or the resort for money-saving packages. Some are only three days, but save hundreds of dollars. Several tour operators offer four-day or longer stays that include airfare, meals and diving or fishing. Rates drop considerably for stays longer than seven days.

Major credit cards are accepted at all of the resorts and large motels. Some of the smaller motels ask for cash only. All hotels listed have air-conditioning and color TV.

Pricing Key	
$$	$80-$99
$$$	$100-$150
$$$$	$151 to $250
$$$$$	$251 and higher

Florida Keys

Amy Slate cozies up to the moray eel for whom she named her resort.

Keys accommodations range from informal housekeeping cottages, simply furnished Bayside motels, spacious condo and house rentals, luxurious resort villages, houseboats, and campgrounds, most of which are packed tight with RVs. All accommodations are air-conditioned and most have cable TV and a refrigerator in the room.

Some of the older mom-and-pop motels on the Bay have been updated and offer a certain island charm that is hard to duplicate in the large resorts. A few are badly in need of renovation and also serve as parking areas for RVs. Send for current brochures.

The Florida Keys area code is 305

■ Key Largo Accommodations

Key Largo and the Upper Keys can be divided into three main areas: Upper Key Largo, where divers and snorkelers settle to explore John Pennekamp Coral Reef State Park; Tavernier, an older settlement that runs from MM 94 to MM 88; and Islamorada, the sportfishing center. A deep-water cut around MM 103 allows boats to travel between the bays and ocean.

For a complete list of home rental agencies, contact the **Key Largo Chamber of Commerce**, 106000 Overseas Hwy., Key Largo FL 33037. ☎ 305-451-1414, US 800-822-1088, fax 305-451-4726; email www.floridakeys.org.

Amy Slate's Amoray Lodge $$-$$$

MM 104, Bayside, Key Largo
☎ 800-426-6729 or 305-451-3595, fax 305-453-9516.

Owner Amy Slate, known for arranging the best underwater weddings in the world, coined the resort's name when a huge moray eel crashed one of her lavish underwater ceremonies. A guest *People Magazine* writer titled a story about the event *That's Amoray*, and the name stuck.

Located on Blackwater Sound, a part of Florida Bay, Amy Slate's Amoray Dive Resort offers 16 ultra-clean, modern one- and two-bedroom apartments with full kitchens. Two-story, two-bath duplexes accommodate up to eight guests. Air-conditioned rooms have ceiling fans.

A bayfront Jacuzzi and pool flank a small sandy area for sunbathing or Bay swimming, which we don't recommend.

Complimentary continental breakfast is served on the sundeck under a thatch-roof chickee hut. Scuba, snorkel and boat trips leave for Pennekamp Park from the resort dock aboard the luxurious 45-ft catamaran, *Amoray Diver*. Within walking distance of several good restaurants. A great choice for Pennekamp divers and snorkelers. A few boat slips are available. No pets.

Anchorage Resort & Yacht Club $$-$$$
MM 107.5, Bayside
107800 Overseas Hwy
Key Largo FL 33037
☎ 305-451-0500, fax 305-451-2565

The Anchorage Resort sits on the northern tip of Key Largo, about nine miles from Key Largo's mainstream of activity. Appealing to fishermen, the resort offers guided, backcountry trips to anglers for tarpon, snook, trout and red fish. Guests stay in one-bedroom suites with full kitchens and screened balconies, TV and VCR. Resort amenities include a gift shop, sun deck, heated swimming, pool, fishing pier, laundry facilities, tennis courts, gas grills and deck. Boat docking. Deluxe. This is a good spot if your vacation is centered around fishing the bays and Everglades. Expect a following of pelicans on the water. No pets.

Baycove Motel $-$$
MM 99.5, Bayside
201 Ocean Drive
Key Largo FL 33037
☎ 305-451-1686

Baycove offers 11 clean, newly remodeled motel rooms and low rates. Boat dock. No pets.

Best Western Suites $$-$$$
MM 100, Oceanside,
201 Ocean Drive
Key Largo FL 33037
☎ 800-462-6079 or 305-451-5081.

Best Western rents clean and comfortable canal-side suites with queen beds, fully equipped kitchens, two remote cable TVs, two bathrooms and a screened porch. These are one-bedroom, split-level apartments, with complimentary continental breakfast. Boat dockage available. Outdoor pool.

Scuba diving and snorkeling tours on property. Snorkeling trips depart the resort dock three times daily. Casino, glass-bottom and fishing boats nearby. Group discounts and dive packages available. No pets.

Florida Bay Club $$$
MM 103.5
103500 Overseas Hwy
PO Box 2520
Key Largo FL 33037
☎ 305-451-0101, fax 305-451-0443
E-mail: flabayclub@mindspring

Florida Bay Club sits on Adam's Cut, a deep-water channel that connects Florida Bay to the ocean and the National Marine Sanctuary. Ideal for boaters, this townhouse complex provides dockage and boat trailer storage at no extra charge. The resort features 2,000-square-foot two-bedroom and 2,800-square-foot three-bedroom townhouses with complete kitchens and private yard with gas grill. Swimming pool and tennis court. Nine-hole miniature golf on-site. Close to Pennekamp Park, restaurants and attractions. Weekly unit rates start at $1,100. See them online at www.keysdirectory.com/floridabay/index.html.

Family Paradise Island (aka Gilberts) Motel & Marina $-$$
107900 Overseas Hwy
Key Largo FL 33037
☎ 305-451-1133
E-mail: gilbertsP12@aol.com

If you love to fish the bays and tow your own boat, Gilbert's Family Paradise Island might be just the place. It's a few miles north of Key Largo's bustling tourist activities, but not too far, just 3½ miles north of John Pennekamp State Park.

This older motel was renovated in 2000 with new furnishings and decor. The property features a marina, fuel, boat service center, with me-

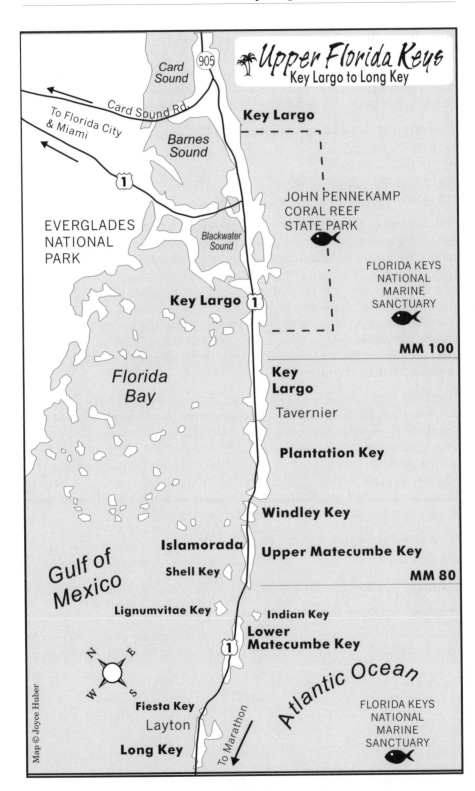

Map © Joyce Huber

Where to Stay

chanics on duty daily, a decent restaurant that serves an early breakfast, plus lunch and dinner, a tiki bar and live entertainment, pool, private beach, boat rentals, Jet Ski rentals and a laundry. Guest rooms on the lower floor have patios directly on the waterfront. You can fish off your patio. View this motel online at www.keysdirectory.com

Holiday Inn Key Largo Resort $$-$$$

MM 99.7, Oceanside,
99701 Overseas Hwy
Key Largo FL 33037
US ☎ 800-THE-KEYS or 305-451-2121

Holiday Inn flanks a huge, busy, marina with a boat ramp and docking for all size craft. The recently renovated resort features 132 guest rooms, each with a coffee maker, hair dryer, mini-fridge, ironing board, iron and cable TV with HBO. The island decor is reflected in huge, floor to ceiling mirrors. Rooms overlook either the gardens or marina. Off the lobby, Bogie's Café serves a tasty breakfast, lunch or dinner. A well-stocked gift shop carries an interesting array of postcards, *African Queen* souvenirs, beach towels, sundries and local books. The resort also features a fitness room and children's playground. Varied children's activities are offered.

Outdoors, guests lounge at two heated, freshwater pools with a cascading waterfall, flanked by a tiki bar that serves light fare all day. Diving, snorkeling, glassbottom boat tours and gambling cruises leave from the adjacent marina. A small snack shop in the lobby offers sandwiches, snacks and cold soft drinks to go. The resort is also home to the steam-powered *African Queen,* used in the 1951 movie starring Humphrey Bogart and Katharine Hepburn, as well as the *Thayer* from the motion picture *On Golden Pond.* No pets.

Howard Johnson's Resort $$

PO Box 1024
MM 102.3, Bayside
Key Largo FL 33037
☎ 800-654-2000 or 305-451-1400

Howard Johnson's Key Largo Resort features clean, standard rooms with two double beds or a king; a soft, white-sand beach on Blackwater

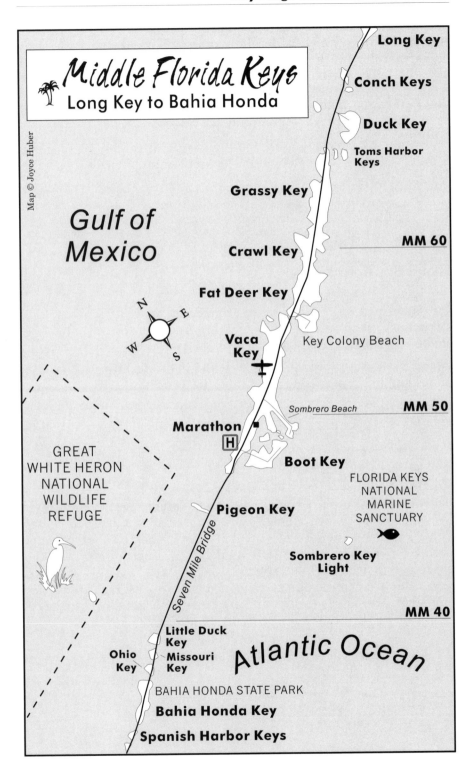

Middle Florida Keys
Long Key to Bahia Honda

Map © Joyce Huber

Gulf of Mexico

Long Key

Conch Keys

Duck Key

Toms Harbor Keys

Grassy Key

MM 60

Crawl Key

Fat Deer Key

Vaca Key

Key Colony Beach

N E W S

Sombrero Beach · MM 50

Marathon ■
Ⓗ

Boot Key

GREAT WHITE HERON NATIONAL WILDLIFE REFUGE

FLORIDA KEYS NATIONAL MARINE SANCTUARY

Pigeon Key

Seven Mile Bridge

Sombrero Key Light

MM 40

Little Duck Key

Ohio Key

Missouri Key

Atlantic Ocean

BAHIA HONDA STATE PARK

Bahia Honda Key

Spanish Harbor Keys

Sound; family restaurant, pool, balconies, beach bar, small dock, dive and other packages. Flowering trees and hibiscus plants grace the grounds. Cable TV. Refrigerators and microwaves. Some small pets are allowed in the ground-floor rooms, but you'll be asked to leave if persistent barking or meowing annoys other guests. Call first. Restaurant serves breakfast, lunch, dinner and snacks. Group rates available.

This resort is heavily promoted in Europe, thus attracting a large number of French and German tourists. Expect to mingle with a robust mix of international guests.

Manatees are often spotted behind the Howard Johnson's Resort in winter.

Island Bay Resort $

MM 92.5, Bayside
PO Box 573
Tavernier FL
☎ 800-654-KEYS or 305-852-4087

Island Bay Resort rents eight rooms with kitchen facilities, a boat dock and ramp, nice sandy beach and cable TV. No pets.

Kelly's Motel and Aqua-Nut Divers

MM 104.2, Bayside
104220 Overseas Hwy
Key Largo FL 33037
☎ 800-226-0415, 305-451-1622

If diving Pennekamp Park is your main interest, consider Kelly's, which can package dive trips with on-premises Aqua Nuts Dive Center. This 33-room dive motel offers breakfast under their tiki hut, a heated pool, swim area, complimentary snorkel gear, locked, dive-gear storage, covered picnic areas, barbecue grills and free kayak usage. Units have cable TV, phones, refrigerators and microwaves. There is a 1950s ambience. The motel sits in a sheltered cove with fast access to the cut that leads to Pennekamp Park. Sporting atmosphere. No pets.

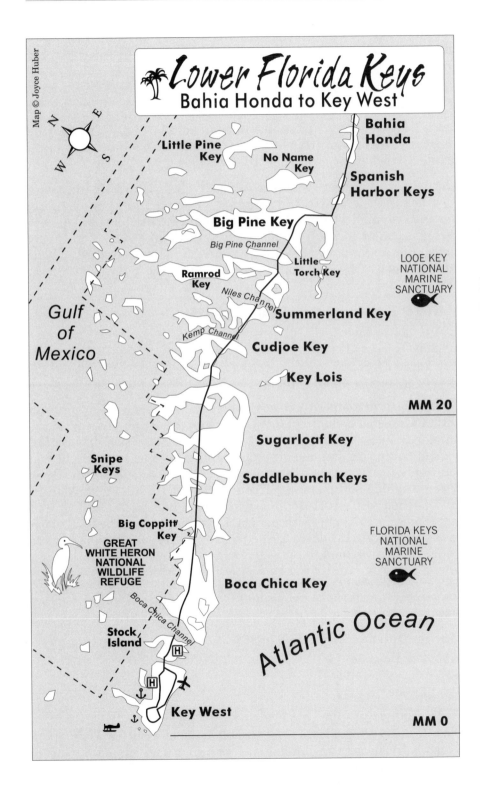

Map © Joyce Huber

Lower Florida Keys
Bahia Honda to Key West

N
E
W
S

Bahia Honda

Little Pine Key

No Name Key

Spanish Harbor Keys

Big Pine Key

Big Pine Channel

Little Torch Key

LOOE KEY NATIONAL MARINE SANCTUARY

Ramrod Key

Niles Channel

Summerland Key

Gulf of Mexico

Kemp Channel

Cudjoe Key

Key Lois

MM 20

Sugarloaf Key

Saddlebunch Keys

Snipe Keys

Big Coppitt Key

FLORIDA KEYS NATIONAL MARINE SANCTUARY

GREAT WHITE HERON NATIONAL WILDLIFE REFUGE

Boca Chica Key

Boca Chica Channel

Stock Island

Atlantic Ocean

H

H

Key West

MM 0

Where to Stay

Largo Lodge $$-$$$

MM 101.5, Bayside
101740 Overseas Hwy
Key Largo FL 33037
☎ 800-IN-THE-SUN (468-4378) or 305-451-0424

Largo Lodge offers six rustic, nicely appointed apartments, all in a lush tropical garden overgrown with giant vines and flowering tropical plants. Guests must be at least 16 years old.

The lodge's small beach, home to a friendly ibis population, is a choice spot for sunset-watching and relaxing. A boat dock and tiny ramp accommodate small, shallow draft runabouts, kayaks or canoes. Maneuvering a trailer through the property's jungle-like vines and lumpy sand paths is reason to pass up their tiny ramp. Opt instead to put your boat in at one of the local marinas, then motor over to the lodge's dock. No pets.

Marriott Key Largo Bay Beach $$$-$$$$

MM 103.8, Bayside
103800 Overseas Hwy
Key Largo FL 33037
☎ 800-932-9332 or 305-453-0000

Focused on sports and superb hospitality, the Marriot welcomes guests with 153 rooms, including 20 two-bedroom suites, an outdoor swimming pool, Jacuzzi, glass-bottom boat and five-star PADI dive center, charter fishing excursions, watersports opportunities, waterfront restaurant, a tiki bar and grill, a boutique and two large helipads, three bars and a nine-hole putting golf course. The spa, a second-story open-air thatched-roof structure, offers massage therapy, facial, foot and body treatments, along with personal training programs. This plush resort sits next to the deepwater cut between the islands that leads to Pennekamp Park, making it a choice base for divers and snorkelers.

The 153 guest rooms feature mini-bars, in-room safes, cable TV with pay-per-view selections, coffee makers, hair dryers, data-ports and voice mail.

Marina Del Mar, Bayside $$-$$$$

MM 99.5, Bayside
99470 Overseas Hwy
Key Largo FL 33037
☎ 800-242-5229, or 305-451-4450, fax 305-451-9650

Close to everything, Marina Del Mar offers 56 modern, bayfront guest rooms, a freshwater swimming pool, private beach and dock. Guests share facilities with Marina Del Mar, Oceanside.

Marina Del Mar $$-$$$$

MM 100, Oceanside
PO Box 1050
Key Largo FL 33037
☎ 305-451-4107, US 800-451-3483, FL 800-451-3483, Canada 800-638-3483, fax 305-451-1891

Tucked away on a deepwater marina in the heart of Key Largo, Marina Del Mar features 130 deluxe rooms, suites and villas. Refrigerators in all rooms. The suites have complete kitchens. Rooms overlook the yacht basin or ocean. Dive shop on premises. Fishing charters. Meeting facilities. Waterfront restaurant and lounge.

Guests of Marina Del Mar, Bayside, and Marina Del Mar, Oceanside, can use the facilities of both resorts.

Ocean Pointe Suite Resort $$$

MM 92.5, Oceanside
500 Burton Drive
Tavernier FL 33070
☎ 800-882-9464 or 305-3000, fax 305-853-3007

Off the main road, just south of Pennekamp Park and the heart of Key Largo, Ocean Pointe's gated property features bright, one- and two-bedroom suites with Jacuzzi tubs and fully equipped kitchens, private balconies, heated swimming pool with whirlpool spa, lighted tennis courts, marina with boat ramp and rental slips, waterfront café and lounge, white sand, suntan beach, watersports equipment. Plenty of parking for boat trailers. Continental breakfast in the dockside café delights guests with stacks of oversized, blueberry muffins and fresh orange juice. Call for money-saving packages. No pets.

Port Largo Villas $$-$$$

MM 100, Oceanside
PO Box 1290, Key Largo FL 33037
☎ 305-451-4847

Sitting in the heart of Key Largo, Port Largo Villas offer 24 spacious, two-bedroom, two-bath units with cable TV, Jacuzzi, tennis court, sundeck. Boat dock and ramp. No pets.

Ramada Inn Key Largo, $$-$$$

MM 99.7, Oceanside
Key Largo FL 33037
☎ 800-THE-KEYS, ext 3
E-mail: frontoffice@ramadakl.net

Sister resort to the Holiday Inn, the Ramada features 90 oversized rooms with either king, queen or two double beds, island decor and bal-

Where to Stay

cony. Sofa beds in some suites. King suites have two TVs, Jacuzzi, two bathrooms and a private patio. Rooms overlook the harbor or Overseas Hwy. Guests at the Ramada and adjacent Holiday Inn may use each other's facilities. Rates include Continental breakfast and tickets to the Sun Cruz casino ship. The resort has a heated outdoor pool, Jacuzzi and close proximity to the 75-slip deep-water marina.

Travelodge Key Largo $-$$

MM 99.2, Oceanside
99202 Overseas Hwy
Key Largo FL 33037
☎ 305-451-2478, fax 305-451-6236

Travelodge features 50 standard guest rooms and two-room family units with cable TV, complimentary breakfast and newspaper daily. Free local calls and incoming faxes. Pool. AARP discount. Good low-budget accommodations, a short drive to shops and restaurants.

Rock Reef Resort $$-$$$

MM 98, Bayside
PO Box 73, Key Largo FL 33037
☎ 800-477-2343 or 305-852-2401

Rock Reef offers clean, comfortable, AAA-approved cottages and apartments on the Bay, with one, two or three bedrooms. Family-owned and -operated. Playground, tropical gardens. Boat dock and ramp. Sandy beach. No pets.

Westin Beach Resort Key Largo $$$-$$$$

MM 97, Bayside
97000 Overseas Hwy., Key Largo FL 33037
☎ 305-852-5553; worldwide 800-539-5274, fax 305-852-3530

This splendid watersports resort features 200 oversized luxury rooms, two restaurants, lounge, nature trails, two pools with waterfall, pool bar and a large dock on the bay. Private beach. Caribbean Watersports at the beach shack offers a variety of activities. Meeting facilities. No pets. Call for special packages and off-season rates.

Stone Ledge Resort $

MM 95.3, Bayside
PO Box 50, Key Largo FL 33037
☎ 305-852-8114

Stone Ledge offers 19 conch-style motel rooms, a small soft-sand swimming beach, boat dock. Ten of the units have kitchens. Refrigerators in all rooms. TV. Gorgeous sunsets from the pier. No pets. No Jet Skis. Sunny and pleasant. Rooms have been recently renovated.

Tropic Vista Motel $

MM 90.5, Plantation Key

PO Box 88, Tavernier FL 33070

☎ 800-537-3253 or 305-852-8799, fax 305-852-8799

Large and small efficiencies with kitchens or simple motel rooms accommodate guests at the Tropic Vista Motel, which sits on a quiet oceanside canal with a dive shop on premises and easy access to the ocean reefs or the bays. Rooms have telephones, cable TV, refrigerators and air-conditioning. A 300-ft deep-water dock runs alongside the motel. Guests enjoy a heated swimming pool, a bubbling Jacuzzi and a lovely patio shaded by coconut palms. A pleasant restaurant on the property serves breakfast, lunch and dinner. Standard rooms. Walk to shopping, restaurants and a marina. Dive packages and sailing charters available. View this resort online at www.keysdirectory.com. Pets allowed in some rooms.

Key Largo RV & Tent Campgrounds

Sites for RVs in these campgrounds range from $38 to $90 per night, plus an 11.5% state tax.

America Outdoors

MM 97.5, Bayside

97450 Overseas Hwy

Key Largo FL 33037

☎ 305-852-8054, fax 305-853-0509

Lush vegetation shades 150 campsites. Sandy beach, laundry, bath houses. Boat dock, ramp and marina. Tent and RV sites. Rates are from $40 per night for tents, from $55 to $80 for full hookup. Group sites from $200. Pets allowed. Monthly rates for RVs from $1,150 to $1,275.

Calusa Condo Camp Resort

MM 101.5, Bayside

325 Calusa

Key Largo FL 33037

☎ 305-451-0232

Based on availability, privately owned condo sites may be rented for tents or RVs. Tent sites are $30 per night, no pets. RV sites inland cost $35 per night; pull-through sites, $45; canalfront, $45; bayfront, $65 per night. Pets allowed in RVs. Must be on leashes and owners must clean up after them. Sites have full hookups with water, electricity and sewer.

The park has new tennis courts, a heated pool, boat dock, but no slips or overnight tie-ups. Boat ramp has a four-foot draft.

Florida Keys RV Resort
MM 106, Oceanside
Key Largo FL 33036
☎ 305 451-4615

Provides cable, water and electric on all sites. Approved by the Good Sam Club for RV owners. Pets OK. Near dive shops.

Key Largo Kampground and Marina
MM 101, Oceanside
Key Largo FL 33036
☎ 800-526-7688 or 305-451-1431

Oceanfront RV and tent sites, boat dock, ramp, laundry and bath house. Two pets allowed. Write PO Box 118-A, Key Largo FL 33037.

■ Islamorada Accommodations

Plantation Key to Long Key

*For a complete list of home rental agencies contact the **Islamorada Chamber of Commerce**, PO Box 915, Islamorada FL 33036. ☎ 305-664-4503 or 800-FAB KEYS. See the resorts online at www.islamoradachamber.com, www.fla-keys. com or www.keysdirectory.com.*

Bayview Inn & Marina $
3 North Conch Ave., Gulfside
Conch Key FL 33050
☎ 800-289-2055 or 305-289-1525
E-mail: info@bayviewinn.com, www.bayviewinn.com

Bayview Inn, off the beaten track, just south of Islamorada and eight miles north of Marathon on Conch Key, offers 10 sparkling-clean guest rooms overlooking the marina, which rents boats, Jet Skis and offers dive tours aboard their 30-ft dive boat. Free dockage. A fine choice for die-hard divers. Near restaurants.

Bud & Mary's Fishing Marina $

MM 79.8, Oceanside
Islamorada FL 33036
☎ 800-742-7945 or 305-664-2461, fax 305-664-5592
E-mail: bnmfm@budnmarys.com

Bud & Mary's rents seven motel units and caters to fishermen, divers and snorkelers. Private beach, 12 charter boats, 25 backcountry guides, rental boats, glass-bottom boat, dive boat and party fishing. No pets.

Breezy Palms Resort $-$$

MM 80, Oceanside
PO Box 767
Islamorada FL 33036
☎ 305-664-2361, fax 305-664-2572

Breezy Palms' 40-unit resort offers one- , two- and three-room villas, beach cottages or studio efficiencies. All come with well-equipped kitchens and attractive furnishings. Maid service. Large swimming beach. Freshwater pool, boat harbor and ramp with a lighted dock for night fishing. No pets.

Caloosa Cove Resort $$$

MM 73.8, Oceanside
73801 Overseas Hwy
Islamorada FL 33036
☎ 888-297-3208 or 305-664-8811, fax 305-664-8856
E-mail: caloosa@terranova.net

Caloosa Cove has 30 deluxe oceanfront condos, one- or two-bedroom, with modern kitchens. Heated pool, lounge, restaurant, tennis, bike rentals, boat rentals, free breakfast and activities. Full-service marina with dockage. No pets. Minimum two-night stay required on weekends.

Cheeca Lodge $$$$

MM 82, Oceanside
PO Box 527
Islamorada FL 33036
☎ 800-327-2888 or 305-664-4651
E-mail: cheecalodg@aol.com

Described as being in "its own neighborhood," Cheeca Lodge resort provides guests a wealth of activities – dive and snorkeling trips, a nine-hole golf course, sailing, fishing, tennis, parasailing, board sailing, plus a staff of expert instructors, captains or pros.

Guests choose from more than 200 oversized guestrooms and villas, most with private balcony overlooking the sea or lush gardens, paddle fans, mini-bar, and TV.

Amenities include a children's recreational camp, shops, gourmet dining at Atlantic Edge Restaurant, the Ocean Terrace Grill or the Light Tackle Lounge, entertainment, palm-lined swimming/snorkeling beach, two freshwater pools and a 525-ft lighted fishing pier. Dockage and marina. Conference center. No pets.

Chesapeake Resort $$-$$$$

MM 83.4, Oceanside
PO Box 909, Islamorada FL33036
☎ 800-338-3395 or 305-664-4662
E-mail: chesapea@aol.com

Adjacent to the Whale Harbor Restaurant and Islamorada docks, the Chesapeake sprawls across six lush, oceanfront acres. Guests select from 65 lovely motel rooms, oceanview villas or suites. A sweeping sand beach encircles a deep-water ocean lagoon and marina. Walk to fishing charter boat docks. No pets.

Coconut Cove Resort and Marina $$-$$$

MM 85, Oceanside
84801 Overseas Hwy
Islamorada FL 33036
☎ 305-664-4055

Nature lovers, movie buffs and adventurous folk feel right at home at the Coconut Cove Resort, which is frequently used in TV and movie clips for its huge tiki bar and surrounding island props. These include old aircraft, a submarine and Hemingway memorabilia. Accommodations feature 10 efficiency apartments set in an oceanfront coconut palm grove. Wildlife flock in and around the property's 125,000-gallon saltwater pond that sparkles with speeding tarpon, tropical fish, rays, exotic wading birds and lush tropical flora.

Dive, snorkeling and eco-tours take off from Coconut's Marina, which offers boat rentals, Jet Skis, ultralight flying lessons and rentals, kayak tours, paddle boats, glass-bottom boats, water skis and more.

Read more about their ultra-light flying lessons in our *Aerial Tours* chapter, page 48.

Days Inn Ocean Front Resort $$-$$$$

MM 82.7, Oceanside
Islamorada FL 33036
☎ 305-664-3681, fax 305-664-9020

Days Inn offers deluxe rooms and suites, some with two bedrooms. Rooms have two double beds or a king. Boat dockage. Wading and sun-tan beach. Boat rentals from on-site Relief Watersports. Bike rentals. No pets.

Holiday Isle Resorts $-$$$$

MM 84, Oceanside
84001 Overseas Hwy., Islamorada FL 33036
☎ 800-327-7070 or 305-664-2321, fax 305-664-2703

Holiday Isle encompasses an entire beach club community, with every imaginable watersport and activity. Guests choose from rooms, efficiencies or suites. The huge, panoramic beach vibrates with reggae music. Vendors offer parasailing, fishing and diving charters, sailing, board sailing, Jet Skiing, inflatable-island rentals, sun lounges and dancing. Fast-food stands line the walkways, selling barbecue, pizza, ice cream, drinks and more. Sit-down diners enjoy a lovely rooftop restaurant and a unique place in the parking lot where you can cook it yourself on slabs of granite. Rooms are luxurious. The beach is open to everyone and is packed early during the high season. No pets.

Hidden Harbor $

2396 Overseas Hwy., Bayside
Marathon FL 33050
☎ 800-362-3495 or 305-743-5376

Located on the Gulf and adjacent to the turtle hospital, Hidden Harbor Motel features 21 clean air-conditioned rooms with cable TV, a freshwater pool, boat docking for craft up to 30 ft, boat trailer parking and close proximity to the Seven-Mile bridge. Some efficiencies. No pets. Guests can tour the neighboring turtle hospital.

El Capitan Resort $$$-$$$$

MM 84, Oceanside
Islamorada FL 33036
☎ 800-327-7070

A part of the Holiday Isle complex, El Capitan has deluxe efficiencies and junior suites for two to six people. Guests share the complex's oceanfront lagoon and beach. Boat dockage. No pets.

Where to Stay

Harbor Lights Motel $$

MM 84.9, Oceanside
Islamorada FL 33036
☎ 800-327-7070 or 305-664-3611

Near the Holiday Isle complex, Harbor Lights rents efficiencies, rooms and cottages with in-room safes, phones and barbecue grills. They provide a bus to the Holiday Isle complex on weekends. Write 84001 US 1, Islamorada FL. ☎ 800-327-7070 or 305-664-3611, fax 305-664-2703.

Howard Johnson's Resort $$-$$$

MM 84.5, Oceanside
84001 US 1, Islamorada FL 33036
US ☎ 800-654-2000 or 305-664-2711, fax 305-664-2703

The resort is on a soft sand beach, and there is restaurant. Guests at Howard Johnson's can use the adjacent Holiday Isle beach or lounge under the palms on the motel's own sand beach and watch the board sails ply back and forth. Boat dock and ramp. No pets.

La Jolla Resort $-$$

MM 82.3, Bayside
82216 Oversesas Hwy
Islamorada FL 33036
☎ 305-664-9213
E-mail: fishtony2@aol.com

A tiki hut and great sunsets over the bay provide a nice tropical atmosphere at this older waterfront motel. Kitchen units are simple, yet comfortable. A boat dock and ramp allow for quick access to the backcountry for fishing. There is a small swimming beach, and grills.

Lime Tree Bay Resort $$-$$$

MM 68.5, Bayside
PO Box 839, Long Key FL 33001
☎ 800-723-4519 or 305-664-4740

Lime Tree is an older motel, yet very comfortable, with beautiful grounds and fantastic sunset views. Guests stay in one- and two-bedroom units, some with kitchens. There is a restaurant, tennis court, boat dock, small beach with a fresh water pool and Jacuzzi. An on-premise watersports operation rents waverunners kayaks, Sunfish, day sailers, pontoon boats, robalos, snorkel gear and a jet boat. Reef tours. No pets.

The Moorings $$$-$$$$

123 Beach Road
Islamorada FL 33036
☎ 305-664-4708

Located next to Cheeca Lodge, the Moorings sits on an old plantation. There are lovely homes and cottages here. Some are renovated 1930s abodes, some are new. All have fully equipped kitchens, ceiling fans, sheets and towels. Rental includes use of board sailers and kayaks, swimming pool, tennis court and barbecue grills.

Hampton Inn & Suites $$$-$$$$

MM 80, Oceanside
Islamorada FL 33036
☎ 800-426-7866 or 305-664-0073
E-mail: hamptoninn@floridakeys.com

Gamefishing dominates the island decor at Islamorada's Hampton Inn, which features 60 suites and 16 guest rooms, with four handicapped-access rooms. One- and two-bedroom suites have full kitchens, sleeper sofas in the living room, two TVs with cable, VCR, and pay-per-view. Popcorn and coffee are supplied every day. Rates include a continental breakfast daily.

Hotel grounds feature a heated pool, suntan deck, tiki bar and spa. A large dock accommodates shallow-draft boats. Activities offered include snorkeling, fishing, boat rentals, kayaking, bikes. There is an Outback Steakhouse on the premises.

Port of Call Townhomes $$$

MM 88.5, Oceanside
Islamorada FL 33036
☎ 305-232-3569, fax 305-232-3188
E-mail: keys@4vacationrentals.com

Plantation Key townhouses start at $1,000 per week or $3,000 per month. Units have three floors, porches, cable TV, two baths, full kitchens with microwave, dishwasher, coffeemaker, washer/dryer. Heated pool on property. Beach, dock. Pets permitted in some units.

Tropical Reef Resort $-$$$

MM 85, Oceanside
84977 Overseas Hwy
Islamorada FL 33036
☎ 305-664-8881 or 800-887-3373, fax 305-664-4891

A variety of rooms and rates attract families to Tropical Reef Resort. The property has three freshwater pools, a children's pool, two

Jacuzzis, a picnic beach with tiki huts and floating breakfast café, boat ramp and harbor. Rainbow Reef Dive Center on premises offers dive and snorkeling tours. No pets.

White Gate Court $-$$$

76010 Overseas Hwy, Bayside
Islamorada FL33036
☎ 800-645-GATE or 305-664-4136
E-mail: whitegatecourt@worldnet.att.net
www.whitegatecourt.com

If you enjoy laid-back vacations, can't bear to leave your dog at home and want to experience the Keys the way they were 50 years ago, this is the place for you. Five 1940s-era Bayside cottages have been lovingly restored with new, comfortable beds and furnishings, fully equipped kitchenettes, cable TV, direct-dial phones, air-conditioning and tile floors. And, as in the 1940s, your pet is welcome and you can tie up your boat at no-extra charge.

This Bayside complex provides gas grills, 200 ft of white sandy bayfront, clear water for swimming and snorkeling, lounge chairs and picnic sets, paddle boats and bicycles. Fun!

Islamorada Campgrounds

Fiesta Key Resort, KOA

MM 70, Bayside
Long Key FL 33001
☎ 305-664-49222

Fiesta Key offers tent sites with and without water from $42, with electricity from $45, RV sites with full hookups from $62 to $80. Motel rooms start at $125, efficiencies at $150. Pets are allowed in the tent and RV sites, but not in the motel. The resort sits on a 28-acre tropical island surrounded by warm Gulf waters. 350 sites. Pool, restaurant, pub, game room, marina, docks and ramp.

Long Key State Recreation Area

MM 66, Oceanside
PO Box 776
Long Key FL 33001
☎ 305-664-4815
www.dep.state.fl.us/parks/

Long Key rents 60 oceanfront tent and RV sites. Sites without electricity cost $23.69, with electricity $25.85. Campsites are fenced off from the rest of the park area. Most are by reservation, but you can stop by and try for an opening. Reservations are taken up to 11 months in advance. The oceanfront campground provides hot showers and an electric dump station.

The park features two nature trails, bike and canoe rental, picnic area, observation tower and guided walks. The beach fronts shallow water that gets uncomfortably hot even for wading during summer. The rest of the year, if you wade out a bit, you can snorkel over turtle grasses and watch the small fish dart about. No pets.

■ Marathon Accommodations

For a complete list of rental units, condos and villas, contact the **Greater Marathon Chamber of Commerce**, 12222 Overseas Hwy., Marathon FL 33050. ☎ 305-743-5417 or 800-842-9580. www.fla-keys.com, www.keysdirectory.com or www.floridakeysmarathon.com.

Banana Bay Resort - Key West & Marathon $-$$$

MM 49.5, Bayside
Marathon FL 33050
☎ 800-226-2621 or 305-743-3500
www.bananabay.com

Sitting on 10 lush acres, Banana Bay Resort, Marathon (sister resort to Banana Bay, Key West) offers all the amenities of a larger resort. Facilities include 60 deluxe guest rooms with either one king or two double beds, a fine restaurant, poolside lounge, waterfront tiki bar, huge pool, outdoor whirlpool, two tennis courts, volleyball courts, conference rooms, a wedding gazebo, 50-slip marina, boat ramp, sandy suntan beach and watersports center.

Activities include boat and WaveRunner rentals, board sailing, sailing dinghies, kayak tours, fishing charters on the reef or bay. A full-service dive shop nearby arranges for dive and snorkeling excursions.

Bonefish Resort $-$$

MM 58, Oceanside
58070 Overseas Hwy
Grassy Key FL 33050
☎ 305-743-7107
E-mail: bonefishgk@aol.com

Favored by fishermen and those on a tight budget, this small family motel features clean, pleasant rooms with cable TV, phones, barbecues, and use of a kayak or row boat. The saltwater flats are too shallow for swimming, but Bonefish guests may use the facilities of the nearby Cabana Club Beach for ocean swimming or in their heated pool. Pets welcome.

Buccaneer Resort $-$$$

MM 48.5, Bayside
2600 Overseas Hwy., Marathon FL 33050
US ☎ 800-237-3329 or 305-743-9071
E-mail: buccaneer@floridakey.com
www.florida.com

A favorite of divers and boaters, the Buccaneer has 76 motel rooms, some with kitchens. A waterfront restaurant, tiki bar and café serve local favorites. Outdoors there's a sandy beach, tennis court, fishing docks and a boat dock.

Conch Key Cottages $$-$$$$

MM 62.3, Oceanside
62250 Overseas Hwy
Marathon FL 33050
☎ 800-330-1877 or 305-289-1377, fax 305-743-8207
E-mail: info@conchkeycottages.com
www.conchkeycottages.com

Sitting on a secluded, private island which, up until the 1970s, could only be reached by boat, Conch Key Cottages charm visitors with rustic 50s-style wooden cottages. They have screened-in porches, huge ceiling fans and terrific island colors. All are air-conditioned, with cable TV, hammock and barbecue. Coin washers and dryers on premises. Boat dock and ramp.

The largest cottage, the King's Crown, has a king-size bed in one bedroom and two queen-size beds in the other. Three cottages built in 1997 feature two bedrooms and two baths, two TVs with cable. Beautiful flowers, palm trees and a small pool flank the boat ramp and marina. There is also a fish-cleaning station with water and electricity.

Conch Key Cottages are off the beaten track. A great choice if you want to relax and soak in the scenery, but quite a distance from Key West and commercial activities.

Continental Inn $$-$$$

MM 53.5, Bayside
121 West Ocean Drive
Key Colony Beach FL 33051
☎ 800-443-7352 or 305-289-0101, fax 305-743-8150
E-mail: continentalinn@aol.com

Sitting on Key Colony Beach, a tiny oceanside cay in Marathon, Continental Inn features attractive, modern one- and two-bedroom condos surrounding a heated freshwater pool and patio. Swim in the ocean from their lovely palm-shaded beach. Lots of small fish to snorkel with off the rocks at the edge of the beach. No pets, boats or trailers.

CocoPlum Beach & Tennis Club $$$-$$$$

MM 54.5, Oceanside
109 Coco Plum Drive
Marathon FL 33050
☎ 800-228-1587 or 305-743-0240, fax 305-743-9351
E-mail: reservations@cocoplum.com
www.cocoplum.com

Sample a taste of oceanfront, tropical living with all the comforts of home in CocoPlum's octagonal-shaped villas. Each two-bedroom, two-bath villa is fully furnished and rimmed with a wrap-around deck and screened patio, elevated off the ground to catch the breezes. The second-floor entry level contains the kitchen, dining room and patio. Convenient kitchens are equipped with microwave ovens, coffee makers, blenders, toasters and dishwashers, cookware, utensils, linens and dinnerware. A washer and dryer are conveniently located on the lower level of each villa.

The upper level houses the two bedrooms, bathrooms and the living room. The master suite has a queen-bed and private bath. Guest bedroom has a double and a twin bed. Living room has a full-sized sofa-bed, a wet-bar, cable TV and VCR.

Outdoors, guests wander through a tropical orchard of banana and citrus trees, play a set on the tennis court or swim in the oceanfront pool or the ocean, which drops off enough to swim in.

 Check the website for specials at Coco Plum.

Where to Stay

Crystal Bay Resort & Marina $-$$$

MM 49, Bayside
4900 Overseas Hwy
Marathon FL 33050
☎ 305-289-8089 or 888-289-8089, fax 305-289-8189
E-mail: info@crystalbayresort or jleggett@bellsouth.net

Crystal Bay offers sparkling clean, air-conditioned efficiencies with cable TV, phone, microwave, refrigerator and coffee maker. Lush tropical plantings shade a small sandy beach and a fishing pier. Children under 12 stay free. Near Bahia Honda Beach.

Hampton Inn & Suites $-$$$$

MM 48, Bayside
1688 Overseas Hwy
Marathon FL 33050
☎ 305-743-9009
E-mail: hamptoninns@aol.com
www.flkeyshampton.com

Marathon's newest resort offers spacious suites and rooms with private balconies, 25-inch remote TVs with 27 channels and HBO. One-bedroom suites have a modern kitchenette and a living room with a sleeper sofa. Handicap-accessible and non-smoking rooms available.

A watersports center on the grounds rents WaveRunners, and small boats. They also run daily reef trips for snorkeling and eco-tours. Ocean tours cut across under the Seven Mile Bridge.

Relax by the heated pool or whirlpool overlooking the Gulf of Mexico. Swimming in the Gulf is undesirable at this location, but a short four-mile drive brings you to Sombrero Beach. Bahia Honda State Park beaches are also nearby. Visit the website or call for specials and packages.

Holiday Inn $$-$$$

MM 54, Oceanside
13201 Overseas Hwy
Marathon FL 33050
☎ 800-224-5053 or 305-289-0222, fax 305-743-5460
www.keysdirectory.com

New owners have completely renovated the guest rooms, restaurant and lounge. Rooms have two double beds or one king. Handicap-access rooms and nonsmoking rooms are available. Pool. No beach.

Watersports are easily arranged with **Abyss Diving** (☎ 800-457-0134), located behind the inn. A boat ramp and marina allow for quick ocean and reef access.

Faro Blanco Marine Resort $$-$$$$

MM 48
1996 Overseas Hwy
Marathon FL 33050
☎ 800-759-3276 or 305-743-9018

Faro Blanco spreads from shore to shore, with the most diverse selection of facilities and guest rooms on the Atlantic and the Gulf. Under new ownership, the resort complex was completely renovated during 2000 and now offers spacious accommodations with bright tropical decor.

There is a full-service marina if you are arriving by yacht and wish to tie up for a stay. The dockmaster stands by on VHF Channel 16. Convenient to fine restaurants and diving.

Hawk's Cay Resort and Marina $$$-$$$$

MM 61, Oceanside
61 Hawk's Cay Blvd
Duck Key FL 33050
☎ 888-443-6393 or 305-742-7000 fax 305-743-3805
www.hawkscay.com

Hawk's Cay maintains 135 deluxe two-bedroom villas, 160 guest rooms and 16 suites. On the premises are a marina, four restaurants, a saltwater swimming lagoon with sandy beach, two heated pools, watersports concession, glass-bottom boat, children's program, fishing charters, a dive shop, tennis courts, bicycle rentals, an interactive dolphin program and 10,000 square feet of meeting space.

Charter fishing and dive boats leave from the marina. Protected boat slips for large and small craft. No pets.

The resort has established a new fly-fishing academy with weekend courses designed for beginning and experienced anglers aged 16 and older. Included is instruction in tying flies and fly-casting, along with the basics of rods, reels, lines and leaders and a half-day fishing excursion. To register for the academy, ☎ 888-809-7305, ext 3570.

Where to Stay

Ocean Beach Club $$-$$$$

MM 53.5, Oceanside
351 East Ocean Drive
Key Colony Beach
Marathon FL 33050
☎ 800-321-7213 or 305-289-0525, fax 305-289-9703
www.fl-web.com/oceanbrach

This modern three-story hotel sits on Key Colony Beach at the Atlantic Ocean's edge, offering suite accommodations, standard rooms and an impressive stretch of sandy beach.

Fish or fish-watch from their 100-ft pier. Guests have caught grunts, snappers, yellowtails and one 300-lb bullshark from this spot. The resort restaurant opens for lunch and dinner, specializing in seafood and steaks. The hotel sits about a mile from Marathon. No pets.

Rainbow Bend Fishing Resort $-$$

MM 58, Oceanside
57784 Overseas Hwy
Marathon FL 33050
☎ 800-929-1505 or 305-289-1505, fax 305-743-4257
E-mail: rainbowbend@fla-keys.com
www.fla-keys.com

Rooms and efficiencies come with free use of a motorboat or sailboat plus complimentary breakfast daily. There is a wide sandy beach, freshwater pool, spa, fishing pier, tackle shop. Dive and fishing charters. Café. Pets OK.

Sombrero Resort & Lighthouse Marina $$-$$$

MM 50, Oceanside
19 Sombrero Blvd.
Marathon FL 33050
☎ 800-433-8660 or 305-743-2250, fax 305-743-2998
www.fl-web.com/sombrero

Centrally located in the Middle Keys, Sombrero Resort offers 123 condos and efficiencies in two three-story buildings, plus 70 marina slips for boats up to 100 ft long. Condos have a living room with sleeper sofa, dining area, kitchen and bedroom with king-sized bed or two doubles and full bath. Rooms were newly painted and carpeted in 1999. A nice sundeck encircles the Junior Olympic heated pool. **Chef's Steakhouse & Bar** on the premises opens nightly from 6 pm to 10 pm. A poolside tiki bar serves frozen island drinks from 12 noon to 11 pm. The gameroom buzzes with video arcade games, billiards and table soccer. Outdoors, four lighted tennis courts, a sauna, small fitness center and marina serve active guests. Tennis lessons available. Swimming beach and golf nearby. Book sunset cruises, snorkeling and kayak rentals from the marina.

The Seahorse Motel $-$$

MM 51, Bayside
7196 Overseas Hwy
Marathon FL 33050
☎ 800-874-1115 or 305-743-6571, fax 305-743-0775
E-mail: seahorse@terranova.net

Save a bundle at the sunny Seahorse Motel. A good choice for budget-conscious vacationers and boaters. Accommodations are clean, simple two-double-bed motel rooms with cable TV and air-conditioning. Some have mini-fridges and a sleeper sofa. A pool, gas grills, patio, picnic tables and playground overlook a canal that leads to the Bay. Boat ramp for small craft. Look for the motel's hot pink roof.

Wellesley Inn Marathon $-$$

MM54, Bayside
13351 Overseas Hwy
Marathon FL 33050

The Wellesley features 80 newly decorated deluxe guest rooms, a garden patio, pool, cable TV, 24-hour Denny's Restaurant, glass-bottom boat, paddle boats and WaveRunner rentals. Scuba and vacation packages, guest laundry. Some rooms have a microwave, refrigerator and coffee maker. No-smoking and handicapped-accessible rooms available. 24-hr message service, dataport in each room. Charter fishing cruises, sunset cruises.

Marathon Campground

Knights Key Campground

MM 47, Oceanside
Marathon FL 33050
☎ 800-348-2267 or 305-743-4343, fax 305-743-2907
www.kylehowell@aol.com

Located on a beautiful spit of land at the Seven Mile Bridge, three miles from shopping, Knights Key Campground offers a variety of oceanfront, harborfront and meadow sites for RVs and tents. Once a junction for the old Flagler Railroad, the surrounding deep water provided a sheltered harbor for Cuban ships to unload goods from the trains. Today, the deep harbor is a swimming area, complete with diving board and a white sand beach. The campground also features a well-stocked stone aquarium, coin laundry, clean bathhouses, boat ramp and a pub-style restaurant. Boaters can rent marina sites with hookups and boat dockage for $61.95 to $66.95 per day. Tent sites, which have tables but no water, are from $26.95 per day – they are near the shower rooms. Rates are based on two adults. Children under 10 are free; additional adults pay $8 per day.

No pets in the tent sites. Pets must be on a six-foot leash and are only allowed in air-conditioned RVs. No cable TV or telephone hookups. No minibikes or motorcycles on park roads. There is a pump and dump station, but no sewer hookups.

■ Big Pine & the Lower Keys Accommodations

Big Pine is centered between Marathon and Key West. A 20-minute drive will get you to either.

For a complete list of Lower Keys accommodations call, write or visit **Lower Keys Chamber of Commerce**, PO Box 430511, Big Pine Key FL 33043. ☎ 800-872-3722 or 305-872-2411. www.fla-keys.com or www.keysdirectory.com.

Big Pine Resort Motel $-$$
MM 30.5, Bayside
30725 Overseas Hwy
Big Pine Key FL 33043
☎ 305-872-9090, fax 305-872-2816
E-mail: bigpinemotel@att.net
www.bigpinemotel.com

Big Pine's proximity to Looe Key Marine Sanctuary and its low rates make it a fine choice for divers on a budget. The motel has 32 recently renovated, large and comfortable rooms, efficiencies and apartments. Adjacent restaurant. No pets.

Dolphin Resort and Marina $-$$$
MM 28.5, Oceanside
Little Torch Key FL 33042
☎ 800-553-0308 or 305-872-2685
E-mail: dolphinresort@earthlink.net
www. dolphinresort.com

Destroyed by Hurricane George in 1997, the resort and marina have since been completely rebuilt, with a new fuel dock, bait shop, store, boat ramp and a fleet of rental boats. Guests stay in modern apartments, most with kitchens and porches. All are air-conditioned and have cable TV.

Dolphin Resort and Marina is close to Looe Key Marine Sanctuary and a 30-minute drive to Key West. A good choice for boaters, fishermen and families who want a laid-back vacation. No pets. ☎ 800-942-5397.

Parmer's Place Resort Motel $-$$$

MM 28.5, Bayside
565 Barry Ave.
Little Torch Key FL 33043
☎ 305-872-2157, fax 305-872-2014
www.parmersplace.com

Nineteen aviaries might make you think Parmer's Place is strictly for the birds, but you'll find the simple air-conditioned motel rooms not only price-worthy, but clean and comfortable. No beach, but a pool in the middle of the property serves swimmers. Boat dockage is limited. Maid service is additional. Complimentary continental breakfast comes with the room.

Guest rooms and efficiencies have TVs and screened-in porches. One handicapped-accessible unit is available. Twenty-five-minute drive to Key West. No phones, no pets.

Little Palm Island $$$$

MM 28.5, Oceanside
Little Torch Key FL 33042
☎ 800-343-8567 or 305-872-2524, fax 305-872-4843
E-mail: getlost@littlepalmisland.com
www.littlepalmisland.com

Located on a five-acre out-island, three miles offshore from Little Torch Key and 28.5 miles east of Key West, Little Palm Island features 28 ultra-plush one-bedroom, thatched-roof bungalow suites scattered among thickets of oleander, hibiscus and Jamaican palms. Each suite has a king-size bed, separate living room, Jacuzzi whirlpool bath, indoor and outdoor shower and private veranda. All are air-conditioned and include ceiling fans, mini-bar, coffee maker, robes, hair dryer, iron, mini-safe and a data-link line. Designed for privacy and seclusion, telephones, televisions and alarm clocks are banned.

A wealth of sports and recreational amenities are offered for resort guests. Among them are the lagoon-like freshwater pool and waterfall, surrounded by an arbor of trees, plants, exotic birds, fish and flowers; and a strip of beach boasting soft white sand. There is complimentary use of the fitness center, a life-size chess set, day sailers, kayaks, and sailboats, as well as rods and reels for fishing and masks and fins for snorkeling. Pontoon and fishing boats can be rented. Canoes and bicycles also available. Arrangements can be made for scuba diving, snorkeling, backcountry and deep-sea fishing instruction, as well as guided nature tours by canoe or sailboat. Several off-shore and mainland excursions are also available. Scuba divers and snorkelers can arrange for trips to nearby Looe Key National Marine Sanctuary.

Ecological preservation is a major priority at Little Palm Island. The resort's environmentally sensitive, low-density development has allowed the preservation of lush foliage and flowers, and an abundance of wildlife, including the Key Deer. There are also many species of fish and marine mammals. Little Palm, which has received numerous awards for its recycling efforts, houses a state-of-the-art waste water treatment plant that uses air and electricity to produce ozone, an activated oxygen that destroys contaminants.

Rates start at $900 per day. Honeymoon packages available.

■ Sugarloaf Key Accommodations

Sugarloaf Lodge $-$$

MM 17, Bayside
Sugarloaf Key FL 33043
☎ 800-553-6097 or 305-745-3211
E-mail: information@sugarloaflodge.com
www.sugarloaflodge.com

At one time or another Sugarloaf Key has been home to smugglers, sponge divers and eccentric entrepreneurs. Today, it appeals to dynamic vacationers who enjoy sea kayaking, canoeing, flying, sky diving, fly fishing and those who want to be close to Key West's action, but not too close (it's a 30-minute drive to Old Town).

Sugarloaf Lodge features clean, simple, waterfront motel rooms with air-conditioning and cable TV. The grounds have tennis courts, shuffleboard, a new chickee bar – perfectly situated for sunset viewing, a miniature golf course, a 3,000-ft airstrip, freshwater pool, restaurant and marina. You can book a scenic flight over the area with Fantasy Dan's at the air strip or sign up for a sky diving lesson. Swim in the pool or the bays.

Looe Key Reef Resort & Dive Center $-$$

MM 27.5
PO Box 509
Ramrod Key FL 33042
☎ 800-942-5397 or 305-872-3786
E-mail: looekeydive@aol.com
www.diveflakeys.com

Located on a canal with boat ramp and dockage, you can board the dive boat right outside your back door and enjoy a day of diving and snorkeling on the reef. Resort rooms are newly renovated, standard motel rooms with air-conditioning, TV, phones and two double beds. The resort features a pool, sundeck, restaurant, tiki bar, and five-star PADI dive center.

■ Lower Keys Campgrounds

Sugarloaf Key KOA $

MM20, Oceanside
Summerland Key FL 33042
☎ 800-562-7731 or 305-745-3549, fax 305-745-9889
E-mail: sugarloaf@koa.net
www.fla-keys.com

Enjoy sea breezes and a palm-shaded beach at Sugarloaf. This KOA oceanfront park has 184 sites on 14 acres, a full-service marina with canoe and boat rentals, a game room, heated pool, hot tub, sandy beach, open-air pub and grill, laundry facilities, boat ramp, dock, and full-service store. Tent sites, which rent for $39.95, have no water or electricity. RV sites have full hookups, some with sewer hookups, run from $52.95 to $72.95 for waterfront. Rates are for two adults. Kids under six stay free. Additional adults pay $9 per night. Cable hookup $4. Electricity to 30 amps. No slide-outs or pull-throughs. Pets must be kept on leashes. Owners must clean up after pets.

Bahia Honda State Recreation Area $

MM 38, Oceanside
Box 782, Big Pine Key FL 33043
☎ 305-872-2353
www.bahiahondapark.com or www.fla-keys.com

Bahia Honda State Recreation Area, the Keys' prettiest park and best beach area, accommodates campers in 80 sites at three oceanside and Bayside areas. All RV sites are back-in, no pull-throughs. Large motor homes – up to 35 ft long – park at the Buttonwood area. Pop-up tents and small truck-top campers can stay in Sandspur and Bayside. Water and electricity are supplied at Buttonwood and Sandspur. Rates are $26. There is a dump station at Buttonwood. Bayside sites have only one rate – $24. To reach the Bayside campground, you need to drive under the Bahia Honda Bridge. Hot showers and a bathhouse

The park caters to 200,000 day visitors per year with a variety of activities, including snorkeling boat trips, snorkeling equipment rentals (you keep the snorkel), kayak rentals, and swimming on the Atlantic

Where to Stay

and Gulf sides – both beaches have sandy bottoms. The park also has a nature trail, marina with overnight slips and a gift shop.

There are also three furnished duplex cabins (six units) in the park that accommodate six people each. These book up as far as 11 months in advance. Linens and utensils are provided. Snacks and limited grocery items are available at the concession building. Shaded picnic tables are at the old bridge and at Sandspur Beach.

The park opens at 8 am and closes at sunset. For further information and occasional discount opportunities, write or visit their website.

■ Key West Accommodations

Key West has three main resort areas – Old Town, the center of activity and where you'll find the island's most posh, oceanfront resort complexes; South Roosevelt Blvd., which runs along the south shore parallel to the Atlantic Ocean; and North Roosevelt Blvd., the commercial strip packed with fast-food joints and strip malls, which runs along the island's northern, Gulf shore. Because the island is just two miles wide and four miles long, no matter where you stay, you can travel to any point within a matter of minutes. Hotel rates vary with the season and special activities.

For a complete list of Key West accommodations including guest houses, condominiums, apartments and vacation homes, contact the **Greater Key West Chamber of Commerce**, Mallory Square, 402 Wall St., Key West FL 33040. ☎ 800-LAST KEY or 305-294-2587. www.keywest.com, www.fla-keys.com or www.keysdirectory.com.

Banana Bay Resort $$-$$$
2319 N. Roosevelt Blvd.
Key West FL 33040
☎ 305-296-6925

Banana Bay's adult resort features deluxe air-conditioned guestrooms, and one-bedroom suites, each with its own patio and parking space. The resort amenities include a freshwater pool, small sandy sunning beach (too shallow for swimming), whirlpool, mini-fitness gym, wedding gazebo, conference room, tiki bar, boat rentals, eco-sail adventures, flats fishing guide, volleyball, and a snorkel boat with two daily reef trips. Within walking distance of restaurants, shops, trolley tours, charter fishing and sailing.

Guest rooms feature private baths, ceiling fans, color TV, phones, refrigerators, wet bars, coffee makers, hair dryers, irons/boards, clock radios, one canopy king or two double beds. Courtyard mini-suites have queen bed, private bath and kitchenette. Cabana and Marina one-bedroom suites rent on a weekly basis, and have a private bedroom with queen bed, bath, living area with pull-out sleeper sofa and kitchenette – ideal for couples who want a little more space. Rates vary, depending on date of arrival and length of stay. Plenty of free parking. Dockage for boats up to 24 ft is $20 per night. Rates include a continental breakfast served beachside daily. No children under 16. No pets.

Best Western Key Ambassador Resort Inn $$-$$$

3755 South Roosevelt Blvd.
Key West FL 33040
☎ 800-432-4315 or 305-296-3500, fax 305-296-9961
E-mail: keyambbw@aol.com
www.keyambassador.com

Each of this Best Western's 100 guest rooms has a private balcony, spacious dressing area, color TV with premium movie channel. Palm-shaded grounds wrap around a large, heated pool and patio, where you can relax for lunch and cocktails at the tiki bar. The grounds also feature a Paracourse Fitness Cluster, which can best be described as an adult jungle gym with pull-up bars, sit-up benches and stretching areas. Room rates include complimentary continental breakfast. Airport van service is provided for guests flying into Key West Airport. No pets.

Best Western Hibiscus Motel $-$$$

1313 Simonton St.
Key West FL 33040
☎ 305-294-3763, 800-228-7364, fax 305-293-9243

A lush, tropical setting on Paradise Island, the grounds are landscaped with over 100 varieties of exotic palms surrounding a beautiful heated pool and Jacuzzi. All newly renovated rooms (including efficiencies) have two queen-size beds, safe, refrigerator and smoke detector.

Blue Lagoon $-$$$

3101 N. Roosevelt Blvd.
Key West FL 33040
☎ 305-296-1043, fax 305-296-6499
E-mail: bluelagkw@aol.com
www.floridakeys.net/bluelagoon

Blue Lagoon offers 72 low-budget rooms furnished with two double- or one queen-size bed. A small beach, pool and cement sundeck face the Gulf. The two-story motel has water views, and complete watersports activities – WaveRunners, parasailing, Key Cats, power boats and ultra-light airplanes. No pets.

Coconut Beach Resort $$-$$$$

1500 Alberta St.
Key West FL 33040
☎ 800-835-0055 or 305-294-0057, fax 305-294-5066
www.coconutbeachresort.com

Experience life in a Key West mansion at this oceanfront Victorian gingerbread resort. Choose from 32 two-bedroom or studio apartments overlooking the Atlantic. Suites are tastefully designed in colorful island decor, with French doors to catch the island breeze and hardwood flooring to add a touch of warmth.

Each unit has panoramic views, high ceilings, or a private balcony. One-bedroom and two-bedroom suites all have their own full kitchen and common balcony. Studios for two hold their own as intimate hideaways. Watch sunsets from the ocean-front Jacuzzi, the pool deck or the beach.

Located on the quiet side of the island next to Louie's Backyard Restaurant and Dog Beach, Coconut Beach blends old island architecture with today's comforts. Each guest gets a key to the pool area. It's a 10-minute walk to Duval Street shops and galleries, a short drive to the heart of Old Town. No pets.

Curry Mansion Inn $$-$$$

511 Caroline St.
Key West FL 33040
☎ 800-253-3466 or 305-294-5349, fax 305-294-4093
E-mail: FrontDesk@CurryMansion.com
www.currymansion.com

Nestled alongside the original 1899 Curry Mansion, the Inn offers 15 elegant romantic rooms, each opening onto a sparkling pool and surrounded by the lush foilage of the Curry Estate.

Like the Mansion, rooms are beautifully decorated in wicker and antiques, with private baths and phones, wet bars, air-conditioning, ceiling fans and cable TV. Other amenities include parking, a hot tub and swimming pool that are open 24 hours a day. Guests enjoy a European breakfast buffet, daily cocktail parties and full access to the 22-room mansion built by Florida's first millionaire family.

Days Inn Key West $-$$

3852 N Roosevelt Blvd
Key West FL 33040
☎ 800-325-2525 or 305-294-3742
www.daysinn.com

Located on the highway at the beginning of Key West as you enter from Stock Island, this discount resort has 133 newly renovated rooms and suites, some with kitchens; seven are handicapped-accessible. Gift shop, restaurant, pool. Weekly/monthly rates available.

El Rancho Motel $-$$$

830 Truman Ave.
Key West FL 33040
☎ 800-294-8783 or 305-294-8700, fax 305-294-0069
E-mail: info@elranchomotel.com
www.elranchokeywest.com

Just two blocks from Duval Street attractions, bars, shops and restaurants, the El Rancho offers 50 recently refurnished, small motel rooms, some low-priced. Each has a private bath, air-conditioner, cable TV and telephone. Standard rooms have one double bed or two twins. Refrigerators in select rooms. The courtyard amenities include a heated pool, sundeck and tiki huts. Short walk to beaches and marina. Three-night minimum stay.

Fairfield Inn by Marriott $$-$$$$

2400 N Roosevelt Blvd.
Key West FL 33040
☎ 800-228-2800 305, 296-5700, fax 305-292-9840
www.keywest.com/fairfieldinn

Fairfield Inn, a short drive from Old Town and the new Seaport District, features 100 bright, comfortable guest rooms and 31 one-bedroom suites with kitchenettes. All have coffee makers, irons, hair dryers and computer dataports.

A complimentary fresh continental breakfast is served daily. Refresh at one of two heated pools or the poolside tiki bar.

The Old Town Trolley makes hourly stops at the main lobby entrance.

Grand Key Resort $$$-$$$$

3990 South Roosevelt Blvd.
Key West FL 33040
☎ 888-310-1540 or 305-293-1818, fax 305-296-6962
E-mail: information@grandkeyresort.com
www.grandkeyresort.com

Adjacent to Key West Airport, Grand Key Resort specializes in eco-tourism, with earth-friendly, luxurious rooms and suites overlooking the Salt Ponds and marshes, where indigenous flora and waterfowl thrive. All sports are booked through the resort desk. No pets.

Hampton Inn Key West $$-$$$

2801 N. Roosevelt Blvd.
Key West FL 33040
☎ 800-960-3054, 305-294-2917, fax 305-296-0221
E-mail: hikwest@aol.com
www.hamptoninnkeywest.com

On the Gulf, across from the commercial strip, the Hampton Inn is a short drive from Old Town. Rooms are clean, spacious and comfortable, with individual climate control, your choice of a king-size or two double beds, and a spacious bathroom, with full bath and shower and hair dryer. There is a safe, coffee maker, dataports, iron and ironing board in each room.

Rates include the breakfast bar, with a variety of foods and beverages, choice of smoking or non-smoking accommodations, free local phone calls and no surcharge for long-distance calls made directly with your calling card, plus an in-room movie channel.

Children 18 years and under, or a third or fourth adult, stay free when sharing a room with the primary guests. Personal amenities kit in each room. No pets. Gulfview dining room, pool and hot tub.

The Gulf is too shallow for swimming at the Hampton Inn.

Harborside Motel & Marina $-$$

903 Eisenhower Drive
Key West FL 33040
☎ 800-501-7823 or 305-294-2780
E-mail: info@keywestharborside.com
www.keywestharborside.com

If deep-sea fishing is your reason for visiting Key West, consider this small motel. It's located at the charter boat marina and offers low-priced, modern, clean motel rooms. Boat dockage. Laundromat. Convenient to everything, the motel is a 10-minute drive to Old Town attractions, restaurants and shops.

Hilton Key West Resort and Marina $$-$$$$

245 Front St.
Key West FL 33040
☎ 800-HILTONS, 445-8667 or 305-294-4000, fax 305-294-4086
E-mail: Bruce_Skwarlo@hilton.com
www.keywestresort.hilton.com

Key West's only AAA Four-Diamond Resort features 216 air-conditioned guest rooms and suites with adjustable thermostats, alarm clock, dataport, TV with premium HBO, ESPN and CNN.

All rooms have coffee-maker, ironing board, iron, two phones (one in the bath), balcony, mini-bar. Suites have bathrobes, sofa bed, local paper daily, wet bar. Romance package available.

A business room, open 9 to 5 daily, offers guests use of computers with limited software and inkjet printers.

Guestrooms and suites wrap around a central pool overlooking the ocean and the Keys' most fabulous sunsets. Scuba and snorkeling trips can be booked from the resort. On-site fitness room.

The best feature of this hotel is its location, smack in the heart of Old Town and one block from Duval Street's famous watering holes, museums and shopping. Self-parking or valet.

Check their website for specials and packages.

Holiday Inn Beachside $$-$$$$

3841 N. Roosevelt Blvd.
Key West FL 33030
☎ 800-HOLIDAY or 305-294-2571
www.basshotels.com

Rebuilt in 2000 after severe hurricane damage, this Gulf-front resort offers 222 lovely rooms, 79 with water views. Amenities include a large freshwater pool, whirlpool, on-site water sports and dive trips, gift shop, full-service restaurant and bar, two lighted tennis courts and full catering facilities. Soft, sand beach, WaveRunners. Convenient by car to both sides of the island and Stock Island. Deluxe. No pets.

Holiday Inn La Concha Hotel $$-$$$$

430 Duval St.
Key West FL 33040
☎ 800-HOLIDAY or 305-296-2991, fax 305-294-3283
E-mail: bspoto@remingtonhotels.com
www.laconchakeywest.com

This historic hotel towers over the center of Old Town. Renovated in 1986, La Concha has 160 romantic rooms, a restaurant, fitness room, whirlpool spa, shops and the best view of the city from the rooftop lounge. Steps away from shopping, dining and all major attractions. Meetings and receptions for up to 200 people. Handicapped-accessible. The publisher received a lengthy complaint from one reader about this hotel in 1999, alleging discrimination and harassment.

Where to Stay

Key Lodge Motel $-$$

1004 Duval St.
Key West FL 33040
☎ 800-845-8384 or 305-296-9915
E-mail: EYWHotels@aol.com
www.keylodge.com

A fine small motel with low rates and clean, comfortable rooms. Conveniently located in the heart of Old Town. Close to the beach, nightlife and attractions.

Ocean Key Resort $$-$$$$

Zero Duval St.
Key West FL 33040
☎ 800-328-9815 or 305-296-7701
E-mail: info@oceankey.com
www.oceankey.com

Renowned for its spectacular Sunset Pier, Ocean Key Resort features 100 beautiful guest rooms and one- and two-bedroom units. Suites all have Jacuzzis, two baths, kitchens, living rooms and private balconies. Two-bedroom suites have a king-size bed in the master bedroom and two twins or one queen in the second bedroom.

Rooms overlook the ocean, Key West Harbor, Mallory Square or Duval Street. All accommodations include hair dryers, coffee makers, irons and ironing boards, ceiling fans, and direct dial/modem-capable phones.

Indulge yourself in great food, cold drinks and live music at Ocean Key's **Sunset Pier Restaurant and Lounge**. Open daily at 7:30 am, the Sunset Pier serves breakfast favorites and Starbucks coffee while you watch cruise ships drift by or view the fishing fleet heading to battle marlin, sailfish and tuna. The main menu starts at 11:30 am, with burgers, snacks, and grilled specialties available throughout the day and night. Walking distance to beach, shops, nightlife and dining. No pets.

Pegasus International Hotel $-$$$

501 Southard St.
Key West FL 33040
☎ 800-397-8148 or 305-294-9323
E-mail: intpegasus@aol.com
www.pegasuskeywest.com

Overlooking the corner of Duval and Southard Streets, this art deco hotel has 30 newly renovated standard rooms with either two double beds or one queen or king-size bed. Each room has a private bath, cable television, direct-dial telephone with dataport; most have a refrigerator and some have a micro-fridge. Complimentary coffee is provided each morning. The hotel's art deco architecture, though typical of South Beach in Miami, is unique in the Keys.

Amenities include free parking, a swimming pool, Jacuzzi and a large sundeck, all located on the second floor of the hotel. Within walking distance from the Pegasus hotel are all the famous bars, restaurants, historic homes and attractions are within walking distance. A good choice if you want to be in the midst of the shopping area.

Pier House Resort & Caribbean Spa $$-$$$$

One Duval St.
Key West FL 33040
☎ 800-327-8340 or 305-296-4600, fax 305-296-7568
E-mail: info@pierhouse.com
www.pierhouse.com

In the heart of Old Town Key West, Pier House rates as one of Key West's finest resorts. Choose from 128 eclectic, romantic guest rooms and 14 suites with private terraces or patios. The private ocean beach is one of only a few that has water deep enough for swimming. Other amenities include a full-service spa, offering body treatments, massages, facials, hair and nail salon and fitness center; a heated pool surrounded by tropical gardens; a beach club bar; four fine restaurants, a wine galley and piano bar; plus a harbour-view café and beachside entertainment. Walking distance to restaurants, shopping, Mallory Square attractions and the Historic Harbor Walk. Parking. No pets. Deluxe. Overlooking the Gulf of Mexico, with spectacular sunset views.

Radisson Resort $$-$$$

3820 N. Roosevelt Blvd
Key West FL 33040
☎ 800-333-3333 or 305-294-5511, fax 305-296-1939
www.radisson.com

Near the entrance to Key West, the Radisson features 145 newly decorated rooms with air-conditioning, refrigerator, coffee maker, hair dryer, iron, ironing board, in-room safe, and two direct-dial phones, one with a fax/computer hookup. Facilities include a restaurant, bar, pool, fitness room and coin laundry. Driving time to Old Town or the beach areas is 10-15 minutes.

Sheraton Suites $$$-$$$$

2001 South Roosevelt Blvd.
Key West FL 33040
☎ 800-452-3224 or 305-292-9800, fax 305-294-6009
E-mail: info@sheratonkeywest.com
www.sheratonkeywest.com

Near Key West Airport, across from Smather's Beach, Sheraton Suites hosts vacationers in 180 oversized guest suites with more than 550 square feet of living space. Some suites are equipped with in-room Jacuzzis. All have a wet bar, microwave oven, in-room coffee and tea service, two entertainment centers, and computer ports. Each suite also offers a hair dryer, iron, ironing board and a copy of *USA Today* delivered at your door each weekday morning.

Outdoors, splash sounds beckon from a lagoon-style pool with cascading waterfalls shadowed by fragrant tropical foliage. The resort's **Crab House Restaurant** serves local specialties and drinks at its pool-side tiki bar. Overall, the resort's wood-frame exterior, complete with Bahama-shuttered windows, captures the essence of historic Key West.

Rates include complimentary shuttle service to and from the airport, plus hourly transportation to Mallory Square and the historic district of Old Key West.

South Beach Oceanfront Motel $-$$

508 South St.
Key West FL 33040
☎ 800-354-4455 or 305-294-5539, fax 305-294-8272
E-mail: sobch508@aol.com
www.oldtownresorts.com/southbeach.htm

The South Beach Oceanfront Motel is nestled on Key West's only natural public beach, located near Fort Taylor and the Southernmost Point. There are 47 rooms, ranging from a standard room to an oceanview with kitchenette and private balcony.

Dive into the motel's newly remodeled Olympic-size pool or stop by the on-site dive shop to sign up for snorkel or scuba trips.

Southernmost Motel in the USA $-$$

1319 Duval St.
Key West FL 33040
E-mail: somostUSA1319@aol.com
www.oldtownresorts.com/southernmost1.htm

Across the street from South Beach, the Southernmost Motel offers low rates, 127 guest rooms, two large pools, Jacuzzi, public beach access, bike and moped rentals, free parking, in-room safes, cable TV. This is Key West's ideal Old Town location. On Duval Street, walk to the beach, shops and nightlife, or relax beside one of the two poolside tiki bars.

Sunrise Suites Resort $$$$

3685 Seaside Drive
Key West FL 33040
888-723-5200, fax 305-296-6968
E-mail: damon@sunrisekeywest.com

Sunrise Suites, near Key West Airport, offers elegantly appointed two-bedroom condos with a king bed in the master and a queen bed in the second, plus two full baths. The resort provides hairdryers, bathrobes and daily newspapers. All rooms have a TV, telephone and dataport. Fully equipped kitchens are separated from the living room by an eating counter. Balconies overlook the Salt Ponds, the Atlantic Ocean – or both.

Sunset Key Guest Cottages $$$$

Sunset Key, Key West FL 33040
☎ 305-292-5300 888-4777 fax 305-292-5395
E-mail: rebecca_hysell@hilton.com
www.hilton.com
Mailing address: 245 Front St., Key West FL 33040

Sunset Key, an island built by the US Navy while dredging Key West's harbor, has been transformed from Tank Island into a luxury resort just 10 minutes by boat from Key West.

Sunset Key Guest Cottages are super-plush, with every imaginable amenity and service.

The cottages, in traditional Key West style, offer panoramic beach-front, ocean or garden views. In-room amenities include fully equipped kitchens, living and dining areas, three full baths, with bathrobes and hair dryers, CD player, stereo system, video player, cable TV, beverage and pantry bar, mini-safe in each bedroom, iron and ironing board, direct-dial phone and ceiling fans.

Services include private chef upon request, in-room dining, grocery delivery, daily maid and turndown, massage therapy, concierge, 24-hour boat transportation from Sunset Key to the Key West Hilton Marina, and CD, video, board game, and literary libraries.

Resort amenities include **Latitudes Beach Café**, a marketessen, **Flippers Pool Bar**, a tropical free-form garden pool, two heated whirlpools, a white sandy beach with beach attendants, cabanas, and lounge chairs. Recipient of the Five Star Diamond Award by the American Academy of Hospitality Sciences.

Travelodge and Suites $$-$$$$

3444 N. Roosevelt Blvd.
Key West FL 33040
☎ 800-578-7878 or 305-296-7593
www.travelodgekeywest.com

Sitting in the midst of the commercial district, across from Florida Bay, this sparkling resort offers 64 rooms, including 24 one-bedroom suites and eight bi-level two- and three-bedroom penthouse suites. All suites include a fully equipped kitchen, with refrigerator, oven, range, dishwasher, toaster, washer and dryer. Penthouse suites include 2,000 square feet of living space with a staircase and cathedral ceilings.

Resort facilities include a heated outdoor pool and Jacuzzi, garage parking, poolside tiki bar. Rates include a complimentary continental breakfast.

Fine dining, casual restaurants, art galleries, museums and boutique shopping are a five-minute drive from the resort.

Wyndham Casa Marina Resort & Beach House $$-$$$$

1500 Reynolds St.
Key West FL 33040
☎ 800-626-0777 or 305-296-3535
E-mail: wcmbh@wyndham.com
www.casamarinakeywest.com

Situated directly on the Atlantic Ocean with 1,100 ft of private oceanfront, this top resort pampers guests in 311 exquisite rooms and suites, featuring every imaginable convenience and service. All rooms have individual climate control, telephone with voice-mail, TV, alarm clock radio, cable movie channels, in-room pay movies, mini-bar, coffee maker, hair dryer, safe. Many rooms with balcony/patio. The resort has two terrific restaurants – **Flagler's Steakhouse** and beachside **Sun Sun Pavilion and Raw Bar**. There are two outdoor pools, a lighted tennis court, an exercise room, whirlpool, volleyball court, sauna and massage services.

Rates include airport transportation, free parking, concierge, activities/tour desk, valet service, babysitting, notary public, gift shop/clothing shop, beauty shop, tennis pro shop.

Sorry, no pets or recreational vehicles allowed.

To get there from Key West International Airport, turn west on Roosevelt Blvd., go one mile to Atlantic Blvd., turn left, and drive one mile to Reynolds St., where you turn right. Hotel is on left.

Wyndham's Reach Resort

1435 Simonton St.
Key West FL 33040
☎ 800-874-4118 or 305-296-5000, fax 305-296-9960
www.keywest.com/reach

Situated in historic Old Town, one block from the Duval Street shopping district on a private beach, Wyndham's Reach Resort has 150 guest rooms, including 79 junior and one-bedroom suites, eight handicapped-accessible rooms, 84 non-smoking rooms, 21 doubles. All rooms have a private balcony, ceiling fan, hair dryer, wet bar, mini-bar, coffeemaker, iron, ironing board, in-room safe, cable television and in-room movies.

Facilities and amenities include a sand beach, use of the Body Shop Health Club, massage studio and full-service spa, outdoor pool and whirlpool. Full watersports equipment available for rental on premises.

The resort's **Sands Restaurant** opens early for breakfast. The **Sand Bar** is open from 11 am-9 pm for beach and poolside lunch, dinner, and beverages. More than 4,500 square feet of meeting space includes an oceanview terrace with a panoramic view of the Atlantic Ocean.

Key West Campgrounds

Boyd's Campground

6401 Maloney Ave.
Stock Island FL
☎ 305-294-1465, fax 305-293-9301
E-mail: boydscamp@aol.com
www.keysdirectory.com

You're just 15 minutes from Key West when you stay on neighboring Stock Island at Boyd's Campground. This Bayside park features all watersports, pool, game room, tiki hut, showers, restrooms, laundry, store, ice, city bus to Key West, telephone, dump station, bottled gas, electric, water, and sewer hookups. Twenty boat slips and launching ramps. Small dogs OK in air-conditioned, hard-shelled campers only. Pool MC/Visa.

Where to Stay

Waterfront Rates: Tents $46; Water and electric $56; Water, electric, sewer hookup and TV $68. Extra trailers $3; boats $6; boat slips $9.

Jabour's Trailer Court – Camping

223 Elizabeth St.
Key West FL 33040
☎ 305-294-5723, fax 305-296-7969
E-mail: info@kwcamp.com
www.kwcamp.com

Jabour's Trailer Court sits next to the fishing charter docks at Key West Bight. You're near all the restaurants and shops on North Roosevelt Boulevard and a few minutes from Mallory Square and Old Town. The park has 74 reservable 20-ft wide pearock sites for motor homes, travel trailers, tents, vans and any other type of camping unit. They also rent rooms and trailers. Rates start at $53 for a motor home or pop-up trailer site; vans without attachments from $37. There are no pull-throughs, but you can call for help with backing up. No standard, double slideouts, no phone hookups, no modem ports, no handicapped access, no gas or propane sold. They do have a dump station, cable TV hookup with 73 channels, tiled bathrooms with individual hot showers, secure combination lock entry, laundry room with coin-operated washer and dryer, plus coin/card pay phones.

In season, tent camp sites for two adults with no car cost $47 per night, with a van or car $57; tent trailer $71. For online photos of the site, visit www.kwcamp.com/tenting.htm.

Extra adults are charged $10 per day; $4 per child.

The pet policy is strictly enforced – no pets allowed in any lodging unit provided by management. Pets under 20 lbs are allowed in air-conditioned, owner-occupied camping units under leash and with owner's hands-on attendance. Pets over 20 lbs in air-conditioned, owner-occupied camping units may be allowed, subject to specific management approval (☎ 305-294-5723). Park management will ask violators to leave immediately with a forfeiture of unused prepaid rent.

■ Dry Tortugas National Park

40001 State 9336
Homestead FL 33034
☎ 305-242-7700 or 305-242-7761
www.nps.gov

If you loved the TV program *Survivor*, and want a similar rugged experience, plan a trip to Garden Key, Dry Tortugas National Park. The best time to go is during April or May. Thirteen campsites are available all year on a first-come, first-served basis for $3 per person per day. Eleven of the campsites can accimmodate up to six people or three tents each. There is one group site for about 40 people; groups of 10 or more must obtain a special permit in advance. The campground has picnic tables and grills. Saltwater flush toilets are available at the dock. All supplies, including fresh water, fuel, ice and food, must be brought in. Visitors must carry out all trash and garbage upon departure.

The seven-island cluster making up the Dry Tortugas National Park lies 70 miles west of Key West. There is usually no problem getting a site. There are no services, no food, no fresh water, no electricity, no medical facilities. Getting there is weather-dependent. Both seaplanes and high-speed ferries serve the area from Key West on calm days. Getting back is also weather-dependent – bring extra fresh water and rations.

The islands were named for once-abundant sea turtles or *tortugas* in the area when early 16th-century explorers provisioned their ships with the fresh turtle meat. They were called dry because there is no fresh water. Before modern navigation systems, the reefs and shoals of the Dry Tortugas were a serious hazard to navigation and are the site of hundreds of shipwrecks. On the positive side, this has created many magnificent dive and snorkeling sites. Corals grew over the wrecks and scores of fish moved in. Birds, who feed on the fish, nest in the area. Besides wildlife, the area is known for its famous bird and marine life, and its legends of pirates and sunken gold. Fort Jefferson, the largest of the 19th-century American coastal forts, is the park's central feature.

Tortugas Ferry operates ***Yankee Freedom II***, a luxurious 100-ft high-speed catamaran cruiser that departs Land's End Marina, Key West for day-tours of the Dry Tortugas. The yacht averages 30 knots, with travel time from Key West to the Tortugas approximately two hours and 15 minutes.

Amenities include air-conditioned cabin, spacious sundeck, complete galley, complimentary breakfast and full bar.

The ferry leaves Key West at 8 am and returns at 7 pm to Key West every day, weather permitting. Current price is $95, with some discounts for seniors, students with ID, military personnel and groups. Rates and schedules subject to change. ☎ 305-294-7009 or 800-634-0939. www.yankeefleet.com. Trips are canceled when winds exceed 25 knots.

Where to Stay

Seaplanes of Key West will drop you off and pick you up for $299. Flights depart Key West Airport. ☎ 305-294-0709. One-way would be $159 (prices fluctuate with gas rates).

Everglades National Park

General Park Information: ☎ 305-242-7700
Lodging: Contact Flamingo Lodge at ☎ 800-600-3813 or 941-695-3101. www.flamingolodge.com.

Dining: Contact Flamingo Lodge Restaurant at ☎ 800-600-3813 or 941-695-3101
Camping: ☎ 800-365-CAMP (2267)

For the northwestern, Ten Thousand Islands region contact:

Everglades Area Chamber of Commerce
PO Box 130
Everglades City FL 33929
☎ 914-695-3941.

Please note that although the park is open year-round, the recreational services are open from mid-November to mid-April.

Flamingo Lodge, Marina & Outpost Resort
#1 Flamingo Lodge Hwy
Flamingo FL 33034
☎ 941-695-3101, fax 941-695-3921
Reservations: ☎ 800-600-3813

Perched on the north shore of Florida Bay, Flamingo Lodge, Marina & Outpost Resort is open year-round and provides the only lodging within Everglades National Park. The inn offers 103 standard rooms and 24 cottages with kitchens. There is a freshwater pool, restaurant and lounge. Rooms are air-conditioned, modern and comfortable. Nearby, you can find fuel, a convenience store, gift shop and full-service marina offering scenic boat tours, boat rentals and fishing charters. The National Park Service operates the Flamingo Campground and Visitor Center. Some services offered vary seasonally. Absolutely no pets. Full service from November 1 through April 30. Open all year

Flamingo Lodge Restaurant, overlooking Florida Bay, serves seafood, steak, chicken, vegetarian dishes and local specialties. The bar offers tropical concoctions such as their Flamingo Sunset, Rum Runner and a Coco Loco. From November 1 to April 30, breakfast is from 7 to 10

am, lunch from 11:30 am to 3 pm, and dinner from 5 to 9 pm. Dinner reservations are recommended. From May to October, the restaurant and lounge are open for lunch and dinner from 11:30 am to 8 pm.

Buttonwood Lounge and Café serves pizza, salads, and sandwiches. It is open from December to April.

Get to Flamingo Lodge by taking Florida's Turnpike or US 1 to Florida City, then follow signs to Everglades National Park and Flamingo. It takes about 45 minutes to drive the 38-mile distance from the main entrance to Flamingo.

■ Camping

Camping is offered year-round at Long Pine Key, Flamingo, and Chekika. Reservations are strongly recommended at Long Pine Key and Flamingo during peak season from November 23 to April 18. Call the reservation agent at ☎ 800-365-2267 up to five months in advance. Both campgrounds are available on a first-come, first-served basis the rest of the year. Chekika camping is first-come, first-served year-round.

Front-country (i.e., regular camping area) fees during peak season are $14 for walk-in sites, $14 for RV sites and $28 for group sites. Park campgrounds at Long Pine Key, Flamingo, and Chekika have drinking water, picnic tables, grills, tent and trailer pads, and rest rooms. Flamingo has cold-water showers, Chekika has hot showers for free, and Flamingo Marina offers hot showers for $3. RVs are welcome, but there are no hook-ups. Campground stays are limited to 14 days during the peak season. Checkout time is 11 am.

Note: Some portions of the Flamingo Campground may be closed for repairs.

- Chekika campers must register before 5 pm, after which time the gates are locked and only registered campers are allowed access.

- RV facilities are located in Florida City and Homestead.

- Pets are allowed at the campgrounds, but not on trails or in the backcountry.

Backcountry Camping

Backcountry Use Permits are required for all overnight use of the backcountry (except on-board boats). Permits are $10 for one to six people; $20 for seven to 12 people; and $30 for 13 or more. These may be obtained in person up to 24 hours before the day your trip begins at either of two locations – the **Gulf Coast Visitor Center** (Everglades City), 7:30 am to 5 pm daily, ☎ 941-695-3311; or the **Flamingo Visitor Center** at the end of the Main Park Road, 7:30 am to 5 pm daily, ☎ 941-695-2945. Both are staffed from mid-November to mid-April. At other times, permit-writing desks may not be staffed, but permits are still required. Follow the self-registration instructions. Be sure to carry your permit or display it on your tent if camping. Upon completion of your trip, turn your permit in to a ranger station or visitor center.

Most campsites are chickees – elevated wooden platforms with a roof and chemical toilet – and accessible only by boat. Length of stay and number of people are restricted.

■ Northern Everglades Accommodations

Ten Thousand Island Region

This jungle-like area of mangrove islands offers fishermen and canoe campers an untouched-wilderness experience. Sightseeing and airboat excursions featuring alligator- , manatee- and frog-watching outings rank high in popularity. Credit cards are not yet accepted everywhere.

Everglades City

Everglades' Rod and Gun Resort Lodge $-$$
PO Box 190
Everglades City FL 33929
☎ 941-695-2101

Burt Reynolds, President Nixon and countless celebrities stayed at this hunting lodge in earlier times. The main house no longer lodges guests, but a few cottages on the property have been renovated for visitors. It's old and the rooms are small and simple, but there's a certain charm to the place. You can sit on the porch of the restaurant and watch herons and egrets fish in the Barron River. If you tow a boat, it's a neat place to tie up and go back to the 1930s. Pets welcome. Rates are under $100, except for Seafood Festival Weekend each February.

Everglades City Motel $
PO Box 361
310 Collier Ave.
Everglades City FL 34139
☎ 941-695-4224

Bank Building, Everglades City (© Jon Huber).

Where to stay

Located on the main road into town, this simple motel has clean rooms with cable TV, air-conditioning and private bath. Visa and MC.

Barron River Resort and Campground $-$$

PO Box 116 Everglades City FL 34139
☎ 941-695-3591 or 800-535-4961

Set on the Barron River with direct access to the 10,000 Islands and the Gulf of Mexico, this motel offers waterfront efficiencies and one- and two-bedroom apartments. The RV Park has 67 large sites with full hookups, cable TV and telephone available on all lots (29 sites are waterfront). Excellent fishing on the docks. Full-service marina, bait and tackle shop and boat rentals.

On the Banks of the Everglades $-$$

201 W. Broadway, PO Box 570, Everglades City FL 34139
☎ 941-695-3151, fax 941-695-3335; toll free 888-431-1977
E-mail: patty@banksoftheeverglades.com
www.banksoftheeverglades.com

Antiques lovers can bunk down in what was the first bank to serve Collier County during the 1920s. Guestrooms on the main floor share baths. Five suites on the second floor have private baths. Breakfast is served each morning on the outdoor patio or in the original bank vault.

Millionaire railroad man and Everglades City Founder Barron G. Collier built this bank building in 1923 as the center of his realm. Rum runners, alligator hunters, fur traders, and other pioneers formed the clientele. Built like a fort, the building survived countless hurricanes. During Hurricane Donna in 1962, five feet of water filled the vault, soaking all the money inside. Employees rushed to pin more than a million dollars on a clothesline to dry, keeping watch all night to prevent any unwanted "withdrawals." Not a single dollar was lost.

The Loan Department (a "fresh-air" room), the Trust Room, the Checking Department and the Stocks & Bonds Room are located on the first floor, where all of the banking trade took place until 1962. Separate ladies' and gents' baths are a few steps from each room.

Second-floor lodging efficiencies are fully furnished, each with a private bath and some with a full kitchen. There are hardwood floors throughout. Choose from the Foreclosure Department, the Mutual Funds Department, and the Mortgage Loan Department.

Most rooms have heat, air-conditioning and TV.

The President's Suite was Barron Collier's Office back in the '20s. It features a private bedroom, full kitchen, private bath, living room and a full-size dining room. Sleeps four.

Be sure to browse some of the original artifacts, including the 3,000-pound cannonball safe, whose combination lock still works. Easy to find, the bank is on the main road at the town circle.

Ivey House Bed & Breakfast

107 Camelia St.
Everglades City FL 34139
☎ 941-695-3299, fax 941-695-4155
E-mail: sandee@iveyhouse.com
www.iveyhouse.com

Originally a boarding house built in the 1920s, Ivey House has become a favorite of canoe and kayak paddlers exploring the region. Comfortable and clean, simple rooms. Complimentary use of bicycles, canoe and kayak rentals and guided river adventures. It's located one block behind the Circle-K Gas Station.

Camping

Outdoor Resorts

Hwy. 29 South
Chokoloskee FL 34139
☎ 941-695-2881

Outdoor Resorts rents motel efficiencies, RVs and two-bedroom condos. One-week minimum. The campground is well-suited for boaters. Forty-eight of the 283 sites have dockage on the bay. Additional dockage is available for 65 boats. All sites are landscaped, with paved drives and patios. Fully equipped marina with boat ramp, bait shop, boat rental, pool, tennis. Pets are allowed in the campground, but not in the motel.

Chokoloskee Island Park

PO Box 430
Chokoloskee FL 34138
☎ 941-695-2414
E-mail: spstrobel@hotmail.com
www.chokoloskee.com

Open all year, this park features full hookups, hot showers, a laundromat and pay phone, plus boat dockage, live bait, boat and motor rentals. Fast access to the Gulf of Mexico. To get there, take SR 29 four miles south of Everglades City, make the first right past the Post Office and follow the signs.

Where to Stay

Index